William Cowper, John Ebenezer Bryant

An Examination of Sir William Hamilton's Philosophy

And of the Principal Philosophical Questions. Vol. 2

William Cowper, John Ebenezer Bryant

An Examination of Sir William Hamilton´s Philosophy
And of the Principal Philosophical Questions. Vol. 2

ISBN/EAN: 9783337069216

Printed in Europe, USA, Canada, Australia, Japan

Cover: Foto ©ninafisch / pixelio.de

More available books at **www.hansebooks.com**

AN EXAMINATION

OF

SIR WILLIAM HAMILTON'S PHILOSOPHY,

AND OF

THE PRINCIPAL PHILOSOPHICAL QUESTIONS
DISCUSSED IN HIS WRITINGS.

BY

JOHN STUART MILL.

IN TWO VOLUMES.

VOL. II.

BOSTON:
WILLIAM V. SPENCER,
134 WASHINGTON STREET.
1865.

CONTENTS OF VOL. II.

CHAPTER XV.
SIR WILLIAM HAMILTON'S DOCTRINE OF UNCONSCIOUS MENTAL MODIFICATIONS........... 5

CHAPTER XVI.
SIR W. HAMILTON'S THEORY OF CAUSATION...... 25

CHAPTER XVII.
THE DOCTRINE OF CONCEPTS, OR GENERAL NOTIONS.. 49

CHAPTER XVIII.
OF JUDGMENT............... 89

CHAPTER XIX.
OF REASONING............... 118

CHAPTER XX.
ON SIR W. HAMILTON'S CONCEPTION OF LOGIC AS A SCIENCE. IS LOGIC THE SCIENCE OF THE LAWS OR FORMS OF THOUGHT?............ 127

CHAPTER XXI.

THE FUNDAMENTAL LAWS OF THOUGHT ACCORDING T SIR W. HAMILTON. . . . .

CHAPTER XXII.

OF SIR W. HAMILTON'S SUPPOSED IMPROVEMENTS I FORMAL LOGIC. . . . .

CHAPTER XXIII.

OF SOME MINOR PECULIARITIES OF DOCTRINE IN SIR W HAMILTON'S VIEW OF FORMAL LOGIC. . . . .

CHAPTER XXIV.

OF SOME NATURAL PREJUDICES COUNTENANCED BY SIR W. HAMILTON, AND SOME FALLACIES WHICH HE CONSIDERS INSOLUBLE. . . . .

CHAPTER XXV.

SIR W. HAMILTON'S THEORY OF PLEASURE AND PAIN. .

CHAPTER XXVI.

ON THE FREEDOM OF THE WILL. . . . .

CHAPTER XXVII.

SIR W. HAMILTON'S OPINIONS ON THE STUDY OF MATHEMATICS. . . . .

CHAPTER XXVIII.

CONCLUDING REMARKS. . . . .

AN EXAMINATION

OF

SIR WILLIAM HAMILTON'S PHILOSOPHY.

CHAPTER XV.

SIR WILLIAM HAMILTON'S DOCTRINE OF UNCONSCIOUS MENTAL MODIFICATIONS.

THE laws of Obliviscence, noticed in the preceding chapter, are closely connected with a question raised by Sir W. Hamilton, and discussed at some length in his Lectures: Whether there are unconscious states of mind; or, as he expresses it in the eighteenth Lecture,[*] "Whether the mind exerts energies, and is the subject of modifications, of neither of which it is conscious." Our author pronounces decidedly for the affirmative, in opposition to most English philosophers, by whom he says, "the supposition of an unconscious action or passion of the mind, has been treated as something either unintelligible or absurd;" and in opposition, no less, to isolated expressions of opinion by our author himself. The following is one: "Every act of mind is an act of consciousness."[†] Here is another:[‡] "We must say of all our states of mind, whatever they may be, that it" (a state of mind)

---

[*] Lectures, i. 338.   [†] Ibid. ii. 277.   [‡] Ibid. ii. 73.

"can be nothing else than it is felt to be. Its very essence consists in being felt; and when it is not felt, it is not." This is one of the numerous inconsistencies in Sir W. Hamilton's professed opinions, which a close examination and comparison of his speculations bring to light, and which show how far he was in reality from being the systematic thinker which, on a first impression of his writings, he seems to be. In one point of view, these self-contradictions are fully as much an honor as a discredit to him; since they frequently arise from his having acutely seized some important psychological truth, greatly in advance of his general mode of thought, and not having brought the remainder of his philosophy up to it. Instead of having reasoned out a consistent scheme of thought, of which every part fits in with the other parts, he seems to have explored the deeper regions of the mind only at the points which had some direct connection with the conclusions he had adopted on a few special questions of philosophy; and from his different explorations, he occasionally, as in the present case, brought back different results. But, in the place where he treats directly of this particular question, he decides unequivocally for the existence of latent mental modifications. The subject is in itself not unimportant, and his treatment of it will serve as an example by which to estimate his powers of thought in the province of pure psychology.

Sir W. Hamilton recognizes three different kinds, or, as he calls them, degrees, of mental latency. Two of these will be seen, on examination, to be entirely irrelevant.

The first kind of latency is that which belongs to all

the parts of our knowledge which we are not thinking of at the very moment. "I know a science, or language, not merely while I make a temporary use of it, but inasmuch as I can apply it when and how I will. Thus the infinitely greater part of our spiritual treasures lies always beyond the sphere of consciousness, hid in the obscure recesses of the mind."* But this stored-up knowledge, I submit, is not an " unconscious action or passion of the mind." It is not a mental state, but a capability of being put into a mental state. When I am not thinking of a thing, it is not present to my mind at all. It may become present when something happens to recall it; but it is not latently present now; no more than any physical thing which I may have hoarded up. I may have a stock of food with which to nourish myself hereafter; but my body is not in a state of latent nourishment by the food which is in store. I have the power to walk across the room, though I am sitting in my chair; but we should hardly call this power a latent act of walking. What required to be shown was, not that I may possess knowledge without recalling it, but that it can be recalled to my mind, I remaining unconscious of it all the time.†

* Lectures, i. 339.
† Sir W. Hamilton deliberately rejects this obvious distinction, and in his Lecture on Memory (Lect. xxx.) maintains that all the knowledge we possess, whether we are thinking of it or not, is at all times present to us, though unconsciously. "This is certainly" (he says) "an hypothesis, because whatever is out of consciousness can only be assumed; but it is an hypothesis which we are not only warranted, but necessitated by the phænomena, to establish." (Lectures, ii. 209.) This confident assertion is supported only by a passage from an author of whom the reader has already heard something, H. Schmid (*Versuch einer Metaphysik*); by whom, however, the conclusion is not elicited from "the phænomena," but drawn, *à priori*, from the assertion that the act of knowledge is "an energy of the self-active powers of a subject one and indivisible; consequently a

"The * second degree of latency exists when the mind contains systems of knowledge, or certain habits of action, which it is wholly unconscious of possessing in its ordinary state, but which are revealed to consciousness in certain extraordinary exaltations of its powers. The evidence on this point shows that the mind frequently contains whole systems of knowledge, which, though in our normal state they have faded into absolute oblivion, may, in certain abnormal states, as madness, febrile delirium, somnambulism, catalepsy, &c., flash out into luminous consciousness, and even throw

part of the ego must be detached or annihilated if a cognition once existent be again extinguished." This palpable begging of the whole point in dispute (which Schmid makes no scruple of propping up by half a dozen other arbitrary assumptions) of course makes it necessary to explain how anything can be forgotten; which Schmid resolves by declaring that nothing ever is; it merely passes into latency. Of all this, not a shadow of evidence is exhibited; anything being set down as fact, which can be educed from the idea of the Ego evolved by Schmid out of the depths of his moral consciousness. His style of philosophizing may be judged from the following specimen: "Every mental activity belongs to the one vital activity of mind in general; it is, therefore, indivisibly bound up with it, and can neither be torn from, nor abolished in it." Therefore he has only to call every impression in memory a "mental activity," to prove that when we have once had it, we can never more get rid of it. If he had but happened to call it a mental *act*, it would have been all over with his argument; for there may surely be passing acts of one permanent activity. Schmid further argues, from the same premises, that feelings, volitions, and desires, are retained in the mind without the medium of memory, that is, we retain the states themselves, not the notions or remembrances of them; from which it follows, that I am at this moment desiring and willing to rise from my bed yesterday morning, and every previous morning since I began to have a will. Schmid has an easy answer to all attempts at explaining mental phænomena by physiological hypotheses, viz., that " Mind, howbeit conditioned by bodily relations, still ever preserves its self-activity and independence." As if to determine whether it does so or not, was not the very point in dispute between him and the physiological hypotheses. These reasonings are quite worthy of Schmid; but it is extremely unworthy of Sir W. Hamilton to accept and indorse them.

* Lectures, i. 339–346.

into the shade of unconsciousness those other systems by which they had, for a long period, been eclipsed and even extinguished." He then cites from various authors some of the curious recorded cases "in which the extinct memory of whole languages was suddenly restored, and, what is even still more remarkable, in which the faculty was exhibited of actually repeating, in known or unknown tongues, passages which were never within the grasp of conscious memory in the normal state." These, however, are not cases of latent states of mind, but of a very different thing — of latent memory. It is not the mental impressions that are latent, but the power of reproducing them. Every one admits, without any apparatus of proof, that we may have powers and susceptibilities of which we are not conscious; but these are capabilities of being affected, not actual affections. I have the susceptibility of being poisoned by prussic acid, but this susceptibility is not a present phænomenon, constantly taking place in my body without my perceiving it. The capability of being poisoned is not a present modification of my body; nor is the capability I perhaps have of recollecting, should I become delirious, something which I have forgotten while sane, a present modification of my mind. These are future contingent states, not present actual ones. The real question is, can I undergo a present actual mental modification without being aware of it?

We come, therefore, to the third case, which is the only one really in point, and inquire, whether there are, in our ordinary mental life, "mental * modifications, *i. e.*, mental activities and passivities, of which we are

* Lectures, I. 317-349.

unconscious, but which manifest their existence by effects of which we are conscious?" Sir W. Hamilton decides that there are; and even "that what we are conscious of is constructed out of what we are not conscious of;" that "the sphere of our conscious modifications is only a small circle in the centre of a far wider sphere of action and passion, of which we are only conscious through its effects."

His first example is taken from the perception of external objects. The facts which he adduces are these. 1st. Every *minimum visibile* is composed of still smaller parts, which are not separately capable of being objects of vision; "they are, severally and apart, to consciousness as zero." Yet every one of these parts " must by itself have produced in us a certain modification, real though unperceived," since the effect of the whole can only be the sum of the separate effects of the parts. 2d. "When we look at a distant forest, we perceive a certain expanse of green. Of this, as an affection of our organism, we are clearly and distinctly conscious. Now, the expanse of which we are conscious, is evidently made up of parts of which we are not conscious. No leaf, perhaps no tree, may be separately visible. But the greenness of the forest is made up of the greenness of the leaves; that is, the total impression of which we are conscious, is made up of an infinitude of small impressions of which we are not conscious." 3d. Our sense of hearing tells the same tale. There is a *minimum audibile;* the faintest sound capable of being heard. This sound, however, must be made up of parts, each of which must affect us in some manner, otherwise the whole which they compose could not affect us. When we hear the distant murmur of the sea, " this murmur is a sum made up of parts, and the sum would be as zero if the parts did not count as something. . . . If the noise of each wave made no impression on our sense, the noise of the sea, as the result of these impressions, could not be realized. But the noise of each several wave, at the distance we suppose, is inaudible; we must, however, admit that they produce a certain modification, beyond consciousness, on the percipient subject; for this is necessarily involved in the reality of their result."[*]

It is a curious question how Sir W. Hamilton failed to perceive that an unauthorized assumption has slipped into his argument. Because the *minimum visibile* consists of parts (as we know through the microscope), and because the minimum visibile produces an impression on our sense of sight, he jumps to the conclusion that each one of the parts does so too. But it is a supposition consistent with what we know of nature, that a certain *quantity* of the cause may be a necessary condition to the production of *any* of the effect. The minimum visibile would on that supposition *be* this certain quantity, and the two halves into which we can conceive it divided, though each contributing its half to the formation of that which produces vision, would not each separately produce half of the vision, the concurrence of both being necessary to produce any vision whatever. And so of the distant murmur of the sea: the agency which produces it is made up of the rolling of many different waves, each of which, if sufficiently near, would affect us with a perceptible sound; but at the distance at which they are, it may require the rolling of many waves to excite an

[*] Lectures, i. 349-351.

amount of vibration in the air sufficient, when enfeebled by extension, to produce any effect whatever on our auditory nerves, and, through them, on our mind. The supposition that each wave affects the mind separately because their aggregate affects it, is therefore, to say the least, an unproved hypothesis.

The counter-hypothesis, that in order to the production of any quantity whatever of the effect, there is needed a certain minimum quantity of the cause, it is the more extraordinary that Sir W. Hamilton should have overlooked, since he has not only himself adopted a similar supposition in some other cases,* but it is a necessary part of his theory in this very case. He will not admit as possible, that less than a certain quantity of the external agent, produces no mental modification; but he himself supposes that less than a certain quantity of mental modification produces no consciousness. Yet if his *à priori* argument is valid for the one sequence, it is valid for the other. If the effect of a whole must be the sum of similar effects produced by all its parts, and if every state of consciousness is the effect of a modification of mind which is made up of an infinitude of small parts, the state of consciousness also must be made up of an infinitude of small states of consciousness, produced by these infinitely small mental modifications respectively. We are not at liberty to adopt the one theory for the first link in the double succession, and the

---

* "In the internal perception of a series of mental operations, a certain time, a certain duration, is necessary for the smallest section of continuous energy to which consciousness is competent. Some minimum of time must be admitted as the condition of consciousness." (Lectures, i. 369.) And again (Lectures, ii. 102): "It cannot certainly be said, that the minimum of sensation infers the maximum of perception; for perception always supposes a certain quantum of sensation."

other theory for the other link. Having shown no reason why either theory should be preferred, our author would have acted more philosophically in not deciding between them. But to accommodate half the fact to one theory and half to the other, without assigning any reason for the difference, is to exceed all rational license of scientific hypothesis.

After these examples from Perception, our author passes to cases of Association: and as he here states some important mental phænomena well and clearly, I shall quote him at some length.*

"It sometimes happens, that we find one thought rising immediately after another in consciousness, but whose consecution we can reduce to no law of association. Now, in these cases we can generally discover by an attentive observation, that these two thoughts, though not themselves associated, are each associated with certain other thoughts; so that the whole consecution would have been regular, had these intermediate thoughts come into consciousness, between the two which are not immediately associated. Suppose, for instance, that A, B, C, are three thoughts, — that A and C cannot immediately suggest each other, but that each is associated with B, so that A will naturally suggest B, and B naturally suggest C. Now, it may happen, that we are conscious of A, and immediately thereafter of C. How is the anomaly to be explained? It can only be explained on the principle of latent modifications. A suggests C, not immediately, but through B; but as B, like the half of the *minimum visibile* or *minimum audibile*, does not rise into consciousness, we

* Lectures, i. 352, 353.

are apt to consider it as non-existent. You are probably aware of the following fact in mechanics. If a number of billiard balls be placed in a straight row and touching each other, and if a ball be made to strike, in the line of the row, the ball at one end of the series, what will happen? The motion of the impinging ball is not divided among the whole row; this, which we might *à priori* have expected, does not happen, but the impetus is transmitted through the intermediate balls which remain each in its place, to the ball at the opposite end of the series, and this ball alone is impelled on. Something like this seems often to occur in the train of thought. One idea mediately suggests another into consciousness, — the suggestion passing through one or more ideas which do not themselves rise with consciousness. The awakening and awakened ideas here correspond to the ball striking and the ball struck off; while the intermediate ideas of which we are unconscious, but which carry on the suggestion, resemble the intermediate balls which remain moveless, but communicate the impulse. An instance of this occurs to me with which I was recently struck. Thinking of Ben Lomond, this thought was immediately followed by the thought of the Prussian system of education. Now, conceivable connection between these two ideas in themselves, there was none. A little reflection, however, explained the anomaly. On my last visit to the mountain, I had met upon its summit a German gentleman, and though I had no consciousness of the intermediate and unawakened links between Ben Lomond and the Prussian schools, they were undoubtedly these, — the German, — Germany, — Prussia, — and, these media being admitted, the connection between the extremes was manifest."

Though our author says that the facts here described can only be explained on the supposition that the intervening ideas never came into consciousness at all, he is aware that another explanation is conceivable, namely, that they were momentarily in consciousness, but were forgotten, agreeably to the law of Obliviscence already spoken of: which, in fact, is the explanation given by Stewart. The same two explanations may be given of his final example, drawn from a class of phænomena also governed by laws of association, "our acquired dexterities and habits."* When we learn any manual operation, suppose that of playing on the pianoforte, the operation is at first a series of conscious volitions, followed by movements of the fingers; but when, by sufficient repetition, a certain facility has been acquired, the motions take place without our being able to recognize afterwards that we have been conscious of the volitions which preceded them. In this case, we may either hold with Sir W. Hamilton, that the volitions (to which may be added the feelings of muscular contraction, and of the contact of our fingers with the keys) are not, in the practised performer, present to consciousness at all; or, with Stewart, that he is conscious of them, but for so brief an interval, that he has no remembrance of them afterwards. The motions, in this case, are said by Hartley to have become secondarily automatic; which our author supposes to be a third opinion, but it is not certain that Hartley meant anything at variance with Stewart's theory.

Let us now consider the reasons given by Sir W. Hamilton for preferring his explanation to Stewart's.

* Lectures, iii. 355.

The first and principal of them is, that to suppose a state of consciousness which is not remembered,* "violates the whole analogy of consciousness." "Consciousness supposes memory; and we are only conscious as we are able to connect and contrast one instance of our intellectual existence with another." "Of consciousness, however faint, there must be some memory, however short. But this is at variance with the phænomenon, for the ideas A and C may precede and follow each other without any perceptible interval, and without any the feeblest memory of B."

Here again I am obliged, not without wonder, to point out the inconclusive character of the argument. When Sir W. Hamilton says that consciousness implies memory, he means, as his words show, that we are only conscious by means of change; by discriminating the present state from a state immediately preceding. Granting this, as with proper explanations I do, all it proves is, that any conscious state of mind must be remembered long enough to be compared with the mental state immediately following it. The state of mind, therefore, which he supposes to have been latent, must, if it passed into consciousness, have been remembered until one other mental modification had supervened; which there is assuredly not a particle of evidence that it was not: for our having totally forgotten it a minute after, is no evidence, but a common consequence of the laws of Obliviscence. It is perhaps true that all consciousness must be followed by a memory, but I see no reason why an evanescent state of consciousness must be followed, if by any, by a more than evanescent memory. "It is a

* Lectures, i. 354, 355.

law of mind," our author says further on,* "that the intensity of the present consciousness determines the vivacity of the future memory. Vivid consciousness, long memory; faint consciousness, short memory." Well, then: in the case supposed, the intensity of consciousness is at the minimum, therefore on his own showing the duration of memory should be so too. If the consciousness itself is too fleeting to fix the attention, so, *à fortiori*, must the remembrance of it. In reality, the remembrance is often evanescent when the consciousness is by no means so, but is so distinct and prolonged as to be in no danger whatever of being supposed latent. Take the case of a player on the pianoforte while still a learner, and before the succession of volitions has attained the rapidity which practice ultimately gives it. In this stage of progress there is, beyond all doubt, a conscious volition, anterior to the playing of each particular note. Yet has the player, when the piece is finished, the smallest remembrance of each of these volitions, as a separate fact? In like manner have we, when we have finished reading a volume, the smallest memory of our successive volitions to turn the pages? On the contrary, we only know that we must have turned them, because, without doing so, we could not have read to the end. Yet these volitions were not latent: every time we turned over a leaf, we must have formed a conscious purpose of turning; but, the purpose having been instantly fulfilled, the attention was arrested in the process for too short a time to leave a more than momentary remembrance of it. The sensations of sight, touch, and the muscles, felt in turning the leaves, were as vivid at the moment as any

* Lectures, i. 368, 369.

of our ordinary sensible impressions which are only important to us as means to an end. But because they had no pleasurable or painful interest in themselves; because the interest they had as means passed away in the same instant by the attainment of the end; and because there was nothing to associate the act of reading with these particular sensations, rather than with other similar sensations formerly experienced; their trace in the memory was only momentary, unless something unusual and remarkable connected with the particular leaves turned over, detained them in remembrance.

If sensations which are evidently in consciousness may leave so brief a memory that they are not felt to leave any memory at all, what wonder that the same should happen when the sensations are of so fugitive a character, that it can be debated whether they were in consciousness at all! However true it may be that there must be some memory wherever there is consciousness, what argument is this against a theory which supposes a low degree of consciousness, attended by just the degree of memory which properly belongs to it?

Imagine an argument in physics, corresponding to this in metaphysics. Some of my readers are probably acquainted with the important experiments of M. Pasteur, which have finally exploded the ancient hypothesis of Equivocal Generation, by showing that even the smallest microscopic animalcules are not produced in a medium from which their still more microscopic germs have been effectually excluded. What should we think of any one who deemed it a refutation of M. Pasteur, that the germs are not discernible by the naked eye? who maintained that invisible animalcules must proceed, if from germs at all, from visible germs? This reasoning would be an exact parallel to that of Sir W. Hamilton.

The only other argument of our author against Stewart's doctrine, is confined to the phænomenon of acquired habits, in which case, he says,* the supposition of real but forgotten consciousness " would constrain our assent to the most monstrous conclusions : " since, in reading aloud, if the matter be uninteresting, we may be carrying on a train of thought (even of "serious meditation") on a totally different subject, and this, too, " without distraction or fatigue : " which, he says, would be impossible, if we were separately conscious of, or (as he rather gratuitously alters the idea) separately attentive to "each least movement in either process." Sir W. Hamilton here loses sight of a part of his own philosophy, which deserves his forgetfulness the less as it is a very valuable part. In one of the most important psychological discussions in his Lectures,† he forcibly maintains that we are capable of carrying on several distinct series of states of consciousness at once ; and goes so far as to contend not only that our consciousness, but what is more than consciousness, our "*concentrated* consciousness, or attention," is capable of being divided among as many as six simultaneous impressions.‡ Returning to the same subject in another place, he quotes from a modern French philosopher, Cardaillac (in a work entitled *Etudes Elémentaires de Philosophie*), an excellent and conclusive passage, showing the great multitude of states, more or less conscious, which often coexist in the mind, and help to determine the subsequent trains of thought or feeling ;

---

* Lectures, i. 360. † Ibid. i. 238–254. ‡ Ibid. p. 254.

and illustrating the causes that determine which of these shall in any particular case predominate over the rest.* Our consciousness, therefore, according to Sir W. Hamilton, ought not to have much difficulty in finding room for the two simultaneous series of states which he quarrels with Stewart's hypothesis for requiring: and we are not bound, under the penalty of "monstrous conclusions," to consider one of these series as latent. Sir W. Hamilton indeed says † truly, that "the greater the number of objects to which our consciousness is simultaneously extended, the smaller is the intensity with which it is able to consider each;" but the intensity of consciousness necessary for reading aloud with correctness in a language familiar to us, not being very considerable, a great part of our power of attention is disposable for "the train of serious meditation" which is supposed to be passing through our minds at the same time. For all this, I would not advise any person (unless one with the peculiar gift ascribed to Julius Cæsar) to stake anything on the substantial value of a train of thought carried on by him while reading aloud a book on another subject. Such thoughts, I imagine, are always the

* Lectures, iii. 250-258. From this long exposition I shall only extract a single passage (p. 258), but I recommend the whole of it to the attentive consideration of readers.

"Thus, if we appreciate correctly the phænomena of Reproduction or Reminiscence, we shall recognize, as an incontestable fact, that our thoughts suggest each other not one by one successively, as the order to which language is astricted might lead us to infer; but that the complement of circumstances under which we at every moment exist, awakens simultaneously a great number of thoughts; these it calls into the presence of the mind, either to place them at our disposal, if we find it requisite to employ them, or to make them co-operate in our deliberations, by giving them, according to our nature and our habits, an influence, more or less active, on our judgments and consequent acts."

† Lectures, i. 237.

better for being revised when the mind has nothing else to do than to consider them.

It is strange, but characteristic, that Sir W. Hamilton cannot be depended on for remembering, in one part of his speculations, the best things which he has said in another; not even the truths into which he has thrown so much of the powers of his mind, as to have made them, in an especial manner, his own.

Notwithstanding the failure of Sir W. Hamilton to adduce a single valid reason for preferring his hypothesis to that of Stewart, it does not follow that he is not, at least in certain cases, in the right. The difference between the two opinions being beyond the reach of experiment, and both being equally consistent with the facts which present themselves spontaneously, it is not easy to obtain sure grounds for deciding between them. The essential part of the phænomenon is, that we have, or once had, many sensations, and that many ideas do, or once did, enter into our trains of thought, which sensations and ideas we afterwards, in the words of James Mill, are "under an acquired incapacity of attending to;"* and that when our incapacity of attending to them has become complete, it is, to our subsequent consciousness, exactly as if we did not have them at all; we are incapable, by any self-examination, of being aware of them. We know that these lost sensations and ideas, for lost they appear to be — leave traces of having existed; they continue to be operative in introducing other ideas — by association. Either, therefore, they have been consciously present long enough to call up associations, but not long enough to be remembered a few moments later,

* Analysis of the Human Mind, i. 33.

or they have been, as Sir W. Hamilton supposes, unconsciously present; or they have not been present at all, but something instead of them, capable of producing the same effects. (I am myself inclined to agree with Sir W. Hamilton, and to admit his unconscious mental modifications, in the only shape in which I can attach any very distinct meaning to them, namely, unconscious modifications of the nerves.) There are much stronger facts in support of this hypothesis than those to which Sir W. Hamilton appeals — facts which it is far more difficult to reconcile with the doctrine that the sensations are felt, but felt too momentarily to leave a recognizable impression in memory. In the case, for instance, of a soldier who receives a wound in battle, but in the excitement of the moment is not aware of the fact, it is difficult not to believe that if the wound had been accompanied by the usual sensation, so vivid a feeling would have forced itself to be attended to and remembered. The supposition which seems most probable is, that the nerves of the particular part were affected as they would have been by the same cause in any other circumstances, but that, the nervous centres being intensely occupied with other impressions, the affection of the local nerves did not reach them, and no sensation was excited. In like manner, if we admit (what physiology is rendering more and more probable) that our mental feelings, as well as our sensations, have for their physical antecedents particular states of the nerves, it may well be believed that the apparently suppressed links in a chain of association, those which Sir W. Hamilton considers as latent, really are so; that they are not, even momentarily, felt; the chain of causation being continued only physically, by one organic state of the nerves succeeding another so rapidly that the state of mental consciousness appropriate to each is not produced.) We have only to suppose, either that a nervous modification of too short duration does not produce any sensation or mental feeling at all, or that the rapid succession of different nervous modifications makes the feelings produced by them interfere with each other, and become confounded in one mass. The former of these suppositions is extremely probable, while of the truth of the latter we have positive proof. An example of it is the experiment which Sir W. Hamilton quoted from Mr. Mill, and which had been noticed before either of them by Hartley. It is known that the seven prismatic colors, combined in certain proportions, produce the white light of the solar ray. Now, if the seven colors are painted on spaces bearing the same proportion to one another as in the solar spectrum, and the colored surface so produced is passed rapidly before the eyes, as by the turning of a wheel, the whole is seen as white. The physiological explanation of this phænomenon may be deduced from another common experiment. If a lighted torch, or a bar heated to luminousness, is waved rapidly before the eye, the appearance produced is that of a ribbon of light; which is universally understood to prove that the visual sensation persists for a certain short time after its cause has ceased. Now, if this happens with a single color, it will happen with a series of colors; and if the wheel on which the prismatic colors have been painted, is turned with the same rapidity with which the torch was waved, each of the seven sensations of color will last long enough to be contemporaneous with all the others, and they will naturally produce by their combination the same color as if they had, from the beginning, been excited simultaneously. If anything similar to this obtains in our consciousness generally (and that it obtains in many cases of consciousness there can be no doubt), it will follow that whenever the organic modifications of our nervous fibres succeed one another at an interval shorter than the duration of the sensations or other feelings corresponding to them, those sensations or feelings will, so to speak, overlap one another, and becoming simultaneous instead of successive, will blend into a state of feeling, probably as unlike the elements out of which it is engendered, as the color white is unlike the prismatic colors. And this may be the source of many of those states of internal or mental feeling which we cannot distinctly refer to a prototype in experience, our experience only supplying the elements from which, by this kind of mental chemistry, they are composed. The elementary feelings may then be said to be latently present, or to be present but not in consciousness. The truth, however, is that the feelings themselves are not present, consciously or latently, but that the nervous modifications which are their usual antecedents have been present, while the consequents have been frustrated, and another consequent has been produced instead.

CHAPTER XVI.

SIR WILLIAM HAMILTON'S THEORY OF CAUSATION.

Sir W. Hamilton commences his treatment of the question of Causation, by warning the reader against " some philosophers who, instead of accommodating their solutions to the problem, have accommodated the problem to their solutions." It might almost have been supposed that this expression had been invented to be applied to Sir W. Hamilton himself. He has defined the problem in a manner in which it has been defined by no one else, for no visible reason but to adapt it to a solution which no one else had thought of.*

" When we are aware," he says,† " of something which begins to exist, we are, by the necessity of our intelligence, constrained to believe that it has a Cause. But what does this expression, that it has a cause, signify? If we analyze our thought, we shall find that it simply means, that as we cannot conceive any new existence to commence, therefore, all that now is seen to arise under a new appearance, had previously an existence under a prior form. We are utterly unable to realize in thought the possibility of the complement of existence being either increased or diminished. We are unable, on the one hand, to conceive nothing becoming something, or, on

---

* When I say no one else, I ought perhaps to except Krug, from whom in another place (Lectures, iv. 135) our author quotes a sentence, containing at least the germ of his own theory.

† Lectures, ii. 377, 378.

the other, something becoming nothing. When God is said to create out of nothing, we construe this to thought by supposing that he evolves existence out of himself; we view the Creator as the cause of the universe. 'Ex nihilo nihil, in nihilum nil posse reverti,' expresses, in its purest form, the whole intellectual phænomenon of causality.

"There is thus conceived an absolute tautology between the effect and its causes. We think the causes to contain all that is contained in the effect, the effect to contain nothing which was not contained in the causes. Take as example: A neutral salt is an effect of the conjunction of an acid and alkali. Here we do not, and here we cannot, conceive that, in effect, any new existence has been added, nor can we conceive that any has been taken away. Put another example: Gunpowder is the effect of a mixture of sulphur, charcoal, and nitre, and those three substances are again the effect, — result, of simpler constituents, either known or conceived to exist. Now, in all this series of compositions, we cannot conceive that aught begins to exist. The gunpowder, the last compound, we are compelled to think, contains precisely the same quantum of existence that its ultimate elements contained prior to their combination. Well, we explode the powder. Can we conceive that existence has been diminished by the annihilation of a single element previously in being, or increased by the addition of a single element which was not heretofore in nature? 'Omnia mutantur; nihil interit,' is what we think — what we must think. This then is the mental phænomenon of causality, — that we necessarily deny in thought that the object which appears to begin to be, really so begins; and that we necessarily identify its present with its past existence."

This being Sir W. Hamilton's idea of what Causality means, he thinks it unnecessary to suppose, with most of the philosophers of the intuitive school, a special principle of our nature to account for our believing that every phænomenon must have a cause. The belief is accounted for, "not* from a power, but from an impotence of mind," namely, from the Law of the Conditioned; or in other words, from the incapacity of the human mind to conceive the Absolute. We are unable to conceive and construe to ourselves an absolute commencement. Whatever we think, we cannot help thinking as existing; and whatever we think as existing, we are compelled to think as having existed through all past, and as destined to exist through all future, time. It does not at all follow that this is really the fact, for there are many things, inconceivable to us, which not only may, but must, be true. Accordingly it may be true that there is an absolute commencement; it may not be true that every phænomenon has a cause. Human volitions, in particular, may come into existence uncaused, and, in Sir W. Hamilton's opinion, they do so. But to us, a beginning and an end of existence are both inconceivable. "We are† unable to construe in thought, that there can be an atom absolutely added to, or an atom absolutely taken away from, existence in general. Make the experiment. Form to yourselves a notion of the universe; now, can you conceive that the quantity of existence, of which the universe is the sum, is either amplified or diminished? You can conceive the creation

* Lectures, ii. 397. † Lectures, ii. 405, 406.

of the world as lightly as you can conceive the creation of an atom. But what is creation? It is not the springing of nothing into something. Far from it: it is conceived, and is by us conceivable, merely as the evolution of a new form of existence, by the fiat of the Deity. Let us suppose the very crisis of creation. *Can we realize it to ourselves, in thought, that the moment after the universe came into manifested being, there was a larger complement of existence in the universe and its Author together, than there was the moment before, in the Deity himself alone?* This we cannot imagine. What I have now said of our conceptions of creation, holds true of our conceptions of annihilation. We can conceive no real annihilation — no absolute sinking of something into nothing. But, as creation is cogitable by us only as an exertion of divine power, so annihilation is only to be conceived by us as a withdrawal of the divine support. All that there is now actually of existence in the universe, we conceive as having virtually existed, prior to creation, in the Creator; and in imagining the universe to be annihilated by its Author, we can only imagine this as the retractation of an outward energy into power."

Had this extraordinary view of Causation proceeded from a thinker of less ability and authority than Sir W. Hamilton, I think there are few readers who, on reaching the sentence which I have marked by italics, would not have set down the entire speculation as a *mauvaise plaisanterie*.

But since any opinion, however strange, of Sir W. Hamilton, must be believed to be serious, and no serious opinion of such a man ought to be dismissed unexamined, I shall proceed to inquire, whether the problem of which he propounds this solution, *is* the problem of Causation, and whether the solution is a true one. To take the last question first; is it a fact that we cannot conceive a beginning of existence? Is it true that whenever we conceive a thing as existing, we are capable of conceiving a time when it did not exist, or a time when it will exist no longer?

If, by incapacity to conceive an absolute commencement, were only meant that we cannot imagine a time when nothing existed; and if our incapacity of conceiving annihilation, only means that we cannot represent to ourselves a universe devoid of existence; I do not deny it. Whatever else we may suppose removed, there always remains the conception of empty space: and Sir W. Hamilton is probably right in his opinion, that we cannot imagine even empty space without clothing it mentally with some sort of color or figure. Whoever admits the possibility of Inseparable Association, can scarcely avoid thinking that these are cases of it; and that we are unable to imagine any object but as occupying space, or to imagine it removed without leaving that space either vacant, or filled by something else. But we can conceive both a beginning and an end to all physical existence. As a mere hypothesis, the notion that matter cannot be annihilated arose early, but as a settled belief, it is the tardy result of scientific inquiry. All that is necessary for imagining matter annihilated is presented in our daily experience. We see apparent annihilation whenever water dries up, or fuel is consumed without a visible residuum. The fact could not offer itself to our immediate perceptions in a more palpable shape, if the annihilation were real. Having an exact type on which to frame the conception of matter annihilated, the vulgar of all countries easily and perfectly conceive it. Those to whom, if to anybody, it is inconceivable, are philosophers and men of science, who, having formed their familiar conception of the universe on the opposite theory, have acquired an inseparable association of their own, which they cannot overcome. To them the vapor which has succeeded to the water dried up by the sun, the gases which replace the fuel transformed by combustion, have become irrevocably a part of their conception of the entire phænomenon. But the ignorant, who never heard of these things, are not in the least incommoded by the want of them; and if they were not told the contrary, would live and die without suspecting that the water, and the wood or coals, were not destroyed.

All this is not denied by Sir W. Hamilton; but his answer to it is, that if the universe were to perish, it would still remain capable of existing, which, it seems, amounts to the same thing. We conceive it as having "virtually existed before it was created," and as virtually existing after it is destroyed. We cannot conceive that there was, at the moment after creation, "a larger complement of existence in the universe and its Author together, than there was the moment before in the Deity himself alone." Creation is to us merely the conversion of power into outward existence; annihilation only "the retractation of an outward energy into power." So that potential existence is exactly the same thing as actual existence; the difference is formal only. Not only is power a real entity, but the power to create a universe *is* the universe: all created things are but a part of its substance, and can be reabsorbed into it. And this is presented to us, not as a recondite ontological theory, forced upon philosophers as an escape from an otherwise insuperable difficulty, but as a statement of what we all think, and cannot but think, from the very constitution of our thinking faculty. Is this the fact? Does any one, except Sir W. Hamilton, think that in computing the sum total of existence, worlds which God might have created but did not, count for exactly as much as they would if he had really created them? There is a corollary from this doctrine which also deserves attention. If the sum of potential and actual existence is always the same, then with every increase of actual existence, there must be a diminution of power: for, if there was once the power without the universe, and is now the same quantity of power and also the universe, what our author nautically terms the "complement of existence" has been increased: which is contrary to the theory. By every exercise, therefore, of creative power, God is less powerful: he has less power now, by a whole universe, than before his power of creating the universe had been transmuted into act; and were he to "retract" the actual existence into potential, he would be more powerful than he now is, by that exact amount. Is this what all mankind think, and are under an original necessity of thinking? Is this the mode in which, by the "law of the Conditioned," every one of us is absolutely necessitated to construe the idea of Creation? Sir W. Hamilton says it is.

By a desperate attempt to put an intelligible meaning into the theory, somebody may interpret it to mean that before the universe existed in fact, it existed as a thought in the Divine Mind; and that the idea of a universe, complete in all its details, is equivalent, in the "complement of existence," to an actual universe. This is not, perhaps, incapable of being maintained; but it affords no escape from the difficulty. For, this idea in the Divine Mind — is the Divine Mind now denuded of it? Has the Deity *forgotten* the universe, from the time when the divine conception was reduced into act? If not, there are now *both* the universe and the idea of the universe; that is, a double "complement of existence" instead of a single.*

But, were it ever so true that we are incapable of conceiving a commencement of anything, and are necessitated to believe that whatever now exists must have existed in the same or another shape through all past time: — that Sir W. Hamilton should imagine *this* to be the law of Cause and Effect, must be accounted one of the most singular hallucinations to be found in the writings of any eminent thinker. According to Sir W.

---

* The curious notion that potential existence is tantamount to actual, reappears in the Appendix to the Discussions (p. 620). "The creation *a Nihilo* means only, that the universe, when created, was not merely put into form, an original chaos, or complement of brute matter, having preceded a plastic energy of intelligence; but that the universe was called into actuality from potential existence by the Divine fiat. The Divine fiat therefore was the proximate cause of the creation; and the Deity containing the cause, contained, potentially, the effect."

It is so frequent in our author's writings to find doctrines of a very decided character laid down in one page, and implicitly or even directly denied in another, that so strange a doctrine as the one in question could not be expected to escape that fate. Accordingly, in p. 703 of the same volume, "the Potential" is defined to be, "what is not at this, but may be at another time." If so, the universe, when it only existed potentially, *was not:* and did not count as part of the "complement" of present existence.

Hamilton, when we say that everything must have a cause, we mean that nothing begins to exist, but everything has always existed. I ask any one, either philosopher or common man, whether he does not mean the exact reverse; whether it is not because things do begin to exist, that a cause must be supposed for their existence. The very words in which the axiom of Causation is commonly stated, and which our author, in the first words of his exposition, adopts, are, that everything which *begins to exist* must have a cause. Is it possible that this axiom can be grounded on the fact that we never suppose anything to begin to exist? Does not he who takes away a beginning of existence, take away all causation, and all need of a cause? Sir W. Hamilton entirely mistakes what it is, which causation is called in to explain. The Matter composing the universe, whatever philosophical theory we hold concerning it, we know by experience to be constant in quantity; never beginning or ending, only changing its form. But its forms have a beginning and ending; and it is its forms, or rather its changes of form, — the end of one form and beginning of another, — which alone we seek a cause for, and believe to have a cause. It is *events*, that is to say, *changes*, not substances, that are subject to the law of Causation. The question for the psychologist is not why we believe that a substance, but why we believe that a change in the form of a substance, must have a cause. Sir W. Hamilton, in a tardy defence of his theory against objections,[*] is forced, in a sort of way, to admit this, and virtually to acknowledge that all which we really consider as caused, we consider as beginning to exist.

---

[*] Appendix on Causation, Lectures, ii. 538.

Nothing is caused but events; and it will hardly be said that we conceive an event as having never had a beginning, but been in existence as an event just as much before it happened as when it did happen. An event then being the only thing which suggests the belief or the idea of having or requiring a cause, Sir W. Hamilton may be charged with the scientific blunder which he imputes, far less justly, to Brown: he "professes to explain the phænomenon of causality, but previously to explanation, evacuates the phænomenon of all that desiderates explanation." *

Sir W. Hamilton was familiar with the teaching of the Aristotelian schools concerning the four Causes — or rather the four meanings of the word Cause, for synonymy and homonymy were, in their classifications, very often confounded: 1, Materia. 2, Forma. 3, Efficiens. 4, Finis: Efficiens being the only one of these which answers either to the common, or to the modern philosophical, notion of Cause. Sir W. Hamilton confounds Materia with Efficiens; or rather ignores Efficiens altogether, and imagines that when the rest of the world are speaking of Efficiens, they mean Materia. It is the very thing which they pre-eminently do not mean. Sir W. Hamilton may choose to call nothing Existence except the permanent element in phænomena; but it is the changeable element, and no other, which is referred to a cause, or which could ever have given the notion of causation.

Sir W. Hamilton says † that the total cause — that the "concurring or co-efficient causes, in fact, constitute the effect." And again,‡ "an effect" is "nothing more than

* Lectures, ii. 384.   † Ibid. i. 59.   ‡ Ibid. p. 97.

the sum or complement of all the partial causes, the concurrence of which constitutes its existence." "An effect* is nothing but the actual union of its constituent entities;" "causes always continue actually to exist in their effects." Because the original matter continues to exist in the matter transformed, the Efficiens which transformed it continues to exist in the fact of the change ! Of course he takes as his example a case in which the material is the prominent thing, that of a salt compounded of an acid and an alkali. "Considering † the salt as an effect, what are the concurrent causes, — the co-efficients, — which constitute it what it is? There are, first, the acid, with its affinity to the alkali; secondly, the alkali, with its affinity to the acid; and thirdly, the translating force (perhaps the human hand) which made their affinities available, by bringing the two bodies within the sphere of mutual attraction. Each of these three concurrents must be considered as a partial cause; for abstract any one, and the effect is not produced." Strange that even this first degree of analysis should not have opened his eyes to the fact, that the moment he admits into *causa efficiens* anything more than *materia*, his theory is at an end. For he will indeed find in the salt, two of his three "co-efficients," the acid and the alkali, with their affinities; but where will he find in it "the translating force, perhaps the human hand"? This essential "concause" does not embarrass him at all; it costs him nothing to make away with it altogether. "This last," he says,‡ "as a transitory condition and not always the same, we shall throw out of account." If we throw out of account all that is transitory, we have no difficulty in proving

---

* Lectures, ii. p. 540.   † Ibid. i. p. 59.   ‡ Ibid. i. 97.

that all that is left is permanent. But the transitory conditions are as much a part of the cause as the permanent conditions. Our author has just before said, that he takes the term causes "as synonymous for all without which the effect would not be;" and if the effect is "the sum or complement" of all the causes, the transitory as well as the permanent elements must be found in it. To exclude all the transitory part of the cause, is to exclude the whole cause, except the materials. Suppose the effect to be St. Paul's: in assigning its causes, the will of the government, the mind of the architect, and the labor of the builders, are all cast out, for they are all transitory, and only the stones and mortar remain.*

It will have been remarked, that in propounding this theory of the belief in Causation, Sir W. Hamilton gives up Causation as a necessary law of the universe; maintaining that a fact is not to be supposed impossible to Nature because we are impotent to conceive it, and indeed regarding the free acts of an intelligent being as an exception to the universality of the law of Cause and Effect. But while in one place he pays this homage to his own principles, in another he entirely takes leave of them, and glides back into the beaten path of the school

* On the same shoal is stranded an argument appended to the same discussion, which our author seems to think of considerable value in the establishment of a First Cause. The progress from cause to effect, he says (Lectures, i. 59, 60), is from the simpler to the more complex. "The lower we descend in the series of causes, the more complex will be the product; the higher we ascend, it will be the more simple." To prove this, he appeals to his example, the composition of a salt. Now, the salt is indeed more complex than either of its chemical ingredients, the acid and the alkali; but need it be, or is it, more complex than the remaining "co-efficient," the human hand, or whatever power, natural or artificial, brings the acid and alkali together? The event which causes, may be in any degree whatever a more complex fact, than the event which is caused by it.

of thought which, erecting human capacities of conception into the measure of the universe, maintains that causes must be, because we are incapable of conceiving phænomena without them. After describing the process of ascending from cause to cause, quite gratuitously, as a progress towards unity, Sir W. Hamilton says,* "Philosophy thus, as the knowledge of effects in their causes, necessarily tends, not towards a plurality of ultimate or first causes, but towards one alone. This first cause, the Creator, it can indeed never reach, as an object of immediate knowledge; but as the convergence towards unity in the ascending series is manifest in so far as that series is within our view" (here he confounds convergence from many to few with convergence towards one), "*and as it is even impossible for the mind to suppose the convergence not continuous and complete*, it follows, unless all analogy be rejected, — unless our intelligence be declared a lie, — that we must, philosophically, believe in that ultimate or primary unity which, in our present existence, we are not destined in itself to apprehend."

A deliverance more radically at variance with the author's own canons, could scarcely have been made. For first, one of the principal of them is, that our inability to conceive a thing as possible, is no argument whatever against its being true. In the second place, the alleged impossibility of conceiving any of the phænomena of the universe to be uncaused, applies equally, on his own showing, to the First Cause itself. For, though he here talks only of one inconceivability, we are, if his theory be correct, under the pressure of two counter-inconceivabilities — being equally unable to conceive an uncaused

* Lectures, i. 60.

beginning, or an infinite regress from effect to cause; it is equally inconceivable to us that there should, as that there should not, be a First Cause. In this difficulty, by what right does he (I mean merely as a philosopher, and on his own principles) select one of the rival inconceivabilities as the real interpreter of Nature, in preference to the other? And, having selected it, why apply it up to a certain point, and there stop? Why must all the phænomena of experience be referred to a single Cause, because we cannot conceive anything uncaused, and that single Cause be proclaimed uncaused, notwithstanding the same impossibility? An argument by Sir W. Hamilton would not be complete unless it wound up with his tiresome final appeal, "unless our intelligence be declared a lie." It is time to understand, once for all, what this means. Does it mean that if our intelligence cannot conceive one thing apart from another, the one thing cannot exist without the other? If yes, what becomes of the Philosophy of the Conditioned? If no, what becomes of the present argument?

Sir W. Hamilton makes a far better figure when arguing against other theories of Causation, than when maintaining his own. He is usually acute in finding the weak points in other people's philosophies; and he brings this talent into play, effectively enough, on the present subject. He is not, indeed, at all successful in combating the doctrine (substantially that of Hume and Brown) that it is experience which proves the fact of causation, and association which generates the idea; for against this he only has to say, that experience and association cannot account for necessity. Now, as to real necessity, we do not know that it exists in the case. Sir W. Hamilton himself is of opinion that it does not, and that there are phænomena (the volitions of rational intelligences) which do not depend on causes. And as for the *feeling* of necessity, or what is termed a necessity of thought, it is (as I have already observed), of all mental phænomena positively the one which an inseparable association is the most evidently competent to generate. I cannot, therefore, attribute any value to Sir W. Hamilton's discussion of this point; but in his refutation of some of the theories of causation, which have originated in his own hemisphere of the intellectual world, he is very felicitous. Take, for example, the doctrine of Wolf and the Leibnitzians (though not of Leibnitz), which " attempts to establish the principle of Causality upon the Principle of Contradiction." " Listen," says our author,* " to the pretended demonstration : — Whatever is produced without a cause, is produced by nothing; in other words, has nothing for its cause. But nothing can no more be a cause than it can be something. The same intuition which makes us aware, that nothing is not something, shows us that everything must have a real cause of its existence. — To this it is sufficient to say, that the existence of causes being the point in question, the existence of causes must not be taken for granted, in the very reasoning which attempts to prove their reality. In excluding causes, we exclude all causes ; and consequently we exclude Nothing, considered as a cause ; it is not, therefore, allowable, contrary to that exclusion, to suppose Nothing as a cause, and then from the absurdity of that supposition to infer the absurdity of the exclusion itself. If everything must have a cause, it follows that upon the

* Lectures, ii. 396, 397.

exclusion of other causes, we must accept of Nothing as a cause. But it is the very point at issue, whether everything must have a cause or not; and therefore it violates the first principles of reasoning to take this quæsitum itself as granted. This opinion," adds our author, " is now universally abandoned."

But there is another theory of Causation which is not abandoned, but has formed for some time past the stronghold of the Intuitive school. This is, that we acquire both our notion of Causation, and our belief in it, from an internal consciousness of power exerted by ourselves, in our voluntary actions: that is, in the motions of our bodies, for our will has no other direct action on the outward world. This relation of the act of will to the bodily movement, it is maintained, is "not a simple relation of succession. The will is not for us a pure act without efficiency; it is a productive energy, so that in volition there is given to us the notion of cause; and this notion we subsequently transport, — project out from our internal activities, into the changes of the external world."

To this doctrine Sir W. Hamilton gives the following conclusive answer.* "This reasoning, in so far as regards the mere empirical fact of our consciousness of causality, in the relation of our will as moving and of our limbs as moved, is refuted by the consideration, that between the overt fact of corporeal movement of which we are cognizant, and the internal act of mental determination of which we are also cognizant, there intervenes a numerous series of intermediate agencies of which we have no knowledge; and consequently, that we can have

* Lectures, ii. 391, 392.

no consciousness of any causal connection between the extreme links of this chain, — the volition to move and the limb moving, as this hypothesis asserts. No one is immediately conscious, for example, of moving his arm through his volition. Previously to this ultimate movement, muscles, nerves, a multitude of solid and fluid parts must be set in motion by the will, but of this motion we know, from consciousness, actually nothing. A person struck with paralysis is conscious of no inability in his limb to fulfil the determination of his will; and it is only after having willed, and finding that his limbs do not obey his volition, that he learns by this experience, that the external movement does not follow the internal act. But as the paralytic learns after the volition that his limbs do not obey his mind, so it is only after the volition that the man in health learns that his limbs do obey the mandates of his will." *

---

* The same argument is restated in the Dissertations on Reid (pp. 866, 867), with some additional development. " Volition to move a limb, and the actual moving of it, are the first and last in a series of more than two successive events, and cannot, therefore, stand to each other, immediately, in the relation of cause and effect. They may, however, stand to each other in the relation of cause and effect, mediately. But then, if they can be known in consciousness as thus mediately related, it is a necessary condition of such knowledge, that the intervening series of causes and effects, through which the final movement of the limb is supposed to be mediately dependent on the primary volition to move, should be known to consciousness immediately under that relation. But this intermediate, this connecting series is, confessedly, unknown to consciousness at all, far less as a series of causes and effects. It follows therefore à fortiori, that the dependency of the last on the first of these events, as of an effect upon its cause, must be to consciousness unknown. In other words: having no consciousness that the volition to move is the efficacious force (power) by which even the event immediately consequent on it (say the transmission of the nervous influence from brain to muscle) is produced, such event being, in fact, itself to consciousness occult; molto minus can we have a consciousness of that volition being the efficacious force by which the ultimate movement of the limb is mediately determined."

With this reasoning, borrowed as our author admits from Hume, I entirely agree; and I wonder that it did not prove to Sir W. Hamilton how little the objection to a doctrine, that it is opposed to our natural beliefs, deserves the exaggerated value he sets upon it; for if there is a natural belief belonging to us, I should suppose it to be, that we are directly conscious of ability to move our limbs. It is, nevertheless, our author's opinion that the belief is groundless, and that we learn even a fact so closely connected with us, in the way in which any bystander learns it; by outward observation.*

Mr. Mansel, who agrees with Sir W. Hamilton in so many of his opinions, separates from him here, and adopts a modified form of the Volitional Theory. He acknowledges the validity of Hume's and Sir W. Hamilton's argument, and does not derive the idea of Power or Causation from mind acting upon body — from my will producing my bodily motions — but from myself producing my will. "In † every act of volition, I am fully conscious that it is in my power to form the resolution or to abstain; and this constitutes the presentative consciousness of free will and of power." And the sole notion we have of causation in the outward universe, as anything more than invariable antecedence and consequence, "is that ‡ of a relation between two objects, similar to that which exists between ourselves and our volitions." Thus interpreted, continues Mr. Mansel,§ it

---

* Sir W. Hamilton adds, as a further objection to the theory, that it does not account for that, in our notion of causation, which is the sole ground for rejecting the Experience theory of it: its "quality of necessity and universality." And this is true: the philosophers who combat the Experience theory of causation by the Volitional one, deprive themselves of a very bad, but still the best argument on their side of the question.

† Prolegomena Logica, p. 139.   ‡ Ibid. p. 140.   § Ibid. pp. 142, 143.

is "an interesting illustration of the universal tendency of men to identify, as far as may be, other agents with themselves, even when the identification tends to the destruction of all clear thinking : — furnishing a psychological explanation of a form of speech which has prevailed and will continue to prevail among all people in all times, but not properly to be called a *necessary truth*, nor capable of any scientific application; inasmuch as, in any such application, it may be true or false, without our being able to determine which, as the object of which it treats never comes within the reach of our faculties. What is meant by *power* in a fire to melt wax? How and when is it exerted, and in what manner does it come under our cognizance? Supposing such power to be suspended by an act of Omnipotence, the Supreme Being at the same time producing the succession of phænomena by the immediate interposition of his own will, — could we in any way detect the change? Or suppose the course of nature to be governed by a pre-established harmony, which ordained that at a certain moment fire and wax should be in the neighborhood of each other, that, at the same moment, fire by itself should burn, and wax by its own laws should melt, neither affecting the other, — would not all the perceptible phænomena be precisely the same as at present? These suppositions may be extravagant, though they are supported by some of the most eminent names in philosophy; but the mere possibility of making them shows that the rival hypothesis is not a necessary truth; the various principles being opposed, only like the vortices of Descartes and the gravitation of Newton, as more or less plausible methods of accounting for the same physical phænomena." Mr. Mansel recognizes the possibility that in some other portion of the universe, phænomena may succeed one another at random, without laws of causation, or by laws which are continually changing. We cannot, he says, *conceive* this state of things, but we can *suppose* it; and this very inability to conceive a phænomenon as taking place without a cause — in other words, this subjective necessity of the law of cause and effect — results, in his opinion, merely from the conditions of our experience. If we were asked, why a physical change must have a cause, "we* should probably reply — Because matter cannot change of itself. But why cannot we think of matter as changing itself? Because *power*, and the *origination of change*, or self-determination, have never been given to us, save in one form, that of the actions of the conscious self. What I am to conceive as taking place, I must conceive as taking place in the only manner of taking place in which it has ever been presented to me." (Here Mr. Mansel exaggerates one of the consequences of the law of Inseparable Association, through his having reached the consequence only empirically, and not analyzed it by the law.) "This reduces the law of Causality, in one sense indeed, to an empirical principle, but to an empirical principle of a very peculiar character; one namely, in which it is psychologically impossible that experience should testify in more than one way. Such principles, however empirical in their origin, are coextensive in their application with the whole domain of thought."

And further on,† "To call the Principle of Causality as thus explained a Law of Thought, would be incor-

---

* Prolegomena Logica, p. 148.   † Ibid. p. 149.

rect. We cannot think the contrary, not because the laws of thought forbid us, but because the material for thought is wanting. Thought is subject to two different modes of restriction : firstly, from its own laws, by which it is restricted as to its form ; and secondly, from the laws of intuition, by which it is restricted as to its matter. The restriction, in the present instance, is of the latter kind. We cannot conceive a course of nature without uniform succession, as we cannot conceive a being who sees without eyes or hears without ears ; because we cannot, under existing circumstances, experience the necessary intuition. But such things may notwithstanding exist ; and under other circumstances, they might become objects of possible conception, the laws of the process of conception remaining unaltered."

In this exposition, which, I do not hesitate to say, contains more sound philosophy than is to be found on the same subject in all Sir W. Hamilton's writings, I must, nevertheless, take exception to the main doctrine — that the type on which we frame our notion of Power or Causation in general, is the power, not of our volitions over matter, but of our Self over our volitions. In common with one half of the psychological world, I am wholly ignorant of my possessing any such power. I can indeed influence my own volitions, but only as other people can influence my volitions, by the employment of appropriate means. Direct power over my volitions I am conscious of none. However possible it may be that I possess this power without knowing it, a fact of consciousness contestable and contested cannot well be the source and prototype of an idea common to all mankind. I agree, however, with Mr. Mansel in the opinion which he shares with Comte, James Mill, and many others who see nothing in causation but invariable antecedence; that we naturally, and unavoidably, form our first conception of all the agencies in the universe, from the analogy of human volitions. The obvious reason is, that nearly everything which is interesting to us, comes, in our earliest infancy, either from our own voluntary motions, or (a consideration too much neglected) from the voluntary motions of others; and, among the few sequences of phænomena which at that time fall within the scope of our perceptions, scarcely any others afford us the spectacle of an apparently absolute commencement; of one thing setting others in motion without being in motion itself — or originating changes in other things, while not itself undergoing any visible change. But as I do not believe, any more than Sir W. Hamilton or Mr. Mansel, that the state of mind called volition carries with it a prophetic anticipation, which can inform us prior to experience that volition will be followed by an effect, I conceive that, no more in this than in any other case of causation, have we evidence of anything more than what experience informs us of: and it informs us of nothing except immediate, invariable, and unconditional sequence.

It is allowed on all hands that part, at least, of our idea of power, is the expectation we feel, that when the cause exists, we shall perceive the effect; but Hume himself admits that in the common notion of power there is an additional element, an animal *nisus*, as he calls it, which would be more properly termed a conception of effort. That this idea of effort enters into our notion of Power, is to my mind one of the strongest proofs that this notion is not derived from the relation of ourselves to our volitions, but from that of our volitions to our actions. The idea of Effort is essentially a notion derived from the action of our muscles, or from that combined with affections of our brain and nerves. Every one of our muscular movements has to contend against resistance, either that of an outward object, or the mere friction and weight of the moving organ; every voluntary motion is consequently attended by the muscular sensation of resistance, and if sufficiently prolonged, by the additional muscular sensation of fatigue. Effort, considered as an accompaniment of action upon the outward world, means nothing, to us, but those muscular sensations. Since we experience them whenever we voluntarily move an object, we by a mere act of natural generalization, the unconscious result of association, on beholding the same object moved by the wind or by any other agent, conceive the wind as overcoming the same obstacle, and figure it to ourselves as putting forth the same effort. Children and savages sincerely mistake it for a conscious effort. We outgrow that belief; but it is not conformable to the mode of action of the human intellect that it should pass, *uno saltu*, from a complete assimilation of the two phænomena, to conceiving them as totally different. The "natural tendency of men" so justly characterized by Mr. Mansel, "to identify, as far as may be, other agents with themselves," does not admit itself baffled, and give up the attempt after the first failure. The consequents being the same, when the mind is no longer able to suppose an exact parity in the antecedents, it still thinks that there must be something in common between them: and when obliged to admit that there is volition in one case, and a mere unconscious object in the other, it interposes between the antecedent and the consequent an abstract entity, to express what is supposed common to the animate and the inanimate agency — through which they both work, and in the absence of which nothing would be effected. This purely subjective notion, the product of generalization and abstraction acting on the real feeling of muscular or nervous effort, is Power. And this, I conceive, is the psychological rationale of Comte's great historical generalization, that the metaphysical conception (as he terms it) of the universe succeeds by a natural law to the Fetish conception, and becomes the agent by which the Fetish theory is transformed into Polytheism, this into Monotheism, and Monotheism itself is frittered away into energies and attributes of Nature, and other subordinate abstractions.

Thus much respecting Causation as a conception of the mind. The law of Cause and Effect in its objective aspect, as the fundamental principle in the order of the universe, the basis of most of our knowledge, and the guide of all our action, has been so fully treated in its numerous bearings in my System of Logic, that it is needless for me to speak further of it here.

CHAPTER XVII.

THE DOCTRINE OF CONCEPTS, OR GENERAL NOTIONS.

WE now arrive at the questions which form the transition from Psychology to Logic — from the analysis and laws of the mental operations, to the theory of the ascertainment of objective truth; the natural link between the two being the theory of the particular mental operations whereby truth is ascertained or authenticated. According to the common classification, from which Sir W. Hamilton does not deviate, these operations are three: Conception, or the formation of General Notions; Judgment; and Reasoning. We begin with the first.

On this subject two questions present themselves: first, whether there are such things as General Notions, and secondly, what they are. If there are General Notions, they must be the notions which are expressed by general terms; and concerning general terms, all who have the most elementary knowledge of the history of metaphysics are aware that there are, or once were, three different opinions.

The first is that of the Realists, who maintained that General Names are the names of General Things. Besides individual things, they recognized another kind of Things, not individual, which they technically called Second Substances, or Universals *a parte rei*. Over and above all individual men and women, there was an entity called Man — Man in general, which inhered in the individual men and women, and communicated to them its essence. These Universal Substances they considered to be a much more dignified kind of beings than individual substances, and the only ones, the cognizance of which deserved the names of Science and Knowledge. Individual existences were fleeting and perishable, but the beings called Genera and Species were immortal and unchangeable.

This, the most prevalent philosophical doctrine of the middle ages, is now universally abandoned, but remains a fact of great significance in the history of philosophy; being one of the most striking examples of the tendency of the human mind to infer difference of things from difference of names, — to suppose that every different class of names implied a corresponding class of real entities to be denoted by them. Having two such different names as "man" and "Socrates," these inquirers thought it quite out of the question that man should only be a name for Socrates, and others like him, regarded in a particular light. Man, being a name common to many, must be the name of a substance common to many, and in mystic union with the individual substances, Socrates and the rest.

In the later middle ages there grew up a rival school of metaphysicians, termed Nominalists, who, repudiating Universal Substances, held that there is nothing general except names. A name, they said, is general, if it is applied in the same acceptation to a plurality of things; but every one of the things is individual. The dispute between these two sects of philosophers was very bitter, and assumed the character of a religious quarrel; authority, too, interfered in it, and as usual on the wrong side. The Realist theory was represented as the orthodox doctrine, and belief in it was imposed as a religious duty. It could not, however, permanently resist philosophical criticism, and it perished. But it did not leave Nominalism in possession of the field. A third doctrine arose, which endeavored to steer between the two. According to this, which is known by the name of Conceptualism, generality is not an attribute solely of names, but also of thoughts. External objects indeed are all individual, but to every general name corresponds a General Notion, or Conception, called by Locke and others an Abstract Idea. General Names are the names of these Abstract Ideas.

Realism being no longer extant, nor likely to be revived, the contest at present is between Nominalism and Conceptualism; each of which counts illustrious names among its modern adherents. Sir W. Hamilton professes allegiance to both, affirming * " that the opposing parties are really at one." But his general mode of thought, and habitual phraseology, are purely Conceptualist. This is already apparent in the passage I shall first quote, which contains his statement of the fact to be explained. It is preceded by a remark on Abstraction which is perfectly just, and throws great light on the processes of human thought. (Abstraction, he says,† is simply the concentration of our attention on a particular object, or a particular quality of an object, and diversion of it from everything else.) There may be abstraction, therefore, without generalization. "The notion of the

* Lectures, ii. 286; and foot-note on Reid, p. 412.
† Lectures, ii. 287.

figure of the desk before me is an abstract idea — an idea that makes part of the total notion of that body, and on which I have concentrated my attention, in order to consider it exclusively. This idea is abstract, but it is at the same time individual; it represents the figure of this particular desk, and not the figure of any other body."

There are, therefore, "individual abstract notions;" but there are also " Abstract General Notions." These are formed " when,* comparing a number of objects, we seize on their resemblances; when we concentrate our attention on these points of similarity, thus abstracting the mind from a consideration of their differences; and when we give a name to our notion of that circumstance in which they all agree. The general notion is thus one which makes us know a quality, property, power, notion, relation; in short, any point of view under which we recognize a plurality of objects as a unity. It makes us aware of a quality, a point of view, common to many things. It is a notion of resemblance; hence the reason why general names or terms, the signs of general notions, have been called *terms of resemblance* (*termini similitudinis*). In this process of generalization, we do not stop short at a first generalization. By a first generalization we have obtained a number of classes of resembling individuals. But these classes we can compare together, observe their similarities, abstract from their differences, and bestow on their common circumstance a common name. On these second classes we can again perform the same operation, and thus ascending the scale of general notions, throwing out of view always a greater

* Lectures, ii. 287-290.

number of differences, and seizing always on fewer similarities in the formation of our classes, we arrive at length at the limit of our ascent in the notion of *being* or *existence*. Thus placed on the summit of the scale of classes, we descend by a process the reverse of that by which we have ascended; we divide and subdivide the classes, by introducing always more and more characters, and laying always fewer differences aside; the notions become more and more composite, until we at length arrive at the individual.

"I may here notice that there is a twofold quantity to be considered in notions. It is evident that, in proportion as the class is high, it will, in the first place, contain under it a greater number of classes, and in the second, will include the smallest complement of attributes. Thus *being* or *existence* contains under it every class; and yet when we say that a thing exists, we say the very least of it that is possible. On the other hand, an individual, though it contain nothing but itself, involves the largest amount of predication. For example, when I say — this is Richard, I not only affirm of the subject every class from existence down to man, but likewise a number of circumstances proper to Richard as an individual. Now, the former of these quantities, the external, is called the Extension of a notion; the latter, the internal quantity, is called its Comprehension or Intension. . . . The internal and external quantities are in the inverse ratio of each other. The greater the extension, the less the comprehension; the greater the comprehension, the less the extension."

As a popular account of Classification, for learners, to be followed by a more scientific exposition, this fully answers its purpose; but it is expressed in the common language of Conceptualists, and we should naturally conclude from it that the author was a Conceptualist. He however asserts the doctrine of the Nominalists, that there are no general notions, and that the notion suggested by a general name is always singular or individual, to be "not only true but self-evident."* And he quotes as "irrefragable" the argument of Berkeley, directed against the very possibility of Abstract Ideas. The passage from Berkeley is in the Introduction to his "Principles of Human Knowledge," and is as follows: —

"It is agreed, on all hands, that the qualities or modes of things do never really exist each of them apart by itself, and separated from all others, but are mixed, as it were, and blended together, several in the same object. But, we are told, the mind, being able to consider each quality singly, or abstracted from those other qualities with which it is united, does by that means frame to itself abstract ideas. For example, there is perceived by sight an object extended, colored, and moved; this mixed or compound idea the mind resolving into its simple constituent parts, and viewing each by itself, exclusive of the rest, does frame the abstract ideas of extension, color, and motion. Not that it is possible for color or motion to exist without extension; but only that the mind can frame to itself by *abstraction* the idea of color exclusive of extension, and of motion exclusive of both color and extension.

"Again, the mind having observed that in the particular extensions perceived by sense, there is something common and alike in all, and some other things peculiar,

* Lectures, ii. 298.

as this or that figure or magnitude, which distinguish them one from another; it considers apart or singles out by itself that which is common, making thereof a most abstract idea of extension, which is neither line, surface, nor solid, nor has any figure or magnitude, but is an idea entirely prescinded from all these. So, likewise, the mind, by leaving out of the particular colors perceived by sense, that which distinguishes them one from another, and retaining that only which is common to all, makes an idea of color in abstract, which is neither red, nor blue, nor white, nor any other determinate color. And, in like manner, by considering motion abstractedly not only from the body moved, but likewise from the figure it describes, and all particular directions and velocities, the abstract idea of motion is framed; which equally corresponds to all particular motions whatever that may be perceived by sense.

"Whether others have this wonderful faculty of abstracting their ideas, they best can tell: for myself I find, indeed, I have a faculty of imagining, or representing to myself, the ideas of those particular things I have perceived, and of variously compounding and dividing them. I can imagine a man with two heads, or the upper part of a man joined to the body of a horse. I can consider the hand, the eye, the nose, each by itself abstracted or separated from the rest of the body. But then whatever hand or eye I imagine, it must have some particular shape and color. Likewise the idea of man that I frame to myself, must be either of a white, or a black, or a tawny, a straight, or a crooked, a tall, or a low, or a middle-sized man. I cannot by any effort of thought conceive the abstract idea above described. And it is equally impossible for me to form the abstract idea of motion distinct from the body moving, and which is neither swift nor slow, curvilinear nor rectilinear; and the like may be said of all other abstract general ideas whatsoever. To be plain, I am myself able to abstract in one sense, as when I consider some particular parts or qualities separated from others, with which though they are united in some object, yet it is possible they may really exist without them. But I deny that I can abstract one from another, or conceive separately, those qualities which it is impossible should exist so separated; or that I can frame a general notion by abstracting from particulars in the manner aforesaid. Which two last are the proper acceptations of *abstraction*. And there are grounds to think most men will acknowledge themselves to be in my case." It is evident, indeed, that the existence of Abstract Ideas — the conception of the class-qualities by themselves, and not as embodied in an individual — is effectually precluded by the law of Inseparable Association.

In what manner Sir W. Hamilton manages to combine two theories, which in words are, and in substance have always been believed to be, directly contradictory of one another, we learn only from his Lectures on Logic. The hearers of those on Metaphysics, unless the Professor supplied oral elucidations which do not appear in the text, must have been considerably puzzled by finding the task of reconciling the two doctrines thrown entirely on themselves. In the Lectures on Logic, however, an attempt is made to perform it for them. It is there stated * that the General Notion, which Sir W.

* Lectures, iii. 128, 129.

Hamilton terms a Concept, and which is the notion we form of some "point of similarity" between individual objects, "is not cognizable in itself, that is, it affords no absolute or irrespective object of Knowledge, but can only be realized in consciousness by applying it, as a term of relation, to one or more of the objects, which agree in the point or points of resemblance which it expresses. . . . The moment we attempt to represent to ourselves any of these concepts, any of these abstract generalities, as absolute objects, by themselves, and out of relation to any concrete or individual realities, their relative nature at once reappears; for we find it altogether impossible to represent any of the qualities expressed by a concept, except as attached to some individual and determinate object, and their whole generality consists in this, that though we must realize them in thought under some singular of the class, we may do it under any. Thus, for example, we cannot actually represent the bundle of attributes contained in the concept *man* as an absolute object by itself, and apart from all that reduces it from a general cognition to an individual representation. We cannot figure in imagination any object adequate to the general notion or term *man;* for the man to be here imagined must be neither tall nor short, neither fat nor lean, neither black nor white, neither man nor woman, neither young nor old, but all and yet none of these at once. The relativity of our concepts is thus shown in the contradiction and absurdity of the opposite hypothesis."

This is sound doctrine, but it is pure Nominalism; as the passage first quoted from our author was pure Conceptualism. It is very necessary that I should quote the

additional elucidations given in the succeeding Lecture.*
A Concept or (General) Notion, he there says, is in
this distinguished from a "Presentation of Perception,
or Representation of Phantasy," that "our knowledge
through either of the latter is a direct, immediate, irrespective, determinate, individual, and adequate cognition; that is, a singular or individual object is known in
itself, by itself, through all its attributes, and without
reference to aught but itself. A concept, on the contrary, is an indirect, mediate, indeterminate, and partial
cognition of any one of a number of objects, but not an
actual representation either of them all, or of the whole
attributes of any one object. . . .

"Formed by comparison," concepts "express only a
relation. They cannot, therefore, be held up as an absolute object to consciousness — they cannot be represented
as universals, in imagination. They can only be thought
of in relation to some one of the individual objects they
classify, and when viewed in relation to it, they can be
represented in imagination; but then, as actually represented, they no longer constitute general attributions;
they fall back into mere special determinations of the individual object in which they are represented. Thus it is,
that the generality or universality of concepts is potential,
not actual. They are only generals, inasmuch as they
may be applied to any of the various objects they contain; but while they cannot be actually elicited into
consciousness, except in application to some one or other
of these, so they cannot be so applied without losing,
pro tanto, their universality. Take, for example, the
concept *horse*. In so far as by *horse* we merely think

* Lectures, iii. 131-137.

of the word, that is, of the combination formed by the letters *h, o, r, s, e*, — this is not a concept at all, as it is a mere representation of certain individual objects. This I only state and eliminate, in order that no possible ambiguity should be allowed to lurk. By *horse*, then, meaning not merely a representation of the word, but a concept relative to certain objects classed under it, — the concept *horse*, I say, cannot, if it remain a concept, that is, a universal attribution, be represented in imagination; but, except it be represented in imagination, it cannot be applied to any object, and except it be so applied, it cannot be realized in thought at all. You may try to escape the horns of the dilemma, but you cannot. You cannot realize in thought an absolute or irrespective concept, corresponding in universality to the application of the word; for the supposition of this involves numerous contradictions. An existent horse is not a relation, but an extended object possessed of a determinate figure, color, size, &c.; *horse*, in general, cannot, therefore, be represented, except by an image of something extended, and of a determinate figure, color, size, &c. Here now emerges the contradiction. If, on the one hand, you do not represent something extended and of a determinate figure, color, and size, then you have, indeed, the image of an individual horse, but not a universal concept coadequate with *horse* in general. For how is it possible to have an actual representation of a figure, which is not a determinate figure? but if of a determinate figure, it must be that of some one of the many different figures under which horses appear; but then, if it be only of one of these, it cannot be the general concept of the others, which it does not represent. In like manner, how is it possible to have the actual representation of a thing colored, which is not the representation of a determinate color, that is, either white, or black, or gray, or brown, &c. ? but if it be any one of these, it can only represent a horse of this or that particular color, and cannot be the general concept of horses of every color. The same result is given by the other attributes; and what I originally stated is thus manifest — that concepts have only a potential, not an actual, universality; that is, they are only universal, inasmuch as they may be applied to any of a certain class of objects, but as actually applied, they are no longer general attributions, but only special attributes."

But if, as our author says, concepts are "incapable of being realized in thought at all," except as representations of individual objects, how are they, even potentially, universal? Being mere mental creations, they *are* nothing except what they can be thought as being; and they cannot be thought as being universal, but only as being part of the thought of an individual object, though the individual object needs not always be the same. This is not a potential universality, though it is a universal potentiality. If, then, the Nominalists are thus completely right, how can it be that the Conceptualists are not wrong?

Our author thinks that the apparent difference between them is a mere case of verbal ambiguity, arising from the " employment of the same terms to express the representations of Imagination, and the notions or concepts of the Understanding." " A relation," he says,* " cannot be represented in Imagination. The two terms — the two relative objects—can be severally imaged in the sen-

---

* Lectures, ii. 312.

sible phantasy, but not the relation itself. This is the object of the Comparative Faculty, or of Intelligence Proper. To objects so different as the images of sense and the unpicturable notions of intelligence, different names ought to be given." "In Germany* the question of nominalism and conceptualism has not been agitated, and why? Simply because the German language supplies terms by which concepts (or notions of thought proper) have been contradistinguished from the presentations and representations of the subsidiary faculties."†
We are therefore to understand that although Imagination cannot figure to itself anything general or universal, Thought proper, or the Comparative Faculty, or the Understanding, can. But I do not believe that Berkeley, whose argument our author declares "irrefragable," or any other of the great Nominalist thinkers whom he enumerates, would have accepted this distinction. They would, I apprehend, have denied that the attributes included in the so-called General Notion can be *thought* separately, any more than they can be imaged separately. But why do I talk of Berkeley? Sir W. Hamilton has himself negatived the distinction in the very passage just quoted, when he says, "The concept *horse* cannot, if it remain a concept, that is, a universal attribution, be represented in imagination; but, *except it be represented in imagination*, it cannot be applied to any object, and except it be so applied, *it cannot be realized in thought*." The simple question is, Can the attributes of horse, as a class, be objects of thought, except as part of a repre-

---

* Lectures, iii. p. 136.
† The words he means are Begriff and Anschauung. See foot-note to Reid, p. 412.

sentation of some individual horse? (If the Concept cannot exist in the mind except enveloped in the miscellaneous attributes of an individual, — which is the truth, and fully recognized as such in the passages quoted from Sir W. Hamilton, — then it can no more be thought separately by the intellect, than depicted separately in the imagination.)

This notion of a Concept as something which can be thought, but "cannot in itself be depicted to sense or imagination,"* is supported, as we saw, by calling it a relation. "As the result of a comparison," a concept "necessarily † expresses a relation; and "a relation cannot be represented in imagination." If a concept is a relation, what relation is it, and between what? "As the result of a comparison," it must be a relation of resemblance among the things compared. I might observe that a Concept, which is defined by our author himself "a bundle of attributes," does not signify the mere fact of resemblance between objects; it signifies our mental representation of that in which they resemble; of the "common circumstance" which Sir W. Hamilton spoke of in his exposition of Classification. The attributes are not the relation, they are the *fundamentum relationis*. This objection, however, I can afford to wave. However inappropriate the expression, let us admit that a concept is a relation. But if a relation cannot be represented in imagination, our author has just

---

* Mansel, Prolegomena Logica, p. 15. What a mere play upon words the distinction is, is shown by Mr. Mansel's saying, a few pages later, (p. 29), "In every complete act of conception, the attributes forming the concept are contemplated as coexisting in a possible object of intuition." So that they *are* "depicted to imagination;" only they are not depicted separately.

† Lectures, iii. 123.

said that "the two terms, the two relative objects," can. The relation, according to him, though it cannot be imagined, can be thought. But can a relation be thought without thinking the related objects between which it exists? Assuredly, no: and this impossibility can the less be denied by Sir W. Hamilton, as it is the basis on which he founds his theory of Consciousness — of the direct apprehension of the Ego and the Non-ego. Consequently, when we think a relation, we must think it as existing between some particular objects which we think along with it: and a Concept, even if it be the apprehending of a relation, can only be thought as individual, not as general.

The true theory of Concepts needs not, I think, be sought farther off than in our author's own account of their origin. "In the formation," he says,* "of a concept or notion, the process may be analyzed into four momenta. In the first place, we must have a plurality of objects presented or represented by the subsidiary faculties. These faculties must furnish the rude material for elaboration. In the second place, the objects thus applied are, by an act of the Understanding, compared together, and their several qualities judged to be similar or dissimilar. In the third place, an act of volition, called Attention, concentrates consciousness on the qualities thus recognized as similar; and that concentration, by attention, on them, involves an abstraction of consciousness from those which have been recognized and thrown aside as dissimilar; for the power of consciousness is limited, and it is clear or vivid precisely in proportion to the simplicity or oneness of the object. Attention

* Lectures, iii. 132, 133.

and Abstraction are the two poles of the same act of thought: they are like the opposite scales in a balance; the one must go up as the other goes down. In the fourth place, the qualities, which by comparison are judged similar, and by attention are constituted into an exclusive object of thought, — these are already, by this process, identified in Consciousness; for they are only judged similar, inasmuch as they produce in us indiscernible effects. Their synthesis in consciousness may however, for precision's sake, be stated as a fourth step in the process. But it must be remembered, that at least the three latter steps are not, in reality, distinct and independent acts, but are only so distinguished and stated, in order to enable us to comprehend and speak about the indivisible operation in the different aspects in which we may consider it." Let me remark, in passing, the fresh illustration afforded in the last sentence, of an important principle, already several times adverted to in the theory of Naming.

The formation, therefore, of a Concept, does not consist in separating the attributes which are said to compose it, from all other attributes of the same object, and enabling us to conceive those attributes, disjoined from any others. We neither conceive them, nor think them, nor cognize them in any way as a thing apart, but solely as forming, in combination with numerous other attributes, the idea of an individual object. But, though thinking them only as part of a larger agglomeration, we have the power of fixing our attention on them, to the neglect of the other attributes with which we think them combined. While the concentration of attention actually lasts, if it is sufficiently intense, we may be temporarily unconscious of any of the other attributes, and may really, for a brief interval, have nothing present to our mind but the attributes constituent of the concept. In general, however, the attention is not so completely exclusive as this; it leaves room in consciousness for other elements of the concrete idea; though of these the consciousness is faint, in proportion to the energy of the concentrative effort, and the moment the attention relaxes, if the same concrete idea continues to be contemplated, its other constituents come out into consciousness. (General concepts, therefore, we have, properly speaking, none; we have only complex ideas of objects in the concrete: but we are able to attend exclusively to certain parts of the concrete idea; and by that exclusive attention, we enable those parts to determine exclusively the course of our thoughts as subsequently called up by association; and are in a condition to carry on a train of meditation or reasoning relating to those parts only, exactly as if we were able to conceive them separately from the rest.

What principally enables us to do this is the employment of signs, and particularly the most efficient and familiar kind of signs, viz., Names. This is a point which Sir W. Hamilton puts well and strongly, and there are many reasons for stating it in his own language.*

" The concept thus formed by an abstraction of the resembling from the non-resembling qualities of objects, would again fall back into the confusion and infinitude from which it has been called out, were it not rendered permanent for consciousness, by being fixed and ratified

* Lectures, iii. 137.

in a verbal sign. Considered in general, thought and language are reciprocally dependent; each bears all the imperfections and perfections of the other; but without language there could be no knowledge realized of the essential properties of things, and of the connection of their accidental states."

The rationale of this is, that when we wish to be able to think of objects in respect of certain of their attributes — to recall no objects but such as are invested with those attributes, and to recall them with our attention directed to those attributes exclusively — we effect this by giving to that combination of attributes, or to the class of objects which possess them, a specific Name. We create an artificial association between those attributes and a certain combination of articulate sounds, which guarantees to us that when we hear the sound, or see the written characters corresponding to it, there will be raised in the mind an idea of some object possessing those attributes, in which idea those attributes alone will be suggested vividly to the mind, our consciousness of the remainder of the concrete idea being faint. As the name has been directly associated only with those attributes, it is as likely, in itself, to recall them in any one concrete combination as in any other. What combination it shall recall in the particular case, depends on recency of experience, accidents of memory, or the influence of other thoughts which have been passing, or are even then passing, through the mind; accordingly the combination is far from being always the same, and seldom gets itself strongly associated with the name which suggests it; while the association of the name with the attributes that form its conventional signification, is constantly becoming stronger. The association of that particular set of attributes with a given word, is what keeps them together in the mind by a stronger tie than that with which they are associated with the remainder of the concrete image. To express the meaning in Sir W. Hamilton's phraseology, this association gives them a unity* in our consciousness. It is only when this has been accomplished, that we possess what Sir W. Hamilton terms a Concept; and this is the whole of the mental phænomenon involved in the matter. We have a concrete representation, certain of the component elements of which are distinguished by a mark, designating them for special attention; and this attention, in cases of exceptional intensity, excludes all consciousness of the others.

Sir W. Hamilton thinks, however, that we can form, though scarcely preserve, concepts without the aid of signs. "Language," he says, † "is the attribution of signs to our cognitions of things. But as a cognition must have been already there, before it could receive a sign, consequently, that knowledge which is denoted by

* One of the best and profoundest passages in all Sir W. Hamilton's writings, is that in which he points out (though only incidentally) what are the conditions of our ascribing Unity to any aggregate. "Though it is only by experience we come to attribute an external unity to aught continuously extended, that is, consider it as a system or constituted whole, still, in so far as we do so consider it, *we think the parts as held together by a certain force*, and the whole, therefore, as endowed with a power of resisting their distraction. It is, indeed, only by finding that a material continuity resists distraction, that we view it as more than a fortuitous aggregation of many bodies, that is, as a single body. The material universe, for example, though not *de facto* continuously extended, we consider as one system in so far, but only in so far, as we find all bodies tending together by reciprocal attraction." Dissertations on Reid, pp. 852, 853.

† Lectures, iii. 138–140.

the formation and application of a word, must have preceded the symbol which denotes it." A sign, however, he continues, in one of his happiest specimens of illustration, "is necessary to give stability to our intellectual progress, — to establish each step in our advance as a new starting point for our advance to another beyond. A country may be overrun by an armed host, but it is only conquered by the establishment of fortresses. (Words are the fortresses of thought.) They enable us to realize our dominion over what we have already overrun in thought; to make every intellectual conquest the basis of operations for others still beyond. Or another illustration: You have all heard of the process of tunnelling, of tunnelling through a sand-bank. In this operation it is impossible to succeed, unless every foot, nay, almost every inch, in our progress, be secured by an arch of masonry, before we attempt the excavation of another. Now, language is to the mind precisely what the arch is to the tunnel. The power of thinking and the power of excavation are not dependent on the word in the one case, on the mason-work in the other; but without these subsidiaries, neither process could be carried on beyond its rudimentary commencement. Though, therefore, we allow that every movement forward in language must be determined by an antecedent movement forward in thought, still, unless thought be accompanied, at each point of its evolution, by a corresponding evolution of language, its further development is arrested. . . . Admitting even that the mind is capable of certain elementary concepts without the fixation and signature of language, still these are but sparks which would twinkle only to expire, and it requires words to give them prominence, and by enabling us to collect and elaborate them into new concepts, to raise, out of what would otherwise be only scattered and transitory scintillations, a vivid and enduring light."

Mr. Mansel, who agrees with Sir W. Hamilton in the essentials of his doctrine of Concepts, goes beyond him on this point, being of opinion that without signs we could not form concepts at all. The objection that we must have had the concept before we could have given it a name, he meets by the suggestion that names when first used are names only of individual objects, but being extended from one object to another under the law of Association by Resemblance, they become specially associated with the points of resemblance, and thus generate the Concept. In Mr. Mansel's opinion,* no one, "without the aid of symbols," can advance "beyond the individual objects of sense or imagination. In the presence of several individuals of the same species, the eye may observe points of similarity between them; and in this no symbol is needed; but every feature thus observed is the distinct attribute of a distinct individual, and however similar, cannot be regarded as identical. For example: I see lying on the table before me a number of shillings of the same coinage. Examined severally, the image and superscription of each is undistinguishable from that of its fellow; but in viewing them side by side, *space* is a necessary condition of my perception; and the difference of locality is sufficient to make them distinct, though similar, individuals. The same is the case with any representative image, whether in a mirror, in a painting, or in the imagination, waking or dreaming. It can

* Prolegomena Logica, pp. 15-17.

only be depicted as occupying a certain place; and thus as an individual, and the representative of an individual. It is true that I cannot say that it represents this particular coin rather than that; and consequently it may be considered as the representative of all, successively, but not simultaneously. To find a representative which shall embrace all at once, I must divest it of the condition of occupying space; and this, experience assures us, can only be done by means of *symbols*, verbal or other, by which the concept is fixed in the understanding. Such, for example, is a verbal description of the coin in question, which contains a collection of attributes freed from the condition of locality, and hence from all resemblance to an object of sense. If we substitute Time for Space, the same remarks will be equally applicable to the objects of our internal consciousness. Every appetite and desire, every affection and volition, as *presented*, is an individual state of consciousness, distinguished from every other by its relation to a different period of time. States in other respects exactly similar may succeed one another at regular intervals; but the hunger which I feel to-day is an individual feeling as numerically distinct from that which I felt yesterday or that which I shall feel to-morrow, as a shilling lying in my pocket is from a similar shilling lying at the bank. Whereas my *notion* of hunger, or fear, or volition, is a general concept, having no relation to one period of time rather than to another, and, as such, requires, like other concepts, a representative sign. Language, taking the word in its widest sense, is thus indispensable, not merely to the communication, but to the formation of Thought."

This is a step in advance of Sir W. Hamilton's doctrine,

but is open to the same criticism, namely, that after showing all Concepts to be concrete and individual, it endeavors to make out, by an indirect process, a sort of abstract existence for them. According to Mr. Mansel, signs are necessary to concepts, because signs alone can give this abstract existence. Signs are wanted, to emancipate our mental apprehension from the conditions of space and time which are in all our concrete representations. The other miscellaneous attributes which have to be cast out, do not, he seems to think, embarrass the formation of the Concept; but it is hampered by the conditions of space and time, and only by means of a sign can we get rid of these. But *do* we get rid of them by employing signs? To take Mr. Mansel's own instance: When we establish our concept of a shilling by a verbal description of the coin, does the description enable us to conceive a shilling as not occupying any space? When we think of a shilling, either by name or anonymously, is not the circumstance of occupying space called up as an inevitable part of the mental representation? Not, indeed, the circumstance of occupying a *given part* of space; but if that is what Mr. Mansel means, it would follow that we need signs to enable us to form a mental representation even of an individual object, provided it be movable: for the same object does not always occupy the same part of space. The truth is, that the condition of space cannot be excluded; it is an essential part of the concept of Body, and of every kind of bodies. But any given space, or any given time, is not a part of the concept, any more than any of the slight peculiarities in which one shilling differs from another are part of the concept of a shilling. Some space and time, and some individual peculiarities, are always thought along with the concept, and make up the whole of which it can only be thought as a part: but these are not directly recalled by the class name, and the attributes composing the concept are. Mr. Mansel, therefore, has not, I conceive, hit the mark: but in the passages which follow, there is real power of metaphysical discrimination.

"Observe * what actually takes place in the formation of language and thought among ourselves. To the child learning to speak, words are not the signs of thoughts, but of intuitions;† the words *man* and *horse* do not represent a collection of attributes, but are only the name of the individual now before him. It is not until the name has been successively appropriated to various individuals, that reflection begins to inquire into the common features of the class. Language, therefore, as taught to the infant, is chronologically prior to thought and posterior to sensation. In inquiring how far the same process can account for the invention of language, which now takes place in the learning it, the real question at issue is simply this: Is the act of giving names to *individual objects of sense* a thing so completely beyond the power of a man created in the full maturity of his faculties, that we must suppose a Divine Instructor performing precisely the same office as is now performed for the infant by his mother or his nurse; teaching him, that is, to associate *this sound* with *this sight?* . . . All concepts are formed by means of signs which have pre-

* Prolegomena Logica, pp. 19, 20, and 29-31.
† By intuitions Mr. Mansel means the Anschauungen of Kant, or what Mr. Mansel himself otherwise calls Presentations of Sense, to which he adds Representations of Imagination.

viously been representative of individual objects only.
. . . Similarities are noticed earlier than differences;
and our first abstractions may be said to be performed
for us, as we learn to give the same name to individuals
presented to us under slight, and at first unnoticed, circumstances of distinction. The same name is thus
applied to different objects, long before we learn to analyze the growing powers of speech and thought, to ask
what we mean by each several instance of its application,
to correct and fix the signification of words used at first
vaguely and obscurely. To point out each successive
stage of the process by which signs of intuition become
gradually signs of thought, is as impossible as to point
out the several moments at which the growing child
receives each successive increase of his stature."

These remarks of Mr. Mansel remove, as it seems to
me, the only real argument for the supposition that Concepts, or what are called General Notions, are formed
without the aid of signs. But the counter-doctrine must
be received with an important reservation. Signs are
necessary, but the signs need not be artificial; there are
such things as natural signs. The only reality there is
in the Concept is, that we are somehow enabled and led,
not once or accidentally, but in the common course of our
thoughts, to attend specially, and more or less exclusively, to certain parts of the presentation of sense or
representation of imagination which we are conscious of.
Now, what is there to make us do this? There must
be something which, as often as it recurs either to our
senses or to our thoughts, *directs* our attention to those
particular elements in the perception or in the idea; and
whatever performs this office is virtually a sign; but it

needs not be a word: the process certainly takes place, to a limited extent, in the inferior animals; and even with human beings who have but a small vocabulary, many processes of thought take place habitually by other symbols than words. It is a doctrine of one of the most fertile thinkers of modern times, Auguste Comte, that besides the logic of signs, there is a logic of images, and a logic of feelings. In many of the familiar processes of thought, and especially in uncultured minds, a visual image serves instead of a word. Our visual sensations — perhaps only because they are almost always present along with the impressions of our other senses — have a facility of becoming associated with them. Hence, the characteristic visual appearance of an object easily gathers round it, by association, the ideas of all other peculiarities which have, in frequent experience, coexisted with that appearance: and, summoning up these with a strength and certainty far surpassing that of the merely casual associations which it may also raise, it concentrates the attention on them. This is an image serving for a sign — the logic of images. The same function may be fulfilled by a feeling. Any strong and highly interesting feeling, connected with one attribute of a group, spontaneously classifies all objects according as they possess or do not possess that attribute. We may be tolerably certain that the things capable of satisfying hunger form a perfectly distinct class in the mind of any of the more intelligent animals; quite as much so as if they were able to use or understand the word food. We here see in a strong light the important truth, that hardly anything universal can be affirmed in psychology except the laws of association. As almost all general propositions which can be laid down respecting Mind, are consequences of these laws, so do these ultimate laws, in varying cases, generate different derivative laws; and are continually raising up exceptions to the empirical generalizations yielded by direct psychical observation, which, so far as true, being mere cases of the wider laws, are always limited by them.

We have now attained a theory of Classification, of Class Notions, and of Class Names, which is clear, free from difficulties, and, in its essential elements, understood and assented to by Sir W. Hamilton. With the exception of a few minor matters, I find no fault in his theory. It is where his theory ends and his practice begins, that I am obliged to diverge from him. His theory is a complete condemnation of his practice. His theory is that of Nominalism; but he affirms, in opposition to every Conceptualist, that Nominalism and Conceptualism are the same, and on this justification expounds all the operations of the intellect in the language, and on the assumptions of Conceptualism. If a Concept does not exist as a separate or independent object of thought, but is always a mere part of a concrete image, and has nothing that discriminates it from the other parts except a special share of attention, guaranteed to it by special association with a name, what is meant by the paramount place assigned to Concepts in all the intellectual processes? Can it be right to found the whole of Logic, the entire theory of Judgment and Reasoning, upon a thing which has merely a fictitious or constructive existence? Is it correct to say that we think by means of Concepts? Would it not convey both a clearer and a truer meaning, to say that we think by means of ideas of concrete phænomena, such as are presented in experience or represented in imagination, and by means of names, which, being in a peculiar manner associated with certain elements of the concrete images, arrest our attention on those elements? Sir W. Hamilton has told us that a concept cannot, as such, be "realized in thought," or "elicited into consciousness." Can it be, that we think and reason by means of that which cannot be thought, of which we cannot become conscious? Of course Sir W. Hamilton did not mean, nor do I, that we cannot think or be conscious of the attributes which are said to compose the concept; but we can only be conscious of them as forming a representation jointly with other attributes which do not enter into the concept. And the difference between the parts of the same representation which are inside and those which are outside what is called the concept, is not that the former are attended to and the latter not, for neither of these is always true. It is, that foreseeing that we shall frequently or occasionally desire to attend only to the former, we have made for ourselves, or have received from our predecessors, a contrivance for being reminded of them, which also serves for fixing our exclusive attention upon them when called to mind. To say, therefore, that we think by means of concepts, is only a circuitous and obscure way of saying that we think by means of general or class names. To give an intelligible idea of the fact, we always need to translate it out of the former language into the latter. It is possible, no doubt, so to define the terms that both expressions shall mean the same thing. But the less appropriate language has the immense disadvantage, that it cannot be used without tacitly assuming that these mere parts of our complex concrete perceptions and ideas have a separate mental existence, which is admitted not to belong to them. No one, more fully than Sir W. Hamilton, recognizes the true theory; but the acknowledgment only serves him as an excuse for delivering himself up unreservedly to all the logical consequences of the false theory. To read the account which he and Mr. Mansel, in common with the great majority of modern logicians, give of our intellectual processes, — which they always make to consist essentially of some operation practised upon concepts, — no one would ever imagine that concepts were not complete, rounded off, distinct and separate possessions of the mind, habitually dealt with by it quite apart from anything else; and this, in the general opinion of Conceptualists, they are: but according to Sir W. Hamilton and Mr. Mansel, they are secretly, all the while, incapable of being thought except as parts of something else which has always to be dealt with along with them, but which these philosophers, in their expositions, suppress as completely as if they had forgotten that its necessary presence is part of their theory. For these and other reasons, I consider it nothing less than a misfortune, that the words Concept, General Notion, or any other phrase to express the supposed mental modification corresponding to a class name, should ever have been invented. Above all, I hold that nothing but confusion ever results from introducing the term Concept into Logic, and that instead of the Concept of a class, we should always speak of the signification of a class name.*

* It is for want of apprehending this view of the matter that Sir W. Hamilton (Lectures, iii. 31, 32) brings a charge of self-contradiction against

The signification of a class name has two aspects, corresponding to the distinction to which Sir W. Hamilton attaches so much importance, between the Extension and the Comprehension of a concept; which is merely a bad expression for the distinction between the two modes of signification of a concrete general name. Most names are still, what according to Mr. Mansel they all were originally, names of objects; and do not cease to be so by becoming class names; but, though names of objects, they become expressive of certain attributes of those objects, and when predicated of an object, they affirm of it those attributes. The name is said, in the language of logicians, to *de*note the objects and *con*note the attributes. *White* denotes chalk and other white substances, and connotes the particular color which is common to them. *Bird* denotes eagles, sparrows, crows, geese, and so forth, and connotes life, the possession of wings, and the other properties by which we are guided in applying the name. The various objects denoted by the class name are what is meant by the Extension of the con-

---

Archbishop Whately, because, having, in the commencement and throughout his treatise on Logic, represented Reasoning as the object-matter of that science, he, in certain passages, says that Logic is entirely conversant with the use of language. This is a contradiction only from Sir W. Hamilton's point of view. If Archbishop Whately's had been the same — if he had thought as Sir W. Hamilton did respecting Concepts, considered as the object-matter of Reasoning — he would have been justly liable to the imputation cast upon him. But the Archbishop's two statements are perfectly consistent, if we suppose his opinion to have been, that the formation of Concepts, and the subsequent process of combining them in arguments, are themselves processes of language. This doctrine (which is in fact Mr. Mansel's) Sir W. Hamilton deems too absurd to be imputed to the Archbishop (Discussions, p. 138). Yet he fancies himself a Nominalist, and does understand and assent to all the arguments of Nominalism. Unfortunately an intelligent assent to one of two conflicting doctrines is in his case no guarantee against holding, for all practical purposes, the other.

cept, while the attributes connoted are its Comprehension. It must be remarked, however, that the Extension is not anything intrinsic to the concept; it is the sum of all the objects, in our concrete images of which, the concept is included: but the Comprehension is the very concept itself, for the concept means nothing but our mental representation of the sum of the attributes composing it.

And here it is important to take notice of a psychological truth, which forms an additional reason for preferring the expression that we think by general names, to that of thinking by concepts. Since the concept only exists as a part of a concrete mental state, if we say that we think by means of it, and not by the whole which it is a part of, it ought at least to be *the* part by which we think. Since that is the only distinction between it and the remainder of the presentation or representation in which it is imbedded, at least that distinction should be real: all which enters into the concept ought to be operative in thought. So far is this from being true, that in our processes of thought, seldom more than a part, sometimes a very small part, of what is comprehended in the concept, is attended to, or comes into play. This is forcibly stated, though in Conceptualist phraseology, by Mr. Mansel. "We can," he says,* "and in the majority of cases do, employ concepts as instruments of thought, without submitting them to the test of even possible individualization.... I cannot *conceive* a triangle which is neither equilateral, nor isosceles, nor scalene; but I can judge and reason about a triangle without at the moment trying to conceive it

* Prolegomena Logica, pp. 31, 32.

at all. This is one of the consequences of the representation of concepts by language. *The sign is substituted for the notion signified;* a step which considerably facilitates the performance of complex operations of thought; but in the same proportion endangers the logical accuracy of each successive step, as we do not, in each, stop to verify our signs. Words, as thus employed, resemble algebraical symbols, which, during the process of a long calculation, we combine in various relations to each other, without at the moment thinking of the original signification assigned to each." The attempt to stand at once on two incompatible theories, leads to strange freaks of expression. Mr. Mansel describes us as thinking by means of concepts which we are incapable of forming, and do not even attempt to form, but use the signs instead. Yet he will not consent to call this thinking by the signs, but insists that it is the concepts which are even in this case the "instruments of thought." It is surely a very twisted logical position which, when he is so entirely right in what he has to say, compels him to use so strangely contorted a mode of saying it.

The same important psychological fact is excellently illustrated by Sir W. Hamilton in one of the very best chapters of his works, the Tenth Lecture on Logic, in which it is stated as follows: * "As a notion or concept is the fictitious whole or unity made up of a plurality of attributes, — a whole, too, often of a very complex multiplicity; and as this multiplicity is only mentally held together, inasmuch as the concept is fixed and ratified in a sign or word; it frequently hap-

* Lectures, iii. 171.

pens that, in its employment, the word does not suggest the whole amount of thought for which it is the adequate expression, but, on the contrary, we frequently give and take the sign, either with an obscure or indistinct consciousness of its meaning, or even without an actual consciousness of its signification at all." The word does not always serve the purpose of fixing our attention on the whole of the attributes which it connotes; some of them may be only recalled to mind faintly, others possibly not at all: a phænomenon easy to be accounted for by the laws of Obliviscence. But the part of the attributes signified which the word does recall, may be all that it is necessary for us to think of, at the time and for the purpose in hand; it may be a sufficient part to set going all the associations by means of which we proceed through that thought to ulterior thoughts. Indeed, it is because part of the attributes have generally sufficed for that purpose, that the habit is acquired of not attending to the remainder. When the attributes not attended to are really of no importance for the end in view, and if attended to would not have altered the results of the mental process, there is no harm done: much of our valid thinking is carried on in this manner, and it is to this that our thinking processes owe, in a great measure, their proverbial rapidity. This kind of thinking was called, by Leibnitz, Symbolical. A passage of one of the early writings of that eminent thinker, in which it is brought to notice, with his accustomed clearness, is translated by Sir W. Hamilton, from whom I requote it.*

"For the most part, especially in an analysis of any

* Lectures, iii. 181.

length, we do not view at once (non simul intuemur) the whole characters or attributes of the thing, but in place of these we employ signs, the explication of which into what they signify we are wont, at the moment of actual thought, to omit, knowing or believing that we have this explication always in our power. Thus, when I think a chiliagon (or polygon of a thousand sides) I do not always consider the various attributes of the side, of the equality, and of the number or thousand, but use these words (whose meaning is obscurely and imperfectly presented to the mind) in lieu of the notions which I have of them, because I remember, that I possess the signification of these words, though their application and explication I do not at present deem to be necessary:— this mode of thinking, I am used to call *blind* or *symbolical:* we employ it in Algebra and in Arithmetic, but in fact universally. And certainly when the notion is very complex, we cannot think at once all the ingredient notions: but where this is possible, — at least, inasmuch as it is possible, — I call the cognition *intuitive.* Of the primary elements of our notions, there is given no other knowledge than the intuitive: as of our composite notions there is, for the most part, possible only a symbolical." *

* It will be remarked that Leibnitz here employs the word Intuitive in a sense entirely different from that which British metaphysicians, and Sir W. Hamilton himself, attach to the word. In Leibnitz's sense, we cognize a thing intuitively in as far as we are conscious of the attributes of the thing itself; symbolically in as far as we merely think of its name, as standing for an aggregate of attributes without having all, or perhaps any of those attributes present to our mind. I cannot help being surprised that Sir W. Hamilton should have regarded this distinction of Leibnitz as coinciding with that of Kant and the modern German thinkers between Begriff and Anschauung, in other words Concept and Presentation. Sir W. Hamilton considers Begriff to be a name for "the symbolical notions

Yet the elements which are thus habitually left out, and of which in the case of a composite notion, if Leibnitz is right, some *must* be left out, are really parts of the signification of the name, and if the word Concept has any meaning, are parts of the concept. Leibnitz, accordingly, knew better than to say, as Mr. Mansel says and Sir W. Hamilton implies, that even in these cases we think by means of the concept. According to him we sometimes think entirely without the concept, generally only by a part of it, which may be the wrong part, or an insufficient part, but which may be, and in all sound thinking is, sufficient. On this point, therefore, a false apprehension of the facts of thought is conveyed by the doctrine which speaks of Concepts as its instrument. Leibnitz would perhaps have said, that the name is the instrument in one of the two kinds of thinking, and the concept in the other. The more reasonable doctrine surely is, that the name is the instrument in both; the difference being, that in one case it does the whole, and in the other only a part, perhaps the minimum, of the work for which it is intended and fitted, that of reminding us of the portions of our concrete mental representations which we expect that we shall have need of attending to.

In summary; if the doctrine, that we think by con-

of the understanding," in contrast with Anschauung, which means "the intuitive presentations of Sense and representations of Imagination." (Lectures, iii. 183.) He is right as to Anschauung, but as for "symbolical notions of the understanding," our thinking is called by Leibnitz symbolical exactly in so far as it takes place without any "notions," any concept or Begriff at all, by virtue of the mere knowledge that there is a Begriff which the word represents, and which we could recall if we wanted it. When thinking is completely symbolical, the meaning of the word is eliminated from thought, and only the word remains: as in Leibnitz's own illustration from algebra.

cepts, means that a concept is the only thing present to the mind along with the individual object which (to use Sir W. Hamilton's language) we think under the concept, this is not true: since there is always present a concrete idea or image, of which the attributes comprehended in the concept are only, and cannot be conceived as anything but, a part. Again, if it be meant that the concept, though only a part of what is present to the mind, is the part which is operative in the act of thought, neither is this true: for what is operative is, in a great majority of cases, much less than the entire concept, being that portion only which we have retained the habit of distinctly attending to. (In neither of these senses, therefore, do we think by means of the concept: and all that is true is, that when we refer any object or set of objects to a class, some at least of the attributes included in the concept are present to the mind; being recalled to consciousness and fixed in attention, through their association with the class-name.)

Before leaving this part of the subject, it seems necessary to remark, that Sir W. Hamilton is by no means consistent in the extension which he gives to the signification of the word Concept. In most cases in which he uses it, he makes it synonymous with General Notion, and allows concepts of classes only, not of individuals.* It is thus that he expressly defines the term. "A Concept," he says,† "is the cognition or idea of the general character or characters, point or points, in which a plurality of objects coincide." "Concept," he says again, ‡ "is convertible with *general notion*, or, more correctly,

---

* Lectures, iii. 119, 121, 127, 128, 130, *cum multis aliis*.
† Ibid. p. 122.   ‡ Discussions, p. 283.

notion simply." He speaks of the extending of the term to our direct knowledge of individuals, as an "abusive employment" of it.* He also says,† "Notions and Concepts are sometimes designated by the style of *general notions, — general conceptions.* This is superfluous, for in propriety of speech, notions and concepts are, in their very nature, general." In certain places, however, he speaks of concepts of individuals. "If I think ‡ of Socrates as son of Sophroniscus, as Athenian, as philosopher, as pugnosed, these are only so many characters, limitations, or determinations which I predicate of Socrates, which distinguish him from all other men, and together make up my *notion* or *concept* of him." And again,§ "When the Extension of a concept becomes a minimum, that is, when it contains no other notions under it, it is called an individual." And further on, ‖ "It is evident that the more distinctive characters the concept contains, the more minutely it will distinguish and determine, and that if it contain a plenum of distinctive characters, it must contain the distinctive, the determining characters of some individual object. How do the two quantities now stand? In regard to the comprehension or depth, it is evident that it is here at its maximum, the concept being a complement of the whole attributes of an individual object, which, by these attributes, it thinks and discriminates from every other. On the contrary, the extension or breadth of the concept is here at its minimum; for, as the extension is great in proportion to the number of objects to which the concept can be applied, and as the

* Lectures, iii. 121. † Ibid. p. 212. ‡ Ibid. p. 78.
§ Ibid. p. 146. ‖ Ibid. p. 148.

object here is only an individual one, it is evident that it could not be less without ceasing to exist at all." But, in the sequel of the same exposition, he again seems to surrender this use of the word Concept as an improper one, saying,* "If a concept be an individual, that is, only a bundle of individual qualities, it is . . . not a proper abstract concept at all, but only a concrete representation of Imagination." And indeed, no other doctrine is consistent with the proposition elsewhere laid down by our author (though founded, as I think, on an error), that the words Conception, Concept, Notion, should be limited to the thought of what cannot be represented in imagination, as the thought suggested by a general term." †

Mr. Mansel, on the contrary, justifies the phrase, concept of an individual, maintaining that "the subjects of all logical judgments are concepts." ‡ "The man," he says,§ "as an individual existing at some past time, cannot become immediately an object of thought, and hence is not, properly speaking, the subject of any logical proposition. If I say, Cæsar was the conqueror of Pompey, the immediate object of my thought is not Cæsar as an individual existing two thousand years ago, but a concept now present in my mind, comprising certain attributes which I believe to have coexisted in a certain man. I may *historically* know that these attributes existed in one individual only; and hence my concept, virtually universal, is actually singular, from the accident of its being predicable of that individual only. But there is no *logical* objection to the theory that the whole history of mankind may be repeated at recurring

* Lectures, iii. 152. † Foot-note to Reid, p. 360.
‡ Prolegomena Logica, p. 63. § Ibid. p. 62.

intervals, and that the name and actions of Cæsar may be successively found in various individuals at corresponding periods of every cycle."

If this be so, one of two things follows. Either, if I met with a person who exactly corresponded to the concept I have formed of Cæsar, I must suppose that this person actually is Cæsar, and lived in the century preceding the birth of Christ; or else, I cannot think of Cæsar as Cæsar, but only as *a* Cæsar; and all those which are mistakenly called proper names are general names, the names of virtual classes, signifying a set of attributes which carry the name with them, wherever they are found. Either theory seems to be sufficiently refuted by stating it. Surely the true doctrine is that of Sir W. Hamilton, that what is called my concept of Cæsar is the presentation in imagination of the individual Cæsar as such. Mr. Mansel might have learned better from Reid, who says, " Most words (indeed all general words) are the signs of ideas; but proper names are not; they signify individual things, and not ideas." * And again, soon after : †
" The same proper name is never applied to several individuals on account of their similitude, because the very intention of a proper name is to distinguish one individual from all others; and hence it is a maxim in grammar that proper names have no plural number. A proper name signifies nothing but the individual whose name it is; and when we apply it to the individual, we neither affirm nor deny anything concerning him." The whole of Reid's doctrine respecting names and general notions is not only far more clear, but nearer to the true doctrine

---

* Essays on the Intellectual Powers, Works, p. 404. By ideas Reid here means (as he fully explains) attributes.
† Ibid. p. 412.

of the connotation of names, than Sir W. Hamilton's or Mr. Mansel's.*

> * Accordingly, when Sir W. Hamilton (foot-note to p. 691) contends, in opposition to Reid, that there are definitions which are not nominal, but *notional,* since they have for their object "the more accurate determination of the contents of a notion," there is no real difference of meaning between them; the contents of a notion being simply the connotation of a name.
>
> Sir W. Hamilton enters, at some length, into the explanation of what is meant by the clearness, and the distinctness, of Concepts. A concept, according to him, is clear, if we can distinguish it as a whole from other concepts; distinct, if we can discriminate the characters or attributes of which it is the sum (Lectures, iii. 158). The last statement is intelligible, but what does the first mean? If we do not know of what characters the concept is composed, seeing that it has no existence but in those characters, how can we know it so as to distinguish it from other concepts? Our author certainly had not a clear conception of what makes a conception clear; and the proof is, that he adopts as part of his text a quotation from Esser's Logic, in which Esser makes the clearness of a concept to depend on our being able to distinguish, not the concept itself, but the objects included under it; on our being able, in short, to apply the class-name correctly. According to Esser, "a concept is said to be clear, when the degree of consciousness by which it is accompanied is sufficient to discriminate" not itself from other concepts, but "what we think in and through it, from what we think in and through other notions:" and "notions absolutely clear" are "notions whose *objects*" (not, as Sir W. Hamilton says, *themselves*) cannot "possibly be confounded with aught else, whether known or unknown." (Lectures, iii. 160, 161.) So that according to Esser the clearness of a concept has reference to its Extension, the distinctness to its Comprehension. This is not the only instance in which our author helps out his own expositions by passages from other authors, written from a point of view more or less different from his own.

CHAPTER XVIII.

OF JUDGMENT.

Though, as has appeared in the last chapter, the proposition that we think by concepts is, if not positively untrue, at least an unprecise and misleading expression of the truth, it is not, however, to be concluded that Sir W. Hamilton's view of Logic, being wholly grounded on that proposition, must be destitute of value. Many writers have given good and valuable expositions of the principles and rules of Logic, from the Conceptualist point of view. The doctrines which they have laid down respecting Conception, Judgment, and Reasoning, have been capable of being rendered into equivalent statements respecting Terms, Propositions, and Arguments: these, indeed, were what the writers really had in their thoughts, and there was little amiss except a mode of expression which attempted to be more philosophical than it knew how to be. To say nothing of less illustrious examples, this is true of all the properly logical part of Locke's Essay. His admirable Third Book requires hardly any other alteration to bring it up to the scientific level of the present time, than to be corrected by blotting out everywhere the words Abstract Idea, and replacing them by "the connotation of the class-name."

We shall, accordingly, proceed to examine the explanation of Judgment, and of Reasoning, which Sir W. Hamilton has built on the foundation of the doctrine of Concepts.

"To judge," he says,* "is to recognize the relation of congruence or of confliction in which two concepts, two individual things, or a concept and an individual, compared together, stand to each other. This recognition, considered as an internal consciousness, is called a Judgment; considered as expressed in language, it is called a Proposition or Predication."

To be certain of understanding this, we must inquire what is meant by a relation of congruence or of confliction between concepts. To consult Sir W. Hamilton's definitions of words is, as we have seen, not a sure way of ascertaining the sense in which he practically uses them; but it is one of the ways, and we are bound to employ it in the first instance. A few pages before, he has given a sort of definition of these terms.† "Concepts, in relation to each other, are said to be either *Congruent* or *Agreeing*, inasmuch as they may be connected in thought; or *Conflictive*, inasmuch as they cannot. The confliction constitutes the *Opposition* of notions." This opposition is twofold. "1°. *Immediate* or *Contradictory* Opposition, called likewise *Repugnance;* and 2°. *Mediate* or *Contrary* Opposition. The former emerges when one concept abolishes directly, or by simple negation, what another establishes; the latter, when one concept does this not directly, or by simple negation, but through the affirmation of something else."

Congruent Concepts, therefore, do not mean concepts which coincide, either wholly or in any of their parts, but such as are mutually compatible; capable of being predicated of the same individual; of being combined in

---

* Lectures, iii. 225, 226.   † Ibid. pp. 213, 214.

the same presentation of sense or representation of imagination. This is more clearly expressed in a passage from Krug, which our author adopts as part of his own exposition.* "Identity is not to be confounded with Agreement or Congruence, nor Diversity with Confliction. All identical concepts are, indeed, congruent, but all congruent notions are not identical. Thus *learning* and *virtue, beauty* and *riches, magnanimity* and *stature*, are congruent notions, inasmuch as, in thinking a thing, they can easily be combined in the notion we form of it, although themselves very different from each other. In like manner, all conflicting notions are diverse or different notions, for unless different, they could not be mutually conflictive; but, on the other hand, all different concepts are not conflictive; but those only whose difference is so great that each involves the negation of the other; as for example, *virtue* and *vice, beauty* and *deformity, wealth* and *poverty*." Thus interpreted, our author's doctrine is, that to judge, is to recognize whether two concepts, two things, or a concept and a thing, are capable of coexisting as parts of the same mental representation. This I will call Sir W. Hamilton's first theory of Judgment; I will venture to add, his best.

But he soon after proceeds to say,† "When two or more thoughts are given in consciousness, there is in general an endeavor on our part to discover in them, and to develop, a relation of congruence or of confliction; that is, we endeavor to find out whether these thoughts will or will not coincide — may or may not be blended into one. If they coincide, we judge, we enounce, their congruence or compatibility; if they do not coincide, we

---

* Lectures, iii. 214. † Ibid. pp. 226, 227.

judge, we enounce, their confliction or incompatibility. Thus, if we compare the thoughts, *water*, *iron*, and *rusting*, find them congruent, and connect them into a single thought, thus, — *water rusts iron*, — in that case we form a judgment.

"But if two notions be judged congruent, — in other words, be conceived as one, — this their unity can only be realized in consciousness, inasmuch as one of these notions is viewed as an attribute or determination of the other. For, on the one hand, it is impossible for us to think as one two attributes, that is, two things viewed as determining, and yet neither determining or qualifying the other; nor, on the other hand, two subjects, that is, two things thought as determined, and yet neither of them determined or qualified by the other."

In this regress from *ignotum* to *ignotius*, the next thing to be ascertained is, what relation between one thought and another is signified by the verb "to determine." Such explanation as our author deemed it necessary to give, may be found a few pages further back. He there stated,* that by determining a notion, he means adding on more characters, by each of which "we limit or determine more and more the abstract vagueness or extension of the notion; until at last, if every attribute be annexed, the sum of attributes contained in the notion becomes convertible with the sum of attributes of which some concrete individual or reality is the complement." Substituting, then, the definition for what it defines, we find our author's opinion to be, that two notions can only be congruent, that is, capable of being blended into one, if we conceive one of them as adding on additional attri-

* Lectures, iii. 194.

butes to the other. This is not yet very clear. We must have recourse to his illustration. "For example,* we cannot think the two attributes *electrical* and *polar* as a single notion, unless we convert the one of these attributes into a subject, to be determined or qualified by the other." Do we ever think the two attributes electrical and polar as a single notion? We think them as distinct parts of the same notion, that is, as attributes which are constantly combined. "But if we do, — if we say, *what is electrical is polar*, — we at once reduce the duality to unity; *we judge that polar is one of the constituent characters of the notion electrical, or that what is electrical is contained under the class of things, marked out by the common character of polarity.*" The last italics are mine, intended to mark the place where an intelligible meaning first emerges. "We may,† therefore, articulately define a judgment or proposition to be the product of that act in which we pronounce that of two notions, thought as subject and as predicate, *the one does or does not constitute a part of the other*, either in the quantity of Extension, or in the quantity of Comprehension."

This is Sir W. Hamilton's second theory of Judgment, enunciated at a distance of exactly three pages from the first, without the smallest suspicion on his part that they are not one and the same. Yet they differ by the whole interval which separates *a part of* from *along with*. According to the first theory, concepts are recognized as congruent whenever they are not mutually repugnant; when they are capable of being objectively realized along with one another; when the attributes comprehended in

* Lectures, iii. 227.   † Ibid. p. 229.

both of them can be simultaneously possessed by the same object. According to the second theory, they are only congruent when the one concept is actually a part of the other. The only circumstance in which the two theories resemble is, that both of them are unfolded out of the vague expression "capable of being connected in thought." They are, in fact, two different and conflicting interpretations of that expression. (How irreconcilable they are, is apparent when we descend to particulars. Krug's examples, learning and virtue, beauty and riches, &c., are congruent in the first sense, since they are attributes which can be thought as existing together in the same subject. But is the concept learning a part of the concept virtue, the concept beauty a part of the concept riches, or *vice versâ?*) Sir W. Hamilton would scarcely affirm that they are in a relation of part and whole in Comprehension; and such relation as they have in Extension is not a relation between the concepts, but between the aggregates of real things of which they are predicable. One of those aggregates might be part of the other, though it is not; but one of the concepts can never be part of the other. No one can ever find the notion beauty in the notion riches, nor conversely.

Our author, having thus gently slid back into the common Conceptualist theory of judgment, that it consists in recognizing the identity or non-identity of two notions, adheres to it thenceforward with as much consistency as we need ever expect to find in him. We may consider as his final theory of Judgment, on which his subsequent logical speculations are built, that a judgment is a recognition in thought, a proposition a statement in words, that one notion is or is not a part of another.

He makes use of the word notion, doubtless, to include the case in which either of the terms of the proposition is singular. The two notions, one of which is recognized as being or not being a part of the other, may be either Concepts, that is, General Notions, or one of them may be a mental representation of an individual object.

The first objection which, I think, must occur to any one, on the contemplation of this definition, is, that it omits the main and characteristic element of a judgment and of a proposition. Do we never judge or assert anything but our mere notions of things? Do we not make judgments and assert propositions respecting actual things? A Concept is a mere creation of the mind: it is the mental representation formed within us of a phænomenon; or rather, it is a part of that mental representation, marked off by a sign, for a particular purpose. But when we judge or assert, there is introduced a new element, that of objective reality, and a new mental fact, Belief. Our judgments, and the assertions which express them, do not enunciate our mere mode of mentally conceiving things, but our conviction or persuasion that the facts as conceived actually exist: and a theory of Judgments and Propositions which does not take account of this cannot be the true theory. In the words of Reid,* " I give the name of Judgment to every determination of the mind concerning *what is true* or *what is false*. This, I think, is what logicians, from the days of Aristotle, have called Judgment." And this is the very element which Sir W. Hamilton's definition omits from it.

I am aware that Sir W. Hamilton would have an apparent answer to this. He would, I suppose, reply,

* Essays on the Intellectual Powers, Works, p. 415.

that the belief of actual reality, implied in assent to a proposition, is not left out of account, but brought to account in another place. The belief, he would say, is not inherent in the judgment, but in the notions which are the subject and predicate of the judgment; these being either mental representations of real objects, which, if represented in the mind at all, must be represented as real, or Concepts formed by a comparison of real objects, which therefore exist in the mind as concepts of realities. Accordingly, when we judge and make assertions respecting objects known to be imaginary, the judgments are accompanied with no belief in any real existence except that of the mental images; what our author calls the "presentations of phantasy." When, indeed, a judgment is formed or an assertion is made respecting something imaginary which is supposed to be real, as for instance concerning a ghost, there is a belief in the real existence of more than the mental image; but this belief is not anything superadded to the comparison of concepts; it already existed in the concepts; a ghost was thought as something having a real existence.

This, at least, is what might be said in behalf of Sir W. Hamilton, though he has not himself said it. But though it evades the objection to omitting the element Belief from the definition of judgment, it does so by an entire inversion of the logical process of definition. The element of Belief, or Reality, may indeed be in the concepts; but it never could have got into the concepts, if it had not first been in the judgments by which the concepts were constructed. If the belief of reality had been absent from those judgments originally, it never could have come round to them through the concepts. Belief is an essential element in a judgment; it may be either present or absent in a concept. Our author, and those who agree with him, postpone this part of the subject until they are treating of the distinction between True and False Propositions. They then say, that if the relation which is judged to exist between the notions, exists between the corresponding realities, the proposition is true, and if not, false. But if the operation of forming a judgment or a proposition includes anything at all, it includes judging that the judgment or the proposition is true. The recognition of it as true is not only an essential part, but the essential element of it as a judgment: leave that out, and there remains a mere play of thought, in which no judgment is passed. It is impossible to separate the idea of Judgment from the idea of the truth of a judgment; for every judgment consists in judging something to be true. The element Belief, instead of being an accident which can be passed in silence, and admitted only by implication, constitutes the very difference between a judgment and any other intellectual fact, and it is contrary to all the laws of Definition to define Judgment by anything else. The very meaning of a judgment, or a proposition, is something which is capable of being believed or disbelieved; which can be true or false; to which it is possible to say yes or no. And though it cannot be believed until it has been conceived, or (in plain terms) understood, the real object of belief is not the concept, or any relation of the concept, but the fact conceived. That fact need not be an outward fact; it may be a fact of internal or mental experience. But even then the fact is one thing, the concept of it is another, and the judgment is concerning the fact, not the concept. The fact may be purely subjective, as that I dreamed something last night; but the judgment is not the cognition of a relation between the presentation *I* and the concept *having dreamed*, but the cognition of the real memory of a real event.

This first, and insuperable objection, the force of which will be seen more and more the further we proceed, is applicable to the Conceptualist doctrine of judgment, howsoever expressed, and to Sir W. Hamilton's as one of the modes of expressing that doctrine. There are other objections special to Sir W. Hamilton's form of it.

In what I have called Sir W. Hamilton's first theory of judgment, we found him saying that the comparison, ending in a recognition of congruence or conflict, may be between "individual things" as well as between concepts. But in his second theory, one at least of the terms of comparison must be a concept. For a judgment, according to this theory, is "the product of that act in which we pronounce that of two notions, thought as subject and predicate, the one does or does not constitute a part of the other." Now, a concept, that is, a bundle of attributes, may be a part of another concept, and may be a part of our mental image of an individual object; but one notion of an individual object cannot be a part of another notion of an individual object. One object may be an integrant part of another, but it cannot be a part in Comprehension or in Extension, as these words are understood of a Concept. St. Paul's is an integrant part of London, but neither an attribute of it, nor an object of which it is predicable.

Since, therefore, a judgment, in Sir W. Hamilton's

second theory, is the recognition of the relation of part and whole, either between two concepts, or between a concept and an individual presentation, the theory supposes that the mind furnishes itself with concepts, or general notions, before it begins to judge. Now, this is not only evidently false, but the contrary is asserted, in the most decisive terms, by Sir W. Hamilton himself. He affirms — and it is denied by nobody — that every Concept is built up by a succession of judgments. We conceive an object mentally as having such and such an attribute, because we have first judged that it has that attribute in reality. Let us see what our author says on this point in his Lectures on Metaphysics. He says that there is a judgment involved in every mental act.

"The fourth * condition of consciousness, which may be assumed as very generally acknowledged, is that it involves judgment. A judgment is the mental act by which one thing is affirmed or denied of another. It may to some seem strange that consciousness, the simple and primary act of intelligence, should be a judgment, which philosophers in general" (including Sir W. Hamilton in his second theory) "have viewed as a compound and derivative operation. This is, however, altogether a mistake. A judgment is, as I shall hereafter show you, a simple act of mind, for every act of mind implies a judgment. Do we perceive or imagine without affirming, in the act, the external or internal existence of the object? Now, these fundamental affirmations are the affirmations — in other words, the judgments — of consciousness."

And in a subsequent part of his Course: "You will †

* Lectures, i. 204. † Ibid. ii. 277, 278.

recollect that, when treating of Consciousness in general, I stated to you that consciousness necessarily involves a judgment; and as every act of mind is an act of consciousness, every act of mind, consequently, involves a judgment. A consciousness is necessarily the consciousness of a determinate something, and we cannot be conscious of anything without virtually affirming its existence, that is, judging it to be. Consciousness is thus primarily a judgment or affirmation of existence. Again, consciousness is not merely the affirmation of naked existence, but the affirmation of a certain qualified or determinate existence. We are conscious that we exist, only in and through our consciousness that we exist in this or that particular state — that we are so and so affected, — so and so active; and we are only conscious of this or that particular state of existence, inasmuch as we discriminate it as different from some other state of existence, of which we have been previously conscious and are now reminiscent; but such a discrimination supposes, in consciousness, the affirmation of the existence of one state of a specific character, and the negation of another. On this ground it was that I maintained, that consciousness necessarily involves, besides recollection, or rather a certain continuity of representation, also judgment and comparison; and consequently, that, *so far from comparison or judgment being a process always subsequent to the acquisition of knowledge through perception and self-consciousness, it is involved as a condition of the acquisitive process.*" But if judgment is a comparison of two concepts, or of a concept and an individual object, and a recognition that one of them is a part of (or even merely congruent with) the other, it *must* be a process "always subsequent to the acquisition of knowledge," or, in other words, to the formation of Concepts. The theory of Judgment in the third volume of the Lectures, belongs to a different mode of thinking altogether from the theory of Consciousness in the first and second; and when Sir W. Hamilton was occupied with either of them he must have temporarily forgotten the other.

But in the third volume itself the same inconsistency is obtruded on us still more openly. We are there told in plain words,* "Both concepts and reasonings may be reduced to judgments: for the act of judging, that is, the act of affirming or denying one thing of another in thought, is that in which the Understanding or Faculty of Comparison is essentially expressed. A concept is a judgment: for, on the one hand, *it is nothing but the result of a foregone judgment, or series of judgments, fixed and recorded in a word*, a sign, and it is only amplified by the annexation of a new attribute, through a continuance of the same process. On the other hand, as *a concept is thus the synthesis or complexion, and the record, I may add, of one or more prior acts of judgment*, it can, it is evident, be analyzed into these again; every concept is, in fact, a judgment or a fasciculus of judgments, — these judgments only not explicitly developed in thought, and not formally expressed in terms."

That the same philosopher should have written these words, and a little more than a hundred pages after should have defined a judgment as the result of a comparison of concepts, either between themselves, or with individ-

* Lectures, iii. 117.

ual objects, is, I think the very crown of the self-contradictions which we have found to be sown so thickly in Sir W. Hamilton's speculations. Coming from a thinker of such ability, it almost makes one despair of one's own intellect and that of mankind, and feel as if the attainment of truth on any of the more complicated subjects of thought were impossible.

It is necessary to renounce one of these theories or the other. Either a concept is not the "synthesis and record of one or more prior acts of judgment," or a judgment is not, at least in all cases, the recognition of a relation of which one or both of the terms are Concepts. The least that could be required of Sir W. Hamilton would be so to modify his doctrine as to admit two kinds of judgment: the one kind, that by which concepts are formed, the other that which succeeds their formation. When concepts have been formed, and we subsequently proceed to analyze them, then, he might say, we form judgments which recognize one concept as a whole, of which another is a part. But the judgments by which we constructed the concepts, and every subsequent judgment by which, to use his own words, we amplify them by the addition of a new attribute, have nothing to do with comparison of concepts: it is the Anschauungen, the intuitions, the presentations of experience, which we in this case compare and judge.*

---

* This mode of escape from contradiction is the one which has, in substance, been resorted to by Mr. Mansel. He distinguishes what he terms Psychological from what he denominates Logical judgments. Psychological judgments merely assert that some object of consciousness, either external or internal, is present: they "may be generally stated in the proposition, This is here." These are the only judgments which are implied in, and necessary to, the formation of Concepts; and these judgments, as they assert a matter of present consciousness, are necessarily true. "But

Take, for instance, Sir W. Hamilton's own example of a judgment, "Water rusts iron:" and let us suppose this truth to be new to us. Is it not like a mockery to say with our author, that we know this truth by comparing "the *thoughts*, water, iron, and rusting"? Ought he not to have said the *facts*, water, iron, and rusting? and even then, is comparing the proper name for the mental operation? We do not examine whether three thoughts agree, but whether three outward facts coexist. If we lived till doomsday we should never find the proposition that water rusts iron in our concepts, if we had not first found it in the outward phænomena. The proposition expresses a sequence, and what we call a causation, not between our concepts, but between the two sensible presentations of moistened iron and rust. When we have already judged this sequence to exist outside us, that is, independently of our intellectual combi-

the psychological judgment must not be confounded with the logical. The former is the judgment of a relation between the conscious subject and the immediate object of consciousness: the latter is the judgment of a relation which two objects of thought bear to each other. . . . The logical judgment necessarily contains two concepts, and hence must be regarded as logically and chronologically posterior to the conception, which requires one only." (Prolegomena Logica, pp. 53–56.)

But the operation by which a concept is built up, supposes much more than a cognition of the present existence of a fact or facts of consciousness, and a judgment in the form, "This is here." It supposes the whole process of comparing facts of consciousness, and recognizing, or, in other words, judging, in what points they resemble. It implies that the mind, in its "psychological" judgments, does to the Intuitions or Presentations, everything which it is supposed to do to the Concepts in the "logical" ones. Consequently the distinction between Mr. Mansel's two kinds of judgments is in their matter only, not in the mental operation, and is therefore, as he would say, extra-logical; to which I will add, insignificant. It will be shown in the text that there is no psychological difference between the two, and that the discrimination of one class of judgments as conversant with Presentations and another with Concepts, and the attribution to the latter class of the name of logical, are founded on a false theory.

nations, we know it, and, once known, it may find its way into our concepts. But we cannot elicit out of a concept any judgment which we have not first put into it; which we have not consciously assented to, in the act of forming the concept. Whenever, therefore, we form a new judgment — judge a truth new to us — the judgment is not a recognition of a relation between concepts, but of a succession, a coexistence, or a similitude, between facts.

This is the smallest sacrifice on the part of Sir W. Hamilton's theory of Judgment, which would satisfy his theory of Consciousness. But when thus reconciled with a part of his system with which it now conflicts, it would not be the better founded. It might still be chased from point to point, unable to make a stand anywhere. For let us next suppose, that the judgment is not new; that the truth, Water rusts iron, is known to us of old. When we again think of it, and think it as a truth, and assent to it, should we even then give a correct account of what passes in our mind, by calling this act of judgment a comparison of our thoughts — our concepts — our notions — of water, rust, and iron? We do not compare our artificial mental constructions, but consult our direct remembrance of facts. We call to mind that we have seen, or learned from credible testimony, that when iron is long in contact with water, it rusts. The question is not one of notions, but of beliefs; belief of past and expectation of future presentations of sense. Of course it is psychologically true that when I believe, I have a notion of that which I believe: but the ultimate appeal is not to the notion, but to the presentation, or intuition. If I am in any doubt, what is the question I ask myself? Is it, — Do I think of, or figure to myself, water as rusting iron? or is it, — Did I ever perceive, and have other people perceived, that water rusts iron? There are persons, no doubt, whose criterion of judgment is the relation between their own concepts, but these are not the persons whose judgments the world has usually found worth adopting. If the question between Copernicus and Ptolemy had depended on whether we *conceive* the earth moving and the sun at rest, or the sun moving and the earth at rest, I am afraid the victory would have been with Ptolemy.

But, again, even if judging were entirely a notional operation, consisting of the recognition of some relation between concepts, it remains to be proved that the relation is that of Whole and Part. Could it, even then, be said, that every judgment in which I predicate one thing of another, on the faith of previous judgments recorded as our author says, in the concepts, consists in recognizing that one of the concepts includes the other as a part of itself? When I judge that Socrates is mortal, or that all men are mortal, does the judgment consist in being conscious that my concept mortal is part of my representation of Socrates, or of my concept man?

This doctrine ignores the famous distinction, admitted, I suppose, in some shape or other, by all philosophers, but most familiar to modern metaphysics in the form in which it is stated by Kant; — the distinction between Analytical and Synthetical judgments. Analytical judgments are supposed to unfold the contents of a concept; affirming explicitly of a class, attributes which were already part of the corresponding concept, and may be brought out into distinct consciousness by mere analysis of it. Synthetical judgments, on the contrary, affirm of a class, attributes which are not in the concept, and which we therefore do not and cannot judge to be a part of the concept, but only to be conjoined in fact with the attributes composing the concept. This distinction, though obtruded upon our author by many of the writers with whom he was familiar, has so little in common with his mode of thought, that he only slightly refers to it, in a very few passages of his works: in one of these, however,* he speaks of it as of something very important, proposes new names for it (Explicative and Ampliative), and discusses, not the distinction itself, but its history; apparently unconscious that his own theory entirely does away with it. According to that, all judgments are analytical, or, in his own phrase, explicative. Even giving up so much of his theory as contradicts his own doctrine on the formation of concepts, the part remaining would compel him to maintain that all judgments which are not new are analytical, and that synthetical judgments are limited to truths, or supposed truths, which we learn for the first time. And this, I presume, was what he had in his mind when he suggested, as proper for synthetical judgments, the name of ampliative.

This discrepancy between our author and almost all philosophers, even of his own general way of thinking, (including, among the rest, Mr. Mansel), arises from the fact, that he understands by concept something different from what they have usually understood by it. The concept of a class, in Sir W. Hamilton's acceptation of the term, includes all the attributes which we have judged, and still judge, to be common to the whole class.

* Dissertations on Reid, pp. 787, 788.

It means, in short, our entire knowledge of the class. But, with philosophers in general, the concept of the class as such, — my concept of man, for example, as distinguished from my mental representation of an individual man, — includes, not all the attributes which I ascribe to man, but such of them only as the classification is grounded on, and as are implied in the meaning of the name. Man is a living being, or Man is rational, they would call analytical judgments, because the attributes life and rationality are of the number of those which are already given in the Concept Man: but Man is mortal, they would account synthetical, because, familiar as the fact is, it is not already affirmed in the very name Man, but has to be superadded in the predicate.

It is quite lawful for a philosopher (though seldom prudent) to alter the meaning of a word, provided he gives fair notice of his intention; but he is bound, if he does so, to remain consistent with himself in the new meaning, and not to transfer to it propositions which are only true in the old. This condition Sir W. Hamilton does not observe. It often happens that different opinions of his belong to different and inconsistent systems of thought, apparently through his retaining from former writers some doctrine, the grounds of which he has, by another doctrine, subverted. His whole theory of Concepts being infected by an inconsequence of this description, the retention of all the Conceptualist conclusions along with Nominalist premises, it is no wonder if further oversights of the same kind meet us in every part of the details. The following is one of the most palpable. As we just mentioned, the concept of a class, in our author's sense, includes all the attributes of the class, so far as the thinker is acquainted with them; the whole of the thinker's knowledge of the class. This is Sir W. Hamilton's own doctrine; but along with it he retains a doctrine belonging to the other meaning of Concept, which I have contrasted with his. "The * exposition of the Comprehension of a notion is called its Definition:" and again,† "Definition is the analysis of a complex concept into its component parts or attributes." But a thing is not analyzed into its component parts if any of the parts are left out. The two opinions taken together lead, therefore, to the remarkable consequence, that the definition of a class ought to include the whole of what is known of the class. Those who mean by the concept not all known attributes of the class, but such only as are included in the connotation of the name, may be permitted to say of a Definition that it is the analysis of the concept; but to Sir W. Hamilton this was not permissible. To crown the inconsistency, he still presents‡ the stock example, Man is a rational animal, as a good definition, and a typical specimen of what a Definition is; as if the notions animal and rational exhausted the whole of the concept Man, according to his meaning of Concept — the entire sum of the attributes common to the class. It would hardly be believed, prior to a minute examination of his writings, how much vagueness of thought, leading to the unsuspecting admission of opposite doctrines in the same breath, lurks under the specious appearance of philosophical precision which distinguishes him.§

* Lectures, iii. 143. † Ibid. p. 151. ‡ Ibid. pp. 143, 144.
§ In his non-recognition of the difference between Analytical and Syn-

To return, from Sir W. Hamilton's self-contradictions, to the merits of the question itself; the word Judgment, by universal consent, is coextensive with the word Proposition: a Judgment must be so defined that a Proposition shall be the expression of it in words. Now, if a Judgment expresses a relation between Concepts (which for the purpose of the present discussion I have conceded) the corresponding Proposition represents that same relation by means of names: the names, therefore, must be signs of the concepts, and the concepts must be the meaning of the names. To make this tenable, the Concept must be so construed as to consist of those attributes only which are connoted by the name. Corporeity, life, rationality, and any other attributes of man which are part of the meaning of the word, insomuch that where those attributes were not, we should withhold the name of man, — these are part of the concept. But

thetical judgments, it is already implied that he never recognizes the Connotation of Names; which in itself is enough to vitiate his whole logical system, and is a great point of inferiority in him to the best Conceptualist thinkers, who do recognize it, though in a misleading phraseology. To the same cause may be ascribed the extremely vulgar character of the explanation of some of the leading metaphysical terms, in his eighth Lecture. For example, the distinction between essential and accidental qualities he defines thus — that the essential qualities of a thing are those "which it cannot lose without ceasing to be." This, which is a retrogression from Conceptualism to Realism, does but prove that he simply transcribed his definition from the Realistic Schoolmen. In a later part of his Lectures (iv. 11), he, *more suo*, forgets this definition, and replaces it by another, drawn from his own thoughts; but in this second definition he betrays that he never saw the genuine meaning which lay under the distinction, so badly expressed by the schoolmen in the language of a false system. Sir W. Hamilton, in distinguishing Essential from Unessential properties, means only the difference between attributes of the whole genus, and those confined to some of its species. Sir W. Hamilton's knowledge of the scholastic writings was extraordinary; but many students of them who had not a tithe of that knowledge, have brought back and appropriated much more of the important materials for thought which those writings abundantly contain.

mortality, and all the other human attributes which are the subject of treatises either on the human body or on human nature, are not in the concept, because we do not affirm them of any individual by merely calling him a man; they are so much additional knowledge. The concept Man is not the sum of all the attributes of a man, but only of the essential attributes — of those which constitute him a man; in other words, those on which the class Man is grounded, and which are connoted by the name — what used to be called the essence of Man, that without which Man cannot be, or, in other words, would not be what he is called. Without mortality, or without thirty-two teeth, he would still be called a man: we should not say, This is not a man; we should say, This man is not mortal, or has fewer than thirty-two teeth.

Instead, therefore, of saying with Sir W. Hamilton, that the attributes composing the concept of the predicate are part of those which compose the concept of the subject, we ought to say, they are either a part, or are invariably conjoined with them, not in our conception, but in fact. Propositions in which the concept of the predicate is part of the concept of the subject, or, to express ourselves more philosophically, in which the attributes connoted by the predicate are part of those connoted by the subject, are a kind of Identical Propositions; they convey no information, but at most remind us of what, if we understood the word which is the subject of the proposition, we knew as soon as the word was pronounced. Propositions of this kind are either definitions, or parts of definitions. These judgments are analytical; they analyze the connotation of the subject-name, and predicate separately the different attributes which the name asserts collectively. All other affirmative judgments are synthetical, and affirm that some attribute or set of attributes is, not a part of those connoted by the subject-name, but an invariable accompaniment of them.*

There remains something to be said on another very prominent feature in Sir W. Hamilton's theory of Judgment. Having said, that in every judgment we compare "two notions, thought as subject and predicate," and pronounce that "the one does or does not constitute a

* This is perfectly understood by Mr. Mansel, who says (Prolegomena Logica, p. 58), "When I assert that A is B, I do not mean that the attributes constituting the concept A are identical with those constituting the concept B, for this is only true in identical judgments; but that the object in which the one set of attributes is found, is the same as that in which the other is found. To assert that all philosophers are liable to error, is not to assert that the signification of the term *philosopher* is identical with that of *liable to error;* but that the attributes comprehended in these two distinct terms are in some manner united in the same subject." What Mr. Mansel here enunciates distinctly, was contained, though less distinctly, in Sir W. Hamilton's first theory of judgment, especially as he illustrated it from Krug. In adhering to that first theory, as well as in limiting the concept to the attributes connoted by the name—for that limitation clearly results from his definition of a Concept (p. 60), in combination with other passages —Mr. Mansel, as it appears to me, is much nearer the truth than Sir W. Hamilton; and would perhaps be nearer still, if he were not entangled in the meshes of the Hamiltonian phraseology.

An example how that phraseology controls him, is his strange assertion (pp. 184, 185) that every concept "must contain a plurality of attributes" as a condition of its conceivability; "for a simple idea, like a *summum genus*, is by itself inconceivable." Inconceivable it truly is, but not in any sense in which conceivability is required of a concept; only in the sense of not being conceivable separately. "Simple ideas are never conceived as such, but only as forming parts of a complex object;" in other words, they are inconceivable in the sense in which, according to Sir W. Hamilton's doctrine and Mr. Mansel's own, all concepts are inconceivable.

From a similar entanglement, although his account of Definition and Division is decidedly better than Sir W. Hamilton's, he follows that philosopher in treating the latter logical operation as a division of the Concept: as if the concept were divided by dividing the things which it is predicable of (pp. 191-194).

part of the other," he adds, "either in the quantity of Extension, or in the quantity of Comprehension."* He develops this distinction as follows : †—

"If the Subject or determined notion be viewed as the containing whole, we have an Intensive or Comprehensive proposition; if the Predicate or determining notion be viewed as the containing whole, we have an Extensive proposition. . . . The relation of subject and predicate is contained within that of whole and part, for we can always view either the determining or the determined notion as the whole which contains the other. The whole, however, which the subject constitutes, and the whole which the predicate constitutes, are different, being severally determined by the opposite quantities of comprehension and of extension; and as subject and predicate necessarily stand to each other in the relation of these inverse quantities, it is manifestly a matter of indifference, in so far as the meaning is concerned, whether we view the subject as the whole of comprehension which contains the predicate, or the predicate as the whole of extension which contains the subject. In point of fact, in single propositions it is rarely apparent which of the two wholes is meant; for the copula *is*, *est*, &c., equally denotes the one form of the relation or the other. Thus, in the proposition *man is two-legged*, — the copula here is convertible with *comprehends or contains in it*, for the proposition means *man contains in it two-legged*, that is, the subject *man* as an intensive whole or complex notion, comprehends as a part the predicate *two-legged*. Again, in the proposition, *man is a biped*, the copula corresponds to *contained under*, for this propo-

---

* Lectures, iii. 229.   † Ibid. pp. 231-233.

sition is tantamount to *man is contained under biped*, — that is, the predicate *biped*, as an extensive whole or class, contains under it as a part the subject *man*. But in point of fact, neither of the two propositions unambiguously shows whether it is to be viewed as of an intensive or of an extensive purport; nor in a single proposition is this of any moment. All that can be said is that the one form of expression is better accommodated to express the one kind of proposition, the other better accommodated to express the other. It is only when propositions are connected into syllogisms, that it becomes evident whether the subject or the predicate be the whole in or under which the other is contained; and it is only as thus constituting two different — two contrasted, forms of reasoning — forms the most general, as under each of these every other is included, — that the distinction becomes necessary in regard to concepts and propositions."

I shall not insist on such of the objections to this passage as have been sufficiently stated; the impropriety, for instance, of saying that the notion Man *contains* the predicate two-legged; when that attribute is evidently not part of the signification of the word; or that the meaning of a proposition is, that an attribute is part of a notion; which, the first time it is observed, it cannot possibly be, and at no time is this the thing asserted by a proposition, unless by those which are avowedly definitions. All these considerations I at present forego: and I will even give our author's theory its necessary correction, by restoring to Propositions the alternative meaning which belongs to them, namely, that a certain attribute is *either* part of a given set of attributes, or invariably coexists with them. Having thus dissociated the doctrine in the quotation from all errors which are incidental and not essential to it, we may state it as follows: — Every proposition is capable of being understood in two meanings, which involve one another, inasmuch as if either of them is true the other is so, but which are nevertheless different; of which only one may be, and commonly is, in the mind; and the words used do not always show which. Thus, All men are bipeds, may either mean, that the objects called men are all of them numbered among the objects called bipeds, which is interpreting the proposition in Extension; or that the attribute of having two feet is one of, or coexists with, the attributes which compose the notion Man; which is interpreting the proposition in Comprehension.

I maintain, that these two supposed meanings of the proposition are not two matters of fact or of thought, reciprocally inferrible from one another, but one and the same fact, written in different ways; that the supposed meaning in Extension is not a meaning at all, until interpreted by the meaning in Comprehension; that all concepts and general names which enter into Propositions, require to be construed in Comprehension, and that their Comprehension is the whole of their meaning.

That the meaning in Extension follows if the meaning in Comprehension is granted, is a point which both sides are agreed in. If the attribute signified by biped is either one of, or always conjoined with, the attributes signified by man, we are entitled to assert that the class Man is included in, is a part of, the class Biped. But my position is, that this second assertion is not a conclusion from, but a mere repetition of, the first. For what is the second assertion, if we leave out of it all reference to the attributes? It can then only mean, that we have ascertained the fact independently of the attributes—that is, that we have examined the aggregate whole "all men," and the still greater aggregate whole "all bipeds," and that all the former were found among the latter. Now, do we assert this? or would it be true? Assuredly no one of us ever represented and contemplated, even with his mind's eye, either of these wholes: still less did we ever compare them as realities, and ascertain that the fact is as stated. Neither could this be done, by anything short of infinite power: for all men and all bipeds, except a comparatively few, have either ceased to exist, or have not yet come into existence. What, then, do we mean by making an assertion concerning all men? The phrase does not mean, all and each of a certain great number of objects, known or represented individually. It means, all and each of an unascertained and indefinite number, mostly not known or represented at all, but which, if they came within our opportunities of knowledge, might be recognized by the possession of a certain set of attributes, namely, those forming the connotation of the word Man. "All men," and "the class man," are expressions which point to nothing but attributes; they cannot be interpreted except in comprehension. To say, all men are bipeds, is merely to say, given the attributes of man, that of being a biped will be found along with them; which is the meaning in Comprehension. If the proposition has nothing to do with the concept Man except as to its comprehension, still less has it with the concept Biped. When I say, All men are bipeds, what has my assertion to do with the class biped as to its

Extension? Have I any concern with the remainder of the class, after Man is subtracted from it? Am I necessarily aware even whether there is any remainder at all? I am thinking of no such matter, but only of the attribute two-footed, and am intending to predicate that. I am thinking of it as an attribute of man, but of what else it may happen to be an attribute does not concern me. Thus, all propositions into which general names enter, and consequently all reasonings, are in Comprehension only. Propositions and Reasonings may be written in Extension, but they are always understood in Comprehension. The only exception is in the case of propositions which have no meaning in Comprehension, and have nothing to do with Concepts — those of which both the subject and the predicate are proper names; such as, Tully is Cicero, or, St. Peter is not St. Paul. These words connote nothing, and the only meaning they have is the individual whom they *d*enote. But where a meaning in Comprehension, or, in other words, in Connotation, is possible, that is always the one intended. And Sir W. Hamilton's distinction (though he lays great stress on it) between Reasoning in Comprehension and Reasoning in Extension, will be found (as we shall see hereafter) to be a mere superfetation on Logic.

It is worth while to add, that even could it be admitted that general propositions have a meaning in Extension capable of being conceived as different from their meaning in Comprehension, Sir W. Hamilton would still be wrong in deeming that the recognition of this meaning depends on, or can possibly result from, a comparison of the Concepts. The Extension of a concept, as I have before remarked, is not, like the Comprehension, intrinsic and essential to the concept; it is an external and wholly accidental relation of the concept, and no contemplation or analysis of the concept itself will tell us anything about it. It is an abstract name for the aggregate of objects possessing the attributes included in the concept; and whether that aggregate is greater or smaller does not depend on any properties of the concept, but on the boundless productive powers of Nature.

CHAPTER XIX.

OF REASONING.

In common with the majority of modern writers on Logic, whose language is generally that of the Conceptualist school, Sir W. Hamilton considers Reasoning, as he considers Judgment, to consist in a comparison of Notions: either of Concepts with one another, or of Concepts with the mental representations of individual objects. Only, in simple Judgment, two notions are compared immediately; in Reasoning, mediately. Reasoning is the comparison of two notions by means of a third. As thus : * "Reasoning is an act of mediate Comparison or Judgment; for to reason is to recognize that two notions stand to each other in the relation of a whole and its parts, through a recognition that these notions severally stand in the same relation to a third." The foundation, therefore, of all Reasoning is "the self-evident† principle that a part of the part is a part of the whole." "Without‡ reasoning we should have been limited to a knowledge of what is given by immediate intuition; we should have been unable to draw any inference from this knowledge, and have been shut out from the discovery of that countless multitude of truths, which, though of high, of paramount importance, are not self-evident." This recognition that we discover a "countless multitude of truths," composing a vast proportion of all

---

* Lectures, iii. 274. † Ibid. p. 271. ‡ Ibid. p. 277.

our real knowledge, by mere reasoning, will be found to jar considerably with our author's theory of the reasoning process, and with his whole view of the nature and functions of Logic, the Science of Reasoning: but this inconsistency is common to him with nearly all the writers on Logic, because, like him, they teach a theory of the science too small and narrow to contain their own facts.

Notwithstanding the great number of philosophers who have considered the definition cited above to be a correct account of Reasoning, the objections to it are so manifest, that until after much meditation on the subject, one can scarcely prevail on one's self to utter them: so impossible does it seem that difficulties so obvious should always be passed over unnoticed, unless they admitted of an easy answer. Reasoning, we are told, is a mode of ascertaining that one notion is a part of another; and the use of reasoning is to enable us to discover truths which are not self-evident. But how is it possible that a truth, which consists in one notion being part of another, should not be self-evident? The notions, by supposition, are both of them in our mind. To perceive what parts they are composed of, nothing surely can be necessary but to fix our attention on them. We cannot surely concentrate our consciousness on two ideas in our own mind, without knowing with certainty whether one of them as a whole includes the other as a part. If we have the notion biped and the notion man, and know what they are, we must know whether the notion of a biped is part of the notion we form to ourselves of a man. In this case the simply Introspective method is in its place. We cannot need to go beyond our consciousness of the notions themselves.

Moreover, if it were really the case that we can compare two notions and fail to discover whether one of them is a part of the other, it is impossible to understand how we could be enabled to accomplish this by comparing each of them with a third. A, B, and C, are three concepts, of which we are supposed to know that A is a part of B, and B of C, but until we put these two propositions together we do not know that A is a part of C. We have perceived B in C intuitively, by direct comparison: but what is B? By supposition it is, and is perceived to be, A and something more. We have therefore, by direct intuition, perceived that A and something more is a part of C, without perceiving that A is a part of C. Surely there is here a great psychological difficulty to be got over, to which logicians of the Conceptualist school have been surprisingly blind.

Endeavoring, not to understand what they say, for they never face the question, but to imagine what they might say, to relieve this apparent absurdity, two things occur to one. It may be said, that when a notion is in our consciousness, but we do not know whether something is or is not a part of it, the reason is that we have forgotten some of its parts. We possess the notion, but are only conscious of part of it, and it does its work in our trains of thought only symbolically. Or, again, it may be said that all the parts of the notion are in our consciousness, but are in our consciousness indistinctly. The meaning of having a distinct notion, according to Sir W. Hamilton, is that we can discriminate the characters or attributes of which it is composed. The admitted fact, therefore, that we can have indistinct notions, may be adduced as proof that we can possess a notion, and not be able to say positively what is included in it. These are the best, or rather the only presentable arguments I am able to invent, in support of the paradox involved in the Conceptualist theory of Reasoning.

It is a great deal easier to refute these arguments than it was to discover them. The refutation, like the original difficulty, is too deep. To begin; a notion, part of which has been forgotten, is to that extent a lost notion, and is as if we had never had it. The parts which we can no longer discern in it are not in it, and cannot therefore be proved to be in it, by reasoning, any more than by intuition. We may be able to discover by reasoning that they ought to be there, and may, in consequence, put them there; but that is not recognizing them to be there already. As a notion in part forgotten is a partially lost notion, so an indistinct notion is a notion not yet formed, but in process of formation. We have an indistinct notion of a class when we perceive in a general way that certain objects differ from others, but do not as yet perceive in what; or perceive some of the points of difference, but have not yet perceived, or have not yet generalized, the others. In this case our notion is not yet a completed notion, and the parts which we cannot discern in it, are undiscernible because they are not yet there. As in the former case, the result of reasoning may be to put them there; but it certainly does not effect this by proving them to be there already.

But even if these explanations had solved the mystery of our being conscious of a whole and unable to be directly conscious of its part, they would yet fail to make intelligible how, not having this knowledge directly, we are able to acquire it through a third notion. By hypothesis we have forgotten that A is a part of C, until we again become aware of it through the relation of each of them to B. We therefore had not forgotten that A is a part of B, nor that B is a part of C. When we conceived B, we conceived A as a part of it; when we conceived C, we conceived B as a part of it. In the mere fact, therefore, of conceiving C, we were conscious of B in it, and consciousness of A is a necessary part of that consciousness of B, and yet our consciousness of C did not enable us to find in it our consciousness of A, though it was really there, and though they both were distinctly present. If any one can believe this, no contradiction and no impossibility in any theory of Consciousness need stagger him. Let us now substitute for the hypothesis of forgetfulness, the hypothesis of indistinctness. We had a notion of C, which was so indistinct that we could not discriminate A from the other parts of the notion. But it was not too indistinct to enable us to discriminate B, otherwise the reasoning would break down as well as the intuition. The notion of B, again, indistinct as it may have been in other respects, must have been such that we could with assurance discriminate A as contained in it. Here then returns the same absurdity: A is distinctly present in B, which is distinctly present in C; therefore A, if there be any force in reasoning, is distinctly present in C; yet A cannot be discriminated or perceived in the consciousness in which it is distinctly present: so that, before our reasoning commenced, we were at once distinctly conscious of A, and entirely unconscious of it. There is no such thing as a reduction to absurdity if this is not one.

The reason why a judgment which is not intuitively

evident, can be arrived at through the medium of premises, is that judgments which are not intuitively evident do not consist in recognizing that one notion is part of another. When that is the case, the conclusion is as well known to us *ab initio* as the premises; which is really the case in analytical judgments. When reasoning really leads to the "countless multitudes of truths" not self-evident, which our author speaks of—that is, when the judgments are synthetical—we learn, not that A is part of C, because A is part of B and B of C, but that A is conjoined with C, because A is conjoined with B, and B with C. The principle of the reasoning is not, a part of the part is a part of the whole, but, a mark of the mark is a mark of the thing marked, *Nota notæ est nota rei ipsius.* It means, that two things which constantly coexist with the same third thing, constantly coexist with one another; the things meant not being our concepts, but the facts of experience on which our concepts ought to be grounded.

This theory of reasoning is free from the objections which are fatal to the Conceptualist theory. We cannot discover that A is a part of C through its being a part of B, since if it really is so, the one truth must be as much a matter of direct consciousness as the other. But we can discover that A is conjoined with C through its being conjoined with B; since our knowledge that it is conjoined with B, may have been obtained by a series of observations in which C was not perceptible. C, we must remember, stands for an attribute, that is, not an actual presentation of sense, but a power of producing such presentations: and that a power may have been present without being apparent is in the common course of things — implying nothing more than that the conditions necessary to determine it into act were not all present. This power or potentiality, C, may in like manner have been ascertained to be conjoined with B, by another set of observations, in which it was A's turn to be dormant, or perhaps to be active, but not attended to. By combining the two sets of observations, we are enabled to discover what was not contained in either of them, namely, a constancy of conjunction between C and A, such that one of them comes to be a mark of the other: though in neither of the two sets of observations, nor in any others, may C and A have been actually observed together; or, if observed, not with the frequency, or under the experimental conditions, which would warrant us in generalizing the fact. This is the process by which we do, in reality, acquire the greater part of our knowledge; all of it (as our author says) which is not "given by immediate intuition." But no part of this process is at all like the operation of recognizing parts and a whole; or of recognizing any relation whatever between Concepts; which have nothing to do with the matter, more than is implied in the fact, that we cannot reason about things without conceiving them, or representing them to the mind.

The theory which supposes Judgment and Reasoning to be the comparison of concepts, is obliged to make the term concept stand for, not the thinker's or reasoner's own notion of a thing, but a sort of normal notion, which is understood as being owned by everybody, though everybody does not always use it: (and it is this tacit substitution of a <u>concept floating in the air</u> for the very concept I have in my own mind, which makes it possible to fancy that we can, by reasoning, find out something to be in a concept, which we are not able to discover in it by consciousness, because, in truth, *that concept is not in consciousness.* But a concept of a thing, which is not that whereby I conceive it, is to me as much an external fact, as a presentation of the senses can be: it is another person's concept, not mine. It may be the conventional concept of the world at large — that which it has been tacitly agreed to associate with the class; in other words, it may be the connotation of the class-name; and if so, it may very possibly contain elements which I cannot directly recognize in it, but may have to learn from external evidence: but this is because I do not know the signification of the word, the attributes which determine its application — and what I have to do is to learn them: when I have done this, I shall have no difficulty in directly recognizing as a part of them, anything which really is so. But with regard to all attributes not included in the signification of the name, not only I do not find them in the concept, but they do not even become part of it after I have learned them by experience; unless we understand by the concept, not, with philosophers in general, only the essence of the class, but with Sir W. Hamilton, all its known attributes. Even in Sir W. Hamilton's sense, they are not found in the concept, but added to it; and not until we have already assented to them as objective facts — subsequently, therefore, to the reasoning by which they were ascertained.

Take such a case as this. Here are two properties of circles. One is, that a circle is bounded by a line, every point of which is equally distant from a certain point within the circle. This attribute is connoted by the name, and is, on both theories, a part of the concept. Another property of the circle is, that the length of its circumference is to that of its diameter in the approximate ratio of 3·14159 to 1. This attribute was discovered, and is now known, as a result of reasoning. Now, is there any sense, consistent with the meaning of the terms, in which it can be said that this recondite property formed part of the concept circle, before it had been discovered by mathematicians? Even in Sir W. Hamilton's meaning of concept, it is in nobody's but a mathematician's concept even now; and if we concede that mathematicians are to determine the normal concept of a circle for mankind at large, mathematicians themselves did not find the ratio of the diameter to the circumference in the concept, but put it there; and could not have done so until the long train of difficult reasoning which culminated in the discovery was complete.

It is impossible, therefore, rationally to hold both the opinions professed simultaneously by Sir W. Hamilton — that Reasoning is the comparison of two notions through the medium of a third, and that Reasoning is a source from which we derive new truths. And the truth of the latter proposition being indisputable, it is the former which must give way. The theory of Reasoning which attempts to unite them both, has the same defect which we have shown to vitiate the corresponding theory of Judgment: it makes the process consist in eliciting something out of a concept which never was in the concept, and if it ever finds its way there, does so after the process, and as a consequence of its having taken place.

CHAPTER XX.

ON SIR WILLIAM HAMILTON'S CONCEPTION OF LOGIC AS A SCIENCE. IS LOGIC THE SCIENCE OF THE LAWS, OR FORMS, OF THOUGHT?

HAVING discussed the nature of the three psychological processes which, together, constitute the operations of the Intellect, and having considered Sir W. Hamilton's theory of each, we are in a condition to examine the general view which he takes of the Science or Art, whose purpose it is to direct our intellectual operations into their proper course, and to protect them against error.

Sir W. Hamilton defines Logic " the Science of the Laws of Thought as Thought." * He proceeds to justify each of the component parts of this definition. And first, is Logic a Science?

Archbishop Whately says that it is both a Science and an Art. He says this in an intelligible sense. He means that Logic both determines what is, and prescribes what should be. It investigates the nature of the process which takes place in Reasoning, and lays down rules to enable that process to be conducted as it ought. For this distinction, Sir W. Hamilton is very severe on Archbishop Whately. In the Archbishop's sense of the words, he says, it never has been, and never could have been, disputed that Logic is both a Science and an Art.

* Lectures, iii. 4.

But* "the discrimination of art and science is wrong. Dr. Whately considers science to be any knowledge viewed absolutely, and not in relation to practice, — a signification in which every art would, in its doctrinal part, be a science; and he defines art to be the application of knowledge to practice, in which sense Ethics, Politics, and all practical sciences, would be arts. The distinction of arts and sciences is thus wrong. But . . . were the distinction correct it would be of no value, for it would distinguish nothing, since art and science would mark out no real difference between the various branches of knowledge, but only different points of view under which the same branch might be contemplated by us, — each being in different relations at once a science and an art. In fact, Dr. Whately confuses the distinction of science theoretical and science practical with the distinction of science and art."

But if the difference between science and art is not the same as that between knowledge theoretical and practical, we are entitled to ask, what is it? If Archbishop Whately has placed the distinction where it is not, does his rather peremptory critic and censor tell us where it is? He declines the problem. "I am well aware that it would be no easy matter to give a general definition of science as contradistinguished from art, and of art as contradistinguished from science; but if the words themselves cannot validly be discriminated, it would be absurd to attempt to discriminate anything by them." In the only other part of his Lectures where the distinction between Art and Science is touched on,† he says that the "apparently vague

* Lectures iii. 11; see also Discussions, pp. 133, 134.
† Lectures, i. 115–119.

and capricious manner in which the terms art and science are applied," is not "the result of some accidental and forgotten usage," but is founded on a "rational principle which we are able to trace." But when the reader is expecting a statement of this rational principle, Sir W. Hamilton puts him off with a merely historical explanation. Without stating what the usage actually is, he derives it from a distinction drawn by Aristotle between "a habit productive," and "a habit practical," which he admits to be "not perhaps beyond the reach of criticism;" which he does not undertake to "vindicate," and which he confesses to have been lost sight of by the moderns ever since they ceased to think "mechanical" arts "beneath their notice," all these being called arts without any reference to Aristotle's supposed criterion.* So that Sir W. Hamilton cannot claim even

* I give the Aristotelian distinction in Sir W. Hamilton's words. "In the Aristotelic philosophy the terms πρᾶξις and πρακτικός, that is, *practice* and *practical*, — were employed both in a generic or looser, and in a special or stricter signification. In its generic meaning, πρᾶξις, *practice*, was opposed to theory or speculation, and it comprehended under it, practice in its special meaning, and another co-ordinate term to which practice, in this its stricter signification, was opposed. This term was ποίησις, which we may inadequately translate by *production*. The distinction of πρακτικός and ποιητικός consisted in this: the former denoted that action which terminated in action, — the latter, that action which resulted in some permanent product. For example, dancing and music are practical, as leaving no work after their performance: whereas painting and statuary are productive, as leaving some product over and above their energy. Now, Aristotle, in formally defining art, defines it as a habit productive, and not as a habit practical, ἕξις ποιητικὴ μετὰ λόγου; and though he has not always himself adhered strictly to this limitation, his definition was adopted by his followers, and the term in its application to the practical sciences (the term practical being here used in its genuine meaning), came to be exclusively confined to those whose end did not result in mere action or energy. Accordingly as Ethics, Politics, &c., proposed happiness as their end, and as happiness was an energy, or at least the concomitant of energy, these sciences terminated in action, and were consequently *practical*, not *pro-*

accordance with usage for the distinction which he seems, but does not distinctly profess, to patronize. Yet the principal fault he finds with Archbishop Whately's distinction, is that it does not agree with usage. According to it, he says,* "ethics, politics, religion, and all other practical sciences, would be arts;" and he speaks of the "incongruity we feel in talking of the art of Ethics, the art of Religion, &c., though these are eminently practical sciences." †

Religion may here be placed out of the question, for if there be incongruity with common feelings in calling Religion an art, there is quite as much in calling it a science, and especially a practical science, as if the theoretical doctrines of religion were no part of religion. If religion is either a science or an art, it must be both, and it is commonly understood to consist preëminently in things different from either, namely, a state of the feelings, and a disposition of the will. As for Ethics and Politics, the one and the other are, like Logic, both sciences and arts. Ethics, so far as it consists of the theory of the moral sentiments, and the investigation of those conditions of human well-being, disclosed by experience, which the practical part of Ethics has for its object to secure, is, in all senses of the word, a science. The rules or precepts of morals are an art. If there is any reluctance felt to speak of an art of morals, it is not because people prefer calling morals a science, but

---

ductive. On the other hand, Logic, Rhetoric, &c., did not terminate in a mere — an evanescent action, but in a permanent — an enduring product. For the end of Logic was the production of a reasoning, the end of rhetoric the production of an oration, and so forth." (Lectures, i. pp. 117, 118.) The English language expresses the same distinction by the two verbs, *to do* and *to make.*

* Discussions, p. 134. † Lectures, i. 116.

because most people are unwilling to look upon it as scientific at all, but prefer to regard it as a matter of instinct, or as depending solely on the state of the will and the affections. In the case of Politics there is not, even to the vulgarest apprehension, any incongruity in the use of the word art; on the contrary, "the art of government" is the vernacular expression, and "science of government" a sort of speculative refinement. Philosophic writers on politics have generally preferred to call their subject a science, in order to indicate that it is a fit subject for speculative thinkers, the word Art being apt to suggest to modern ears (it did not to the ancients) something which is the proper business only of practitioners. In reality Politics includes both a science and an art. The Science of Politics treats of the laws of political phænomena; it is the science of human nature under social conditions. The Art of Politics consists (or would consist if it existed) of rules founded on the science, for the right guidance and government of the affairs of society.

But, says Sir W. Hamilton, if the difference between Science and Art were merely that between affirmations and precepts, the distinction would be of no value, since it would "mark out no real difference between the various branches of knowledge, but only different points of view under which the same branch might be contemplated by us, — each being in different relations at once a science and an art." Was it from Sir W. Hamilton we should have expected to hear that a distinction is of no value, because it does not mark a difference between two things, but a difference in the point of view in which we may regard the same thing? How often has he told us, of many of the most important distinctions in philosophy, that they are precisely of this character! The remark, moreover, in the particular case, is so extremely superficial, that, coming from an author of whom it was by no means the habit to look only at the surface of things, it is one of the strongest of the many proofs which appear in his works, how little thought he had bestowed upon the sciences or arts, beyond his own speciality. The reason why systems of precepts require to be distinguished from systems of truths, is, that an entirely different classification is required for the purposes of theoretical knowledge, and for those of its practical application. Take the art of navigation, for example: where is the single science corresponding to this art, or which could with any propriety be included under the same name with it? Navigation is an art dependent on nearly the whole circle of the physical sciences: on astronomy, for the marks by which it determines the ship's place on the ocean; on optics, for the construction and use of its instruments; on abstract mechanics, to understand and regulate the ship's movements; on pneumatics, for the laws of winds; on hydrostatics, for the tides and currents, and the waves as influenced by wind; on meteorology for the weather; on electricity, for thunderstorms; on magnetism, for the use of the compass; on physical geography, and so on nearly to the end of the list. Not only has each one of all these sciences furnished its contingent towards the rules composing the one art of navigation, but many single rules could only have been framed by the union of considerations drawn from several different sciences. For the purposes of the Art, the rules by themselves are sufficient, wherever it has been found practicable to make them sufficiently precise. But if the learner, not content with knowing and practising the rules, wishes to understand their reasons, and so possess science as well as art, he finds no one science, corresponding in its object-matter with the art; he must extract from many sciences those truths of each, which have been turned to practical account for the furtherance of navigation. All this is obvious to any one (not to say a person of Sir W. Hamilton's sagacity), who has sufficiently reflected on the sciences and arts, to be aware of the relation between them. Archbishop Whately's distinction, therefore, in no way merits the contemptuous treatment which it receives in the Lectures, and still more in the Discussions. It is eminently practical, it conforms to the natural and logical order of thought, and accords better with the ends and even with the custom of language, than any other mode in which Arts can be distinguished from Sciences. Sir W. Hamilton, though he condemns it, has not ventured to set up any competing distinction in its place, but (as we have seen) almost intimates that no satisfactory one can be found.

Next after the question whether Logic is a science, comes the consideration of its object-matter as a science, namely, "the Laws of Thought as Thought." "The consideration of this head," says our author,* "divides itself into three questions — 1. What is Thought? 2. What is Thought as Thought? 3. What are the Laws of Thought as Thought?" These three questions are successively discussed.

To the question, "What is Thought?" Sir W. Ham-

* Lectures, iii. 12.

ilton answers — It is not the direct perception of an object, nor its representation in memory or imagination, nor its mere suggestion by association, but is a product of intelligence. Intelligence acts only by comparison. "All thought* is a comparison, a recognition of similarity or difference, a conjunction or disjunction, in other words, a synthesis or analysis of its objects. In Conception, that is, in the formation of Concepts (or general notions), it compares, disjoins or conjoins, attributes; in an act of Judgment, it compares, disjoins or conjoins, concepts; in Reasoning, it compares, disjoins or conjoins, judgments. In each step of this process there is one essential element; to think, to compare, to conjoin or disjoin, it is necessary to recognize one thing *through* or *under* another, and therefore, in defining Thought proper, we may either define it as an act of Comparison, or as a recognition of one notion as *in* or *under* another. It is in performing this act of thinking a thing under a general notion, that we are said to understand or comprehend it. For example: An object is presented, say a book: this object determines an impression, and I am even conscious of the impression, but without recognizing to myself what the thing is; in that case, there is only a perception, and not properly a thought. But suppose I do recognize it for what it is, in other words, compare it with and *reduce it under* a certain concept, class, or complement of attributes, which I call *book;* in that case, there is more than a perception, — there is a thought."

Further on, he again † defines an act of thought as "the recognition of a thing as coming *under* a concept;

---

* Lectures, iii. 13, 14.   † Ibid. p. 15.

in other words, the marking an object by an attribute or attributes previously known as common to sundry objects, and to which we have accordingly given a general name." And subsequently,* as "the comprehension of a thing under a general notion or attribute;" and again,† "the cognition of any mental object by another in which it is considered as included; in other words, thought is *the knowledge of things under conceptions.*" And again,‡ "Thought is the Knowledge of a thing *through* a concept or general notion, or of one notion *through* another."

From these different expressions we may infer, that the author confines the name Thought to cases where there is a judgment; and, it would seem, a judgment affirming more than mere existence. We think an object, or make anything an object of Thought, when we are able to predicate something of it; to affirm that it is something in particular; that it is a certain sort of thing; that it belongs to a class — has something which is (or may be) common to it with a number of other things; that it has, in short, a certain attribute, or attributes. This is intelligible, and unobjectionable: but our author's technical expressions, instead of facilitating the understanding of it, tend, on the contrary, very much to confuse it. Like the transcendental metaphysicians generally, Sir W. Hamilton, when he attempts to state the nature of a mental phænomenon with peculiar precision, does it by a peculiarly unprecise employment of the common prepositions. What light is thrown upon the simple process of referring objects to a class, by calling it the recognition of one thing through, or in,

* Lectures, iii. 21.   † Ibid. p. 40.   ‡ Ibid. p. 43.

or under, another? What distinct signification is conveyed by the phrases, "thinking a thing under a general notion," "reducing it under a concept," "knowing things under, or through, conceptions"? To find the meaning of the explanation we have to resort to the thing explained. The only passage in which the author speaks distinctly, is that in which he paraphrases these expressions by the following: "the marking an object by an attribute or attributes previously known as common to sundry objects, and to which we have accordingly given a general name." To think of an object, then, is to mark it by an attribute or set of attributes, which has received a name, or (what is much more essential) which gives a name to the object. It gives to the object the concrete name, to which its own abstract name, if it has an abstract name, corresponds: but it is not indispensable that the attribute should have received a name, provided it gives one to the object possessing it. An animal is called a bull, in sign of its possessing certain attributes, but there does not exist an abstract word *bullness*. Having, then, in Sir W. Hamilton's language, thought the object, by marking it with a name derived from an attribute, it is perhaps an allowable, though an obscure, expression, to say that we know the thing through the attribute, or through the notion of the attribute: but what is meant by saying that we know it, or think it *under* the attribute? We know it and think it simply as possessing the attribute. The other phrase, while seeming to mean more, means less. Again, when we are asserted to "know one notion through another;" when, for example, we think, or judge, that men, meaning all men, are mortal; is this to know the notion Man through the notion Mortal? The knowledge we really have, is that the objects Men have the attribute mortality; in other words, that the outward facts by which we distinguish men, exist along with subjection to the outward fact, death. (If there is a recommendation I would inculcate on every one who commences the study of metaphysics, it is, to be always sure what he means by his particles.) A large portion of all that perplexes and confuses metaphysical thought, comes from a vague use of those small words.

After this definition of Thought, our author proceeds to explain what he means by Thought as Thought. He means,* "that Logic is conversant with the form of thought, to the exclusion of the matter." We have here arrived at one of the cardinal points in Sir W. Hamilton's philosophy of Logic. However he may vary on other doctrines, to this he is constant, that the province of Logic is the form, not the matter, of thought. It is a pity that the only terms he can find to denote the distinction, are a pair of the obscurest and most confusing expressions in the whole range of metaphysics. Still more unfortunate is it, that, thinking it necessary to employ such terms, he has never, in unambiguous language, explained their meaning. When Archbishop Whately, in somewhat similar phraseology, tells us that Logic has to do with the form of the reasoning process, but not with its matter, we know what he means. It is, that Logic is not concerned with the actual truth either of the conclusion or of the premises, but considers only whether the one follows from the other; whether the conclusion must be true if the premises are true. Sir W. Hamilton is

* Lectures, iii. 15.

not content to mean only this. He means much more; but if we wish to know what, the only information he here gives us is a quotation from a German philosopher, Esser. "We are able, by abstraction, to distinguish from each other, — 1°. The object thought of; and 2°. The kind and manner of thinking it. Let us, employing the old established technical expressions, call the first of these the *matter*, the second the *form*, of the thought. For example, when I think that the book before me is a folio, the matter of the thought is book and folio, the form of it is a judgment." Thus far Esser. The Form, therefore, of Thought, with which alone Logic is conversant, is not the object thought of, but "the kind and manner of thinking it." It is not necessary to show that this explanation is insufficient. But to find any other, we must have recourse, not to Sir W. Hamilton, but to Mr. Mansel. One of the chapters of Mr. Mansel's "Prolegomena Logica" is entitled "On the Matter and Form of Thought." It commences as follows : * —

"The distinction between Matter and Form in common language relatively to works of Art, will serve to illustrate the character of the corresponding distinction in Thought. The term Matter is usually applied to whatever is given to the artist, and consequently, as given, does not come within the province of the art itself to supply. The Form is that which is given in and through the proper operation of the art. In Sculpture, for example, the Matter is the marble in its rough state as given to the sculptor; the Form is that which the sculptor in the exercise of his art communi-

* Prolegomena Logica, pp. 226, 227.

cates to it." Let me here ask, had the block of marble no form at all when it came out of the quarry? "The distinction between Matter and Form in any mental operation is analogous to this. The former includes all that is given *to*, the latter all that is given *by*, the operation. In the division of notions, for example, whether performed by an act of pure thinking or not, the generic notion is that given to be divided; the addition of the difference in the act of division constitutes the species. And accordingly, Genus is frequently designated by logicians the *material*, Difference the *formal*, part of the Species." (An illustration which, whatever else it may do, does not illustrate.) "So likewise in any operation of pure thinking, the Matter will include all that is given to and out of the thought; the Form is what is conveyed in and by the thinking act itself."

This is a fair account of the meaning of Matter and Form in the Kantian philosophy, and the philosophies which descend genealogically from the Kantian. But this meaning must always be taken with, and interpreted by, the characteristic doctrine of the Kantian metaphysics, that the mind does not perceive, but itself creates, all the most general attributes which, by a natural illusion, we ascribe to outward things; which attributes, consequently, are called, by that philosophy, Forms. Extension and Duration, for example, it calls Forms of our sensitive faculty; Substance, Causality, Quantity, forms of our Understanding, which is our faculty of thought. These, however, are not what Sir W. Hamilton and Mr. Mansel mean, when they say that Logic is the science of the form of thought. They do not mean that it is the science of Substance, Causality, and Quantity. The truth is, that as soon as the word Form is stretched beyond its proper signification of bodily figure, it becomes entirely vague: every thinker uses it in a sense of his own. The only bond connecting its various meanings, is the negative one of opposition to Matter. Whenever anything is called Form, there is something which, relatively to it, is regarded as Matter: and whenever anything is called Matter, there is something capable of being superinduced upon it, which when superinduced will be styled its Form. How completely the notion of Form accompanies that of Matter as its relative opposite, we have an illustrious example in Aristotle, when he defines the Soul as the Form of the Body; so, at least, Sir W. Hamilton translates ἐντελεχεια.* It would be quite warranted by the practice of metaphysicians, to call any compound the form of its component elements; water, for instance, the form of hydrogen and oxygen. And since there is nothing that may not be regarded as matter relatively to something which can be constructed out of it, and which is form relatively to it, but matter relatively to some other thing, we have form within form, like a nest of boxes. Kant actually calls the conclusion of a syllogism the form of it, the premises being its matter: so that in every train of reasoning, the successive conclusions pass over one by one from Form to Matter. Without going this length, Sir W. Hamilton,† after Krug, con-

* See Reid, p. 202, and Sir W. Hamilton's foot-note. A still odder example is given by Reid in his Essays on the Active Powers (Works, pp. 649, 650). "In the scholastic ages, an action good in itself was said to be *materially* good, and an action done with a right intention was called *formally* good. This last way of expressing the distinction is still familiar among theologians."

† Lectures, iii. 287, 288. So also Mr. Mansel, Prolegomena Logica, p. 235.

siders the propositions and terms as the matter of the syllogism, and the mode in which they are connected as its form. Yet propositions and terms (*i. e.*, concepts) are classed by him as Forms of Thought. Thus it is impossible to draw any line between the Matter of Thought and its Form, or to convey any distinct conception of the province of a science by saying that it is conversant with the one and not with the other. We may, however, in a general way, understand Sir W. Hamilton to mean, that Logic is not concerned with the actual contents of our knowledge — with the particular objects, or truths, which we know — but only with our mode of knowing them; with what the mind does when it knows, or thinks, irrespectively of the particular things which it thinks about: with the theory of the act or fact of thinking, so far as that fact is the same in all our Thought, or can be reduced to universal principles.

But the fact of thinking is a psychological phænomenon; and Logic is a different thing from Psychology. It is for the purpose of marking this difference that Sir W. Hamilton adds a third point to his definition of Logic, calling it the science not simply of Thought as Thought, but of the Laws of Thought as Thought. For Psychology also treats of thought, considered merely as thought; and professes to give an account of Thought as a mental operation. In what, then, consists the difference between the two? I cannot venture to state it in any but our author's own words.*

" The phænomena of the formal, or subjective phases of thought, are of two kinds. They are either such as

* Lectures, iii 24.

are contingent, that is, such as may or may not appear; or they are such as are necessary, that is, such as cannot but appear. These two classes of phænomena are, however, only manifested in conjunction; they are not discriminated in the actual operations of thought; and it requires a speculative analysis to separate them into their several classes. In so far as these phænomena are considered merely as phænomena, that is, in so far as philosophy is merely observant of them as manifestations in general, they belong to the science of Empirical or Historical Psychology. But when philosophy, by a reflective abstraction, analyzes the necessary from the contingent forms of thought, there results a science, which is distinguished from all others by taking for its object-matter the former of these classes; and this science is Logic. Logic, therefore, is at last fully and finally defined as the science of the necessary forms of thought."

If language has any meaning, this passage must be understood to say, that the "laws" or "forms" which are the province of Logic, are certain "phænomena" of thought, distinguished from its other phænomena by being necessarily present in it, — "such as cannot but appear," — while the remaining phænomena "may or may not appear." If this be meant, we are landed in a strange conclusion. There is a science, Psychology, which is the science of all mental phænomena, and among others, of the phænomena of Thought, and yet another science, Logic, is required to teach us its *necessary* phænomena. There is a portion of the properties of Thought which are expressly excluded from the science which treats of Thought, to be reserved as the matter of another science, and these are precisely its Necessary properties. Those which are merely contingent, "such as may or may not appear"—the properties which are not common to all thought, or do not belong to it at all times—these, it seems to be said, Psychology knows something about: but the Necessary properties, "such as cannot but appear"—the properties which all thoughts possess, which thought must possess, without the possession of which it would not be thought—these Psychology knows not of, and it is the office of a different science to investigate them. We may next expect to be told, that the science of dynamics knows nothing of the laws of motion, the composition of forces, the theory of continuous and accelerating force, the doctrines of Momentum and Vis Viva, &c.; it only knows of wind power and water power, steam power and animal power, and the accidents by flood and field which accompany them and disturb their operation.

This, however, supposes that our author means what he expressly says. It assumes that by the "Laws of Thought," and the "Necessary Forms of Thought," he means the modes in which, and the conditions subject to which, by the constitution of our nature, we cannot but think. But when we turn over a few pages, to the place where he is preparing to treat of those laws or necessary forms one by one — it appears that this is an entire mistake. Laws now no longer mean necessities of nature; they are laws in a totally different sense; they mean precepts: and the "necessary forms of thought" are not attributes which it must, but only which it ought to possess. "When* I speak of laws, and of their absolute necessity in relation to thought, you must not suppose

---

* Lectures, iii. 78.

that these laws and that necessity are the same in the world of mind as in the world of matter. For free intelligences, a law is an ideal necessity given in the form of a precept, which we ought to follow, but which we may also violate if we please; whereas, for the existences which constitute the universe of nature, a law is only another name for those causes which operate blindly and universally in producing certain inevitable results. By *law of thought*, or by *logical necessity*, we do not, therefore, mean a physical law, such as the law of gravitation, but a general precept which we are able certainly to violate, but which if we do not obey, our whole process of thinking is suicidal, or absolutely null. These laws are, consequently, the primary conditions of the possibility of valid thought; and . . . the whole of Pure Logic is only an articulate development of the various modes in which they are applied." *

So that, after all, the real theory of Thought — the laws, in the scientific sense of the term, of Thought as Thought — do not belong to Logic, but to Psychology: and it is only the *validity* of thought which Logic takes cognizance of. It is not with Thought as Thought, but

* It might have been supposed that the double meaning of the word law, though in the last century it could blind even a Montesquieu, had been sufficiently written about since that time, to be understood by minds of far less calibre than Sir W. Hamilton's: yet in this passage he does not recognize it, but seems rather to think that the difference between a law in the scientific, and a law in the legislative or ethical sense, does not turn on an ambiguity of the word, but on the difference between "the world of mind" and "the world of matter:" a "free intelligence" knowing only precepts, which it has power to disobey, and not being ruled, like the physical world, by laws from which it cannot escape. Yet Sir W. Hamilton is the same philosopher who is forever telling us of necessities of thought which are absolutely irresistible to us — from which we can by no mental effort emancipate ourselves; and upon this alleged fact the larger half of his philosophy is grounded. When we find all this forgotten, we almost fancy

only as Valid thought, that Logic is concerned. There is nothing to prevent us from thinking contrary to the laws of Logic : only, if we do, we shall not think rightly, or well, or conformably to the ends of thinking, but falsely, or inconsistently, or confusedly. This doctrine is at complete variance with the saying of our author in his controversy with Whately, that Logic is, and never could have been doubted to be, in Whately's sense of the terms, both a Science and an Art. For the present definition reduces it to the narrowest conception of an Art — that of a mere system of rules. It leaves Science to Psychology, and represents Logic as merely offering to thinkers a collection of precepts, which they are enjoined to observe, not in order that they may think, but that they may think correctly, or validly.

It appears to me, however, that our author, though inconsistent with himself, is much nearer the mark in this mode of regarding Logic than in the previous one. I conceive it to be true that Logic is not the theory of Thought as Thought, but of valid thought; not of thinking, but of correct thinking. It is not a Science distinct from, and co-ordinate with, Psychology. So far

that we have opened a volume of some other writer by mistake. Treating of the same question in another place, our author remembers his own philosophy much better. In the Lecture in which he divides mental science into the "Phænomenology of Mind" and its "Nomology," the former a classification and analysis of our mental faculties, the latter an investigation of their "laws" (Lectures, i. 121, *et seqq.*), the word Laws always stands for "necessary and universal facts," "the Laws by which our faculties are governed," not precepts by which they ought to be governed: and of these necessary and universal facts it is expressly said that the Laws of Thought, with which Logic is concerned, are a part. They are classed with "the laws of Memory," "the laws of Association," "the laws which govern our capacities of enjoyment," all of which are correctly described as necessary facts, and not as precepts. The whole of this is thrown to the winds when the time comes for taking up Logic as a separate science.

as it is a science at all, it is a part, or branch, of Psychology; differing from it, on the one hand, as a part differs from the whole, and on the other, as an Art differs from a Science. Its theoretic grounds are wholly borrowed from Psychology, and include as much ot that science as is required to justify the rules of the art. Logic has no need to know more of the Science of Thinking, than the difference between good thinking and bad. A consequence of this is, that the Necessary Laws of Thought, those which our author in his first doctrine reserved especially to Logic, are precisely those with which Logic has least to do, and which belong the most exclusively to Psychology. What is common to all thought, whether good or bad, and inseparable from it, is irrelevant to Logic, unless by the light it may indirectly throw on something besides itself. The properties of Thought which concern Logic, are some of its contingent properties; those, namely, on the presence of which depends good thinking, as distinguished from bad.

I therefore accept our author's second view of the province of Logic, which makes it a collection of precepts or rules for thinking, grounded on a scientific investigation of the requisites of valid thought. It is this doctrine which governs his treatment of the details of Logic, and it is by this that we must interpret the assertion that Logic has for its only subject the Form of Thought. By the Form of Thought we must understand Thinking itself; the whole work of the Intellect. The Matter of Thought is the sensations, perceptions, or other presentations (intuitions, as Mr. Mansel calls them), in which the intellect has no share; which are supplied to it, independently of any action of its own. What the mind adds to these, or puts into them, is Forms of Thought. Logic, therefore, is concerned only with Forms, since, being rules for thinking, it can have no authority but over that which depends on thought. Logic and Thinking are coextensive; it is the art of Thinking, of all Thinking, and of nothing but Thinking. And since every distinguishable variety of thinking act is called a Form of Thought, the Forms of Thought compose the whole province of Logic; though it would be hardly possible to invent a worse phrase for expressing so simple a fact.

But what *are* the Forms of Thought? Kant, as already observed, gives to that expression a very wide extent. He holds that every attribute which we ascribe to external objects is a Form of Thought, being created, not simply discerned, by our thinking faculty. Neither Sir W. Hamilton nor Mr. Mansel goes this length; and at all events they do not consider the theory of the various attributes of bodies to be a part of Logic. It was incumbent on them, therefore, to state clearly what are the Forms of Thought with which Logic is concerned, and for which it supplies precepts. This question is never put, in an express form, by Sir W. Hamilton: but the answer, which he rather leaves to be picked up than directly presents, may be gathered from his classification of our intellectual operations. These he reduces to three, Conception, Judgment, and Reasoning. He must have recognized, therefore, that number of general Forms of Thought. The Forms of Thought are Conception, Judgment, and Reasoning: Logic is the science of the Laws (meaning the rules) of these three operations. If, however, we rigorously hold our author to this short list, we shall perpetually mistake his meaning:

for (as already observed) the mode in which the word Form is used, allows of form within form to an unlimited extent. Every concept, judgment, or reasoning, after having received its form from the mind, may again be contemplated as the Matter of some further mental act; and the product of that further act (according to Kant), or the relation of the product to the matter (according to Sir W. Hamilton and Mr. Mansel), is again a Form of Thought; as we find, to our confusion, when we proceed further, and the more profusely, the further we proceed. We have, first, however, to consider a proposition of Sir W. Hamilton, which qualifies his definition of the province of Logic. He says:*

"Logic considers Thought, not as the operation of thinking, but as its product; it does not treat of Conception, Judgment, and Reasoning, but of Concepts, Judgments, and Reasonings."

Let me begin by saying, that I give my entire adhesion to this distinction, and propose to reform the definition of Logic accordingly. It does not, as we now see, relate to the Laws of Thought as Thought, but to those of the Products of Thought. Instead of the Laws of Conception, Judgment, and Reasoning, we must speak of the Laws of Concepts, Judgments, and Reasonings. This would be mere nonsense in the scientific sense of the word law: for a product, as such, can have no laws but those of the operation which produces it. But understanding by laws, as it seems we are intended to do, Precepts, Logic becomes the science of the precepts for the formation of concepts, judgments, and reasonings: or rather (a science of precepts being an improper

* Lectures, iii. 73.

expression) the science of the conditions on which right concepts, judgments, and reasonings depend. Thus, Logic is the Art of Thinking, which means of correct thinking, and the Science of the Conditions of correct thinking. This seems to me a sufficiently accurate definition of it. But, in attempting a deeper metaphysical analysis of the distinction he has just drawn, our author raises fresh difficulties. He says : *

"The form of thought may be viewed on two sides, or in two relations. It holds, as has been said, a relation both to its subject and to its object, and it may accordingly be viewed either in the one of these relations or in the other. In so far as the form of thought is considered in reference to the thinking mind, — to the mind by which it is exerted, — it is considered as an act, or operation, or energy; and in this relation it belongs to Phænomenal Psychology. Whereas, in so far as this form is considered in reference to what thought is about, it is considered as the product of such an act, and in this relation it belongs to Logic. Thus Phænomenal Psychology treats of thought proper as conception, judgment, reasoning : Logic, or the Nomology of the Understanding, treats of thought proper as a concept, as a judgment, as a reasoning."

Just when the puzzled reader fancied that he had at last arrived at something clear, comes an explanation which throws all back into darkness. The learner who had been wandering in the mazes of "Thought as Thought," laws which are not laws, and "Forms of Thought," in which Form stands for something which he never before heard of in connection with that word, at last descried what seemed to be firm ground : he was told that Con-

* Lectures, iii. 73, 74.

ception, Judgment, and Reasoning are acts of the mind, that Concepts, Judgments, and Reasonings are products of those acts, and that Psychology is conversant with the former and Logic with the latter. And now it turns out that the products *are* the acts. The two series of things are one and the same series. They are both of them only "Thought proper." (The product is another word for the act itself, considered in one of its aspects— "in reference to what thought is about.") It is curious that this should occur only a few pages after Whately has been rebuked for reducing a distinction to inutility, by making it coincide with a difference not between things, but between the aspects in which the same thing is regarded.

Sir W. Hamilton, therefore, is of opinion that the thinking act, though verbally, is not psychologically different from the thought itself. He does not hold, with Berkeley, that an Idea is a concrete object distinct from the mind, and contained in it, like furniture in a house; nor with Locke (if that was Locke's opinion), that it is a modification of the mind, but a modification distinct from the mind's act in cognizing it; but with Brown, that a sensation is only myself feeling, and a thought only myself thinking. Concepts, Judgments, and Reasoning, are only acts of conceiving, judging, and reasoning; acts of thought, considered not in their relation to the thinking mind, but to their object, to "what thought is about." *

---

* Sir W. Hamilton holds a corresponding theory in regard to the identity of an imagination with the imagining act. "A representation considered as an object is logically, not really, different from a representation considered as an act. Here object and act are merely the same indivisible mode of mind viewed in two different relations. Considered by reference to a mediate object represented, it is a representative object; considered by

But what *is* thought about? Not about Concepts, for all our thoughts are not about the thinking act. It must be about the objective presentation, the Anschauung, or Intuition, which the Concept represents, or from which it has been abstracted. According, therefore, to the doctrine here distinctly laid down by Sir W. Hamilton, there are but two things present in any of our intellectual operations; on one hand, the mind itself thinking (that is, conceiving, judging, or reasoning), and, on the other, a mental presentation or representation of the phænomenal Reality which it conceives, or concerning which it judges or reasons. I can understand that the thinking act, or in other words, the mind in a thinking state, may be contemplated in its relation to the Reality thought of, and may receive a name which connotes that Reality; but how does this entitle us to call it a *product* of thought? How can the act of thought, or the mind thinking, be looked upon, even hypothetically, as a product of thinking? How can Concepts, Judgments, and Reasonings, be regarded as products of thought, when they are the thought itself? Can they be both the act and something resulting from the act? Are they results and products of themselves?

I conceive that there is a way out of this difficulty; a sense in which the two assertions can be reconciled, though it has not been pointed out by Sir W. Hamilton,

reference to the mind representing and contemplating the representation, it is a representative act. A representative object being viewed as posterior in the order of nature, but not of time, to the representative act, is viewed as a *product;* and the representative act being viewed as prior in the order of nature, though not of time, to the representative object, is viewed as a producing process." (Dissertations on Reid, p. 809.) Sir W. Hamilton has not explained how, in the order of nature, or in any other order, a thing can be prior, or posterior, or prior and posterior, to itself.

and is hardly compatible with some of his opinions. There is a difference between what can properly be called Acts of the mind, and the other mental phænomena which may be termed its passive States. And I know but one way of conceiving the distinction, in which it can possibly be upheld, namely, by considering as Acts only those mental phænomena which are results of Volition. Now, the first formation of a Concept, and generally (though not always) any fresh operation of judgment or reasoning, requires a mental effort, a concentration of consciousness upon certain definite objects, which concentration depends on the will, and is called Attention. When this takes place, the mind is properly said to be active. But after frequent repetition of this act of will, the associations to which it has given rise are sufficiently rivetted to do their work spontaneously; the effort of attention, after becoming less and less, is finally null, and the operation, originally voluntary, becomes, in Hartley's language, secondarily automatic. When this transition has been completed, what remains of the mental phænomenon has lost the character of an Act, and become numbered among passive States. It is now either a mere mental representation of an object, differing from those copied directly from sense, only in having certain of its parts artificially made intense and prominent; or it is a *fasciculus* of representations of imagination, held together by the tie of an association artificially produced. When the mental phænomenon has assumed this passive character, it comes to be termed a Concept, or, more familiarly and vaguely, an Idea, and to be felt as if it were, not the mind modified, but something in the mind: and in this ultimate phasis of its existence we may properly consider it, not as an act, but as the product of a previous act; since it now takes place without any conscious activity, and becomes a subject on which fresh activity may be exercised, by an act of voluntary attention concentrating consciousness on it, or on some particular part of it. This explanation, which I leave for the consideration of philosophers, would not have suited Sir W. Hamilton, since it would have required him to limit the extent which he habitually gave to the expression "mental act." It has been said, not without reason, of Condillac and others, that their psychological explanations treat our mental nature as entirely passive, ignoring its active side. The contrary error may with equal reason be imputed to Sir W. Hamilton, that of ignoring the passive side. Every phænomenon of mind, down to the mere reception of a sensation, he regards as an act; therein differing from Kant, and annihilating the need and use of the word, the sole function of which is to distinguish what the mind originates, from what something else originates in the mind.

To return to the definition of Logic, as the science of the Forms of Thought, considered in relation, not to the thinking act itself, but, so far as they are distinguishable from it, to the products of thought. The products of thought are Concepts, Judgments, and Reasonings, and the Forms of Thought are Conception, Judgment, and Reasoning. Logic is the science of those Forms, so far as concerns the rules for the right formation of the products; or, as our author elsewhere phrases it, the science of the "formal conditions" of valid thinking. These modes of expression have a rare power of darkening the subject, but I am endeavoring to give them an intelligible interpretation, by means of that which they profess to explain. If, then, all thinking consists in adding, to given matter, a Form derived from the mind itself, what shall we say of the division, on which so much stress is laid, of Thinking itself into two kinds, Formal and Material Thinking, the first of which alone belongs to Logic, or at all events to pure Logic? Mr. Mansel has written a volume for the express purpose of showing that Logic is only concerned with Formal Thinking; and Sir W. Hamilton's division of Logic into Pure and Modified, agrees with Mr. Mansel's distinction. Yet, according to the definition we have just considered, all thinking whatever is Formal Thinking; since all thinking is either conceiving, judging, or reasoning, and these are the Forms of Thought. If Logic investigates the conditions requisite for the right formation of concepts, of judgments, and of reasonings, it investigates all the conditions of right thought, for there are no other kinds of thought than these; and if it does all this, what is left for the so-called Material Thinking which Logic is said not to be concerned with?

The answer to this question affords an additional specimen of the incurable confusion, in which the processes of thought are involved by the unhappy misapplication to them of the metaphorical word Form. Though Concepts, Judgments, and Reasonings, are said to be the forms of thought, and the only forms which thought takes, or rather gives, the metaphysicians who deal in Forms are in the habit of using phrases which signify that Concepts, Judgments, and Reasonings, though themselves Forms, have also, in themselves, a formal part and a material. Different concepts, judgments, and reasonings, have different matter, according to what it is that the conception, the judgment, or the reasoning, is about: and as whatever part of anything is not its Matter, is always styled its Form, whatever is common to all Concepts, or whatever belongs to them irrespectively of all differences in their matter, is said to be their Form; and so of Judgments and of Reasonings. Thus, the difference between an affirmative and a negative judgment is a difference of form, because a judgment may be either affirmative or negative whatever be the matter to which it relates. The difference between a categorical and a hypothetical syllogism is a difference of form, because it neither depends on, nor is at all affected by, any differences in the matter. Logic, according to Mr. Mansel — pure Logic, according to Sir W. Hamilton — is conversant only with the Forms of Concepts, Judgments, and Reasonings, not with their Matter. Not only is it concerned exclusively with the Forms of thought, but exclusively with the Forms of those Forms. And here I fairly renounce any further attempt to deduce Sir W. Hamilton's or Mr. Mansel's conceptions of Logic from their definitions of it. I collect it from the general evidence of their treatises, and I proceed to show why I consider it to be wrong.

Logic, Sir W. Hamilton has told us, lays down the laws or precepts indispensable to Valid Thought; the conditions to which thought is bound to conform, under the penalty of being invalid, ineffectual, not accomplishing its end. And what is, peculiarly and emphatically, the end of Thinking? Surely it is the attainment of Truth. Surely, if not the sole, at all events the first and most essential constituent of valid thought, is that its results should be true. Concepts, Judgments, and Reasonings, should agree with the reality of things, meaning by things the Phænomena or sensible presentations, to which those mental products have reference. A Concept, to be rightly framed, must be a concept of something real, and must agree with the real fact which it endeavors to represent, that is, the collection of attributes composing the concept must really exist in the objects marked by the class-name, and in no others. A Judgment, to be rightly framed, must be a true judgment, that is, the objects judged of must really possess the attributes predicated of them. A Reasoning, to be rightly framed, must conduct to a true conclusion, since the only purpose of reasoning is to make known to us truths which we cannot learn by direct intuition. Even those who take the most limited view of Logic, allow that the conclusion must be true conditionally — provided that the premises are true. The most important, then, and at bottom the only important quality of a thought being its truth, the laws or precepts provided for the guidance of thought must surely have for their principal purpose that the products of thinking shall be true. Yet with this, according to Mr. Mansel, Logic has no concern; and Sir W. Hamilton reserves it for a sort of appendix to the science, under the title of Modified Logic. Questions of truth and falsity, according to both writers, regard only Material Thinking, while Formal Thinking is the province of Logic. The only precepts for thinking with which Logic concerns itself, are those which have some other purpose than the conformity of our thoughts to the fact. Yet every possible precept for thought, if it be an honest one, must have this for at least its ultimate object. What, then, is excluded from Logic, and what is left in it, by the doctrine that it is only concerned with Formal Thinking? What is excluded is the whole of the evidences of the validity of thought. What is included is part of the evidences of its invalidity.

In no case can thinking be valid unless the concepts, judgments, and conclusions resulting from it are conformable to fact. And in no case can we satisfy ourselves that they are so, by looking merely at the relations of one part of the train of thought to another. We must ascend to the original sources, the presentations of experience, and examine the train of thought in its relation to these. But we can sometimes discover, without ascending to the sources, that the process of thought is *not* valid; having been so conducted that it cannot possibly avail for obtaining concepts, judgments, or conclusions in accordance with fact. This, for example, is the case, if we have allowed ourselves to travel from premises to a conclusion through an ambiguous term. The process then gives no ground at all for believing the conclusion to be true : it is perhaps true, but we have no more reason to believe so than we had before. Or again, the concept, the judgment, or the reasoning may involve a contradiction, and so cannot possibly correspond to any real state of facts. It is with this part of the subject only, in the opinion of these philosophers, that Logic concerns itself. According to Mr. Mansel,[*] Logic "accepts, as logically valid, all such concepts, judgments, and reasonings, as do not, directly or indirectly, imply contradictions; pronouncing them thus

[*] Prolegomena Logica, p. 265.

far to be legitimate as thoughts, that they do not in ultimate analysis destroy themselves . . . leaving to this or that branch of material science to determine how far the same products of thought are guaranteed by the testimony of this or that special experience." Mr. Mansel has not here conceived his own view of the subject with his usual precision. He narrows the field of Logic more than he intends. That to which he confines the name of Logic, accepts as valid all concepts and judgments that do not imply contradictions, but by no means all reasonings. It rejects these not only when self-contradictory, but when simply inconclusive. It condemns a reasoning, not only if it draws a conclusion inconsistent with the premises, but if it draws one which the premises do not warrant; not only if the conclusion must, but if it may, be false though the premises be true. For the notion of true and false *will* force its way even into Formal Logic, whatever pains Sir W. Hamilton and Mr. Mansel give themselves to make the notions of consistent and inconsistent, or of thinkable and unthinkable, do duty instead of it. The ideas of truth and falsity cannot be eliminated from reasoning. We may abstract from actual truth, but the validity of reasoning is always a question of conditional truth — whether one proposition must be true if others are true, or whether one proposition can be true if others are true. When Judgments or Reasonings are in question, "the conditions of the thinkable" are simply the conditions of the believable.

What Mr. Mansel and Sir W. Hamilton really mean, is to segregate from the remainder of the theory of the investigation of truth, as much of it as does not require any reference to the original sufficiency of the groundwork of facts, or the correctness of their interpretation, and call this exclusively Logic, or Pure Logic. They assume that concepts have been formed and judgments made somehow; and if there is nothing within the four corners of the concept or the judgment which proves it absurd, that is, no self-contradiction, they do not question it further. Whether it is grounded on fact or on mere supposition, and if on fact, whether the fact is represented correctly, they do not ask; but think only of the conditions necessary for preventing errors from getting into the process of thought, which were not in the notions or the premises from whence it started. The theory of these conditions (of which the doctrine of the Syllogism is the principal part) Mr. Mansel calls Logic, and Sir W. Hamilton Pure Logic. The expression "Formal Logic," which is sometimes applied to it, is perhaps as distinctive and as little misleading as any other, and is that which, for want of a better, I am content to use. That this part of Logic should be distinguished and named, and made an object of consideration separately from the rest, is perfectly natural. What I protest against, is the doctrine of Sir W. Hamilton, Mr. Mansel, and many other thinkers, that this part is the whole; that there is no other Logic, or Pure Logic, at all; that whatever is more than this, belongs not to a general science and art of Thinking, but (in the words of Mr. Mansel) to this or that material science.

This doctrine assumes, that with the exception of the rules of Formal, that is, of Syllogistic Logic, no other rules can be framed which are applicable to thought generally, abstractedly from particular matter: That a general theory is possible respecting the relations which the parts of a process of thought should bear to one another, but not respecting the proper relations of all thought to its matter: That the problem which Bacon set before himself, and led the way towards resolving, is an impossible one: That there is not, and cannot be, any general Theory of Evidence: That when we have taken care that our notions and propositions concerning Things shall be consistent with themselves and with one another, and have drawn no inferences from them but such the falsity of which would be inconsistent with assertions already made, we have done all that a philosophy of Thought can do — and the agreement and disagreement of our beliefs with the laws of the thing itself, is in each case a special question, belonging to the science of that thing in particular: That the study of nature, the search for objective truth, does not admit of any rules, nor its attainment of any general test. For if there are such rules, if there is such a test, and the consideration of it does not belong to Logic, to what science or study does it belong? There is no other science, which, irrespectively of particular matter, professes to direct the intellect in the application of its powers to any matter on which knowledge is possible. These philosophers must therefore think that there can be no such rules, or that if there are, they can only be of the vaguest possible description. Sir W. Hamilton says as much. "If we* abstract from the specialities of particular objects and sciences, and consider only the rules which ought to govern our procedure in reference to the object-matter of the sciences in general, — and this is all that a universal Logic can propose, — these rules are few in number, and their

---

* Lectures, iv. 232 (Appendix I.).

applications simple and evident. A Material or Objective Logic, except in special subordination to the circumstances of particular sciences, is therefore of very narrow limits, and all that it can tell us is soon told." It is very true that all Sir W. Hamilton can tell us of it is soon told. Nothing can be more meagre, trite, and indefinite than the little which he finds to say respecting what he calls Modified Logic. And no wonder, when we consider the following extraordinary deliverance, which I quote from the conclusion of his Thirtieth Lecture on Logic. Speaking of Physical Science generally, Sir W. Hamilton thus expresses himself : * —

"In this department of Knowledge there is chiefly demanded a patient habit of attention to details, in order to detect phænomena; and, these discovered, their generalization is usually so easy that there is little exercise afforded to the higher energies of Judgment and Reasoning. It was Bacon's boast that Induction, as applied to nature, would equalize all talents, level the aristocracy of genius, accomplish marvels by co-operation and method, and leave little to be done by the force of individual intellects. This boast has been fulfilled; Science has, by the Inductive Process, been brought down to minds, who previously would have been incompetent for its cultivation, and physical knowledge now usefully occupies many who would otherwise have been without any rational pursuit."

Sir W. Hamilton had good reason for confining his own logical speculations to a minor and subordinate department of the Science and Art of Thinking, when he was so destitute, as this passage proves, of the pre-

* Lectures, iv. 138.

liminary knowledge required for making any proficiency in the other and higher branch. Every one who has obtained any knowledge of the physical sciences from really scientific study, knows that the questions of evidence presented, and the powers of abstraction required, in the speculations on which their greater generalizations depend, are such as to task the very highest capacities of the human intellect; and a thinker, however able, who is too little acquainted with the processes actually followed in the investigation of objective truth, to be aware of this fact, is entitled to no authority when he denies the possibility of a Philosophy of Evidence and of the Investigation of Nature; inasmuch as his own requirements do not furnish him with the means of judging whether it is possible or not.*

If any general theory of the sufficiency of Evidence and the legitimacy of Generalization be possible, this must be Logic κατ' ἐξοχήν, and anything else called by the name can only be ancillary to it. For the Logic called Formal only aims at removing one of the obstacles to the attainment of truth, by preventing such mistakes as render our thoughts inconsistent with themselves or

* Accordingly all that Sir W. Hamilton has to say concerning the requisites of a legitimate Induction, is that there must be no instances to the contrary, and that the number of observed instances must be "competent." (Lectures, iv. 168, 169.) If this were all that "a Material or Objective Logic" could "tell us," Sir W. Hamilton's treatment of it would be quite justified. The point of view of a complete Induction, namely, one in which the nature of the instances is such, that no other result than the one arrived at is consistent with the universal Law of Causation, had never risen above Sir W. Hamilton's horizon. The same low reach of thought, not for want of power, but of the necessary knowledge, shows itself in every part of the little he says concerning the investigation of Nature. For example, he implicitly follows the mistake of Kant in affirming an intrinsic difference between the inferences of Induction and those of Analogy. Induction, he says (Lectures, iv. 165, 166), infers that "if a number of objects of the same class possess in common a certain attribute,

with one another: and it is of no importance whether we think consistently or not, if we think wrongly. It is only as a means to material truth, that the formal, or, to speak more clearly, the conditional, validity of an operation of thought is of any value: and even that value is only negative: we have not made the smallest positive advance towards right thinking, by merely keeping ourselves consistent in what is, perhaps, systematic error. This by no means implies that Formal Logic, even in its narrowest sense, is not of very great, though purely negative, value. On the contrary, I subscribe heartily to all that is said of its importance by Sir W. Hamilton and Mr. Mansel. It is good to have our path clearly marked out, and a parapet put up at all the dangerous points, whether the path leads us to the place we desire to reach, or to another place altogether. But to call this alone Logic, or this alone Pure Logic, as if all the rest of the Philosophy of Thought and Evidence were merely an adaptation of this to something else, is to ignore the end to which all rules laid down for our thinking operations are meant to be subservient. The

. . . this attribute is possessed by all the objects of that class;" while Analogy infers that "if . . . two or more things agree in several internal and essential characters . . . they agree, likewise, in all other essential characters, that is, they are constituents of the same class." A little more familiarity with the subject would have shown him that the two kinds of argument are homogeneous, and differ only in degree of evidence. The type of them both is, the inference that things which agree with one another in certain respects, agree in certain other respects. Any argument from known points of agreement to unknown, is an inference of analogy; and induction is no more. Induction concludes that if a number of As have the attribute B, all things which agree with them in being As agree with them also in having the attribute B. The only peculiarity of Induction, as compared with other cases of analogy, is, that the known points of agreement from which further agreement is inferred, have been summed up in a single word and made the foundation of a class. For further explanations, see my System of Logic, Book iii. chap. xx.

purpose of them all, is to enable us to decide whether anything, and what, is proved true. Formal Logic conduces indirectly to this end, by enabling us to perceive, either that the process which has been performed is one which could not possibly prove anything, or that it is one which will prove something to be true, unless the premises happen to be false. This indirect aid is of the greatest importance; but it is important because the end, the ascertainment of truth, is important; and it is important only as complementary to a still more fundamental part of the operation, in which Formal Logic affords no help.

I do not deny the scientific convenience of considering this limited portion of Logic apart from the rest — the doctrine of the Syllogism, for instance, apart from the theory of Induction; and of teaching it in an earlier stage of intellectual education. It can be taught earlier, since it does not, like the inductive logic, presuppose a practical acquaintance with the processes of scientific investigation; and the greatest service to be derived from it, that of keeping the mind clear, can be best rendered before a habit of confused thinking has been acquired. Not only, however, is it indispensable that the larger Logic, which embraces all the general conditions of the ascertainment of truth, should be studied in addition to the smaller Logic, which only concerns itself with the conditions of consistency; but the smaller Logic ought to be, at least finally, studied as part of the greater — as a portion of the means to the same end; and its relation to the other parts — to the other means — should be distinctly displayed. If Thought be anything more than a sportive exercise of the mind, its purpose is to enable us to know what can be known respecting the facts of the universe: its judgments and conclusions express, or are intended to express, some of those facts: and the connection which Formal Logic, by its analysis of the reasoning process, points out between one proposition and another, exists only because there is a connection between one objective truth and another, which makes it possible for us to know objective truths which have never been observed, in virtue of others which have. This possibility is an eternal mystery and stumbling-block to Formal Logic. The bare idea that any new truth can be brought out of a Concept—that analysis can ever find in it anything which synthesis has not first put in — is absurd on the face of it; yet this is all the explanation that Formal Logic, as viewed by Sir W. Hamilton, is able to give of the phænomenon; and Mr. Mansel expressly limits the province of Logic to analytic judgments — to such as are merely identical. But what the Logic of mere consistency cannot do, the Logic of the ascertainment of truth, the Philosophy of Evidence in its larger acceptation, can. It can explain the function of the Ratiocinative process as an instrument of the human intellect in the discovery of truth, and can place it in its true correlation with the other instruments. It is therefore alone competent to furnish a philosophical theory of Reasoning. Such partial account as can be given of the process by looking at it solely by itself, however useful and even necessary to accurate thought, does not dispense with, but points out in a more emphatic manner the need of, the more comprehensive Logic of which it should form a part, and which alone can give a meaning or a reason of existence to the Logic styled Formal, or to the reasoning process itself.

CHAPTER XXI.

THE FUNDAMENTAL LAWS OF THOUGHT ACCORDING TO SIR WILLIAM HAMILTON.

HAVING marked out, as the sole province of Logic, the "Laws of Thought," Sir W. Hamilton naturally proceeds to specify what these are. The "Fundamental Laws of Thought," of which all other laws that can be laid down for thought are but particular applications, are, according to our author, three in number: the Law of Identity; the Law of Contradiction; and the Law of Excluded Middle. In his Lectures he recognized a fourth, "the Law of Reason and Consequent," which seems to be compounded of the Law of Causation, and the Leibnitzian "Principle of Sufficient Reason." But as, in his later speculations, he no longer considered this as an ultimate law, it needs not be further spoken of.

These three laws he otherwise denominates "The Conditions of the Thinkable:"* from which it might have been supposed that he regarded them as Laws of Thought in the scientific sense of the word law; conditions to which thought *cannot but* conform, and apart from which it is impossible. One would have said, à priori, that he could not mean anything but this: since otherwise the expression "Conditions of the Thinkable"

---

* Lectures, iii. 79. In the Appendix to the Lectures (iv. 244, 245) he calls them the Laws of the Thinkable; and the laws of Conception, Judgment, and Reasoning he distinguishes from them under the name of "the laws of Thinking in a strict sense."

is perverted from its meaning. Nevertheless, this is not what he means, at least in this place. It is on this very occasion that he disclaims, as applicable to laws of thought, the scientific meaning of the term, and declares them to be (like the laws made by Parliament) general precepts; not necessities of the thinking act, but instructions for right thinking. Yet it would not have been claiming too much for these three laws, to have regarded them as laws in the more peremptory sense; as actual necessities of thought. Our author could hardly have meant that we are able to disbelieve that a thing is itself, or to believe that a thing is, and at the same time that it is not. He not only, like other people, constantly assumes this to be an impossibility, but makes that impossibility the ground of some of his leading philosophical doctrines; as when he says that it is impossible for us to doubt the actual facts of consciousness "because the doubt implies a contradiction."* It is true that a person may, in one sense, believe contradictory propositions, that is, he may believe the affirmative at some times and the negative at others, alternately forgetting the two beliefs. It is also true that he may yield a passive assent to two forms of words, which, had he been fully conscious of their meaning, he would have known to be, either wholly or in part, an affirmation and a denial of the same fact. But when once he is made to see that there is a contradiction, it is totally impossible for him to believe it.

Now, to compel people to see a contradiction where a contradiction is, constitutes the entire office of Logic in the limited sense in which Sir W. Hamilton conceives it:

* Foot-note to Reid, p. 113, and in many other places.

and he is quite right in regarding the whole of Logic in that narrow sense, as resting on the three Laws specified by him. To call them the Fundamental Laws of Thought is a mere misnomer; but they are the laws of Consistency. All inconsistency is a violation of some one of these laws; an unconscious violation, for knowingly to violate them is impossible.

Something remains to be said respecting the three Laws considered singly, as well as respecting our author's mode of regarding them.

The Law or Principle of Identity (*Principium Identitatis*) is no other than the time-honored axiom, "Whatever is, is," or, in another phraseology, "A thing is the same as itself:" the proposition which Locke, in his chapter on Maxims, treated with so much disrespect. Sir W. Hamilton, probably finding it difficult to establish the "principle of all logical affirmation" on such a basis as this, presents the axiom* in a modified shape, as an assertion of the identity between a whole and its parts; or rather between a whole Concept, and its parts in comprehension — the attributes which compose it; for Logic, as conceived by him, has nothing to do with any wholes but Concepts, abstracting altogether (as he asserts) from the reality of the things conceived.†

---

* Lectures, iii. 79, 80.

† We here see our author by implication admitting that a Concept has no parts except its parts in Comprehension; what he elsewhere calls its parts in Extension being in no sense parts of the Concept, but parts of something else, namely, of the aggregate of concrete objects to which the Concept corresponds. Had Sir W. Hamilton adhered to this rational doctrine, he must have given up his Judgments in Extension: instead of which he not only retains them, but considers them as also founded on the Principle of Identity: though he has expressly limited that principle in a manner inconsistent with founding any judgments on it save Judgments in Comprehension. This contradiction was worth pointing out, but is not

Although our author still so far defers to the old version of the Principle of Identity, as to say that it is "expressed in the formula A is A, or $A = A$," I must admit that while paying this tribute of respect to our ancient friend, he has taken a very substantial and useful liberty with him, and has made him mean much more than he ever meant before. The only fault that can be found (but that is a serious one) is, that if we accept this view of the maxim, we shall require many ".principles of logical affirmation" instead of one. For if we are to make a separate principle for every mode in which we have occasion to re-affirm the same thing in different words, we need a large number of them. If we require a special principle to entitle us, when we have affirmed a set of attributes jointly, to affirm over again the same attributes severally, we require also a long list of such principles as these: When one thing is before another, the other is after. When one thing is after another, the other is before. When one thing is along with another, the other is along with the first. When one thing is like, or unlike, another, the other is like (or unlike) the first: in short, as many fundamental principles as there are kinds of relation. For we have need of all these changes of expression in our processes of thought and reasoning. What is at the bottom of them all is, that Logic (to borrow a phrase from our author) postulates to be allowed to assert the same meaning in any words which will, consistently with their signification, express it. The use and meaning of a Fundamental Law of Thought is, that it asserts in general terms the

worth insisting on, since it may be rectified by extending the scope of the First Law to the identity of *any* whole with its parts, instead of limiting it to the identity of a Concept with its parts in Comprehension only.

right to do something, which the mind needs to do in cases as they arise. It is in this sense that the Dictum de Omni et Nullo is called the fundamental law of the Syllogism. But, for this purpose, it is necessary that the Law or Postulate should be stated in so comprehensive and universal a manner as to cover every case in which the act authorized by it requires to be done. Looked at in this light, the Principle of Identity ought to have been expressed thus: Whatever is true in one form of words, is true in every other form of words which conveys the same meaning. Thus worded, it fulfils the requirements of a First Principle of Thought; for it is the widest possible expression of an act of thought which is always legitimate, and continually has to be done.

Understood in this sense, the Principle of Identity absorbs into itself a Postulate of Logic on which Sir W. Hamilton lays great stress, and which he did good service in making prominent, though we shall hereafter find that he sometimes misapplies it. He expresses it as follows:* "The only postulate of Logic which requires an articulate enouncement is the demand, that before dealing with a judgment or reasoning expressed in language, the import of its terms should be fully understood; in other words, Logic postulates to be allowed to state explicitly in language, all that is implicitly contained in the thought." There cannot be a more just demand: but let us carefully note the terms in which our author enunciates it, that he may be held to them afterwards. Everything may be stated explicitly in language, which is "implicitly contained in the thought," that is (according to his own interpretation), in the "import of the

* Lectures, iii. 114.

terms" used. In other words, we have a right to assert explicitly, what has already been asserted in terms which really mean, though they do not explicitly declare it. Observe, what has been already asserted; not what can be *inferred* from something that has been asserted. One proposition may imply another, but unless the implication is in the very meaning of the terms, it avails nothing. It may be impossible that the one proposition should be true without the other being true also, and yet Logic cannot "postulate" to be allowed to affirm this last; she must be required to prove it. Interpreted in this, its true sense, Sir W. Hamilton's postulate is legitimate, but is only a particular case of the Principle of Identity in its most generalized shape. It is a case of postulating to be allowed to express a given meaning in another form of words.

As already mentioned, Sir W. Hamilton represents the Principle of Identity to be " the principle of all logical affirmation." This I can by no means admit, whether the Principle in question is taken in Sir W. Hamilton's narrower, or in my own wider sense. The reaffirmation in new language of what has already been asserted — or (descending to particulars and adopting our author's phraseology) the thinking of a Concept through an attribute which is a part of itself — can, as I formerly observed, be admitted as a correct account of the nature of affirmation, only in the case of Analytical Judgments. In a Synthetical Judgment, the attribute predicated is thought not as part of, but as existing in a common subject along with, the group of attributes composing the Concept: and of this operation of thought it is plain that no principle of Identity can give any account, since there is a new element introduced, which is not identical with any part of what pre-existed in thought. This is clearly seen by Mr. Mansel, who expressly limits the dominion of the Law of Identity to analytical judgments;* and, with perfect consistency, regards these as the only judgments with which Logic, as such, is concerned. If, then, the Law of Identity is to be upheld as the principle "of all logical affirmation," we must understand that logical affirmation does not mean all affirmation, but only affirmations which communicate no fact, and merely assert that what is called by a name, is what the name declares it to be.

If our author had stated the Law of Identity to be the principle not of "logical affirmation," but of affirmative Reasoning, he would have said something far more plausible, and which had been maintained by many of his predecessors. The truth is, however, that as far as that law is a principle of reasoning at all, it is as much a principle of negative, as of affirmative reasoning. In proving a negative, as much as in proving an affirmative, we require the liberty of exchanging a proposition for any other that is æquipollent with it, and of predicating separately of any subject, all attributes which have been predicated of it jointly. These liberties the mind rightfully claims in all its intellectual operations. The Principle of Identity is not the peculiar groundwork of any special kind of thinking, but an indispensable postulate in all thinking.

The second of the "Fundamental Laws" is the Law or Principle of Contradiction (*Principium Contradictionis*); that two assertions, one of which denies what

* Prolegomena Logica, pp. 196, 197.

the other affirms, cannot be thought together. Most people would have said, cannot be believed together; but our author resolutely refuses to recognize belief as any element in the scientific analysis of a proposition. "This law," he says, "is the principle of all logical negation and distinction,"* and "is logically expressed in the formula, What is contradictory is unthinkable." † To this he subjoins, as an equivalent mathematical formula, "A=not A=o, or A—A=o:" a misapplication and perversion of algebraical symbols, not to be omitted among other evidences how little familiar he was with mathematical modes of thought.

Concerning the name of this law, Sir W. Hamilton observes ‡ that "as it enjoins the absence of contradiction as the indispensable condition of thought, it ought to be called, not the Law of Contradiction, but the Law of Non-Contradiction, or of *non-repugnantia*." It seems that no extent and accuracy of knowledge concerning the opinions of predecessors, can preserve a thinker from giving an erroneous interpretation of their meaning by antedating a confusion of ideas which exists in his own mind. The Law of Contradiction does not "enjoin the absence of contradiction;" it is not an injunction at all. If those who wrote before Sir W. Hamilton of the Law or Principle of Contradiction, had meant by those terms what he did, namely, a rule or precept, it would have been, no doubt, absurd in them to have given the name Law of Contradiction, to a Precept of Non-Contradiction. But I venture to assert that when they spoke of the Law of Contradiction (which most of them, I believe, never did, but called it the Principle) they were no more

* Lectures, iii. 82.   † Ibid. p. 81.   ‡ Ibid. p. 82.

dreaming of enjoining anything, than when they spoke of the Law or Principle of Identity they intended to enjoin identity. They used those terms in their proper scientific, and not, as Sir W. Hamilton does, in their moral or legislative sense. By the Law of Identity they meant one of the properties of identity, namely, that a proposition which is identical must be true. And by the Law of Contradiction they meant one of the properties of contradiction, namely, that what is contradictory cannot be true. We should express their meaning better, if instead of the word Law, we used the expressions, Doctrine of Identity, and Doctrine of Contradiction. This is what they had in their minds, and even expressed by their words; for the word Principle, with them, meant a particular kind of Doctrine, namely, one which is the groundwork and justifying authority, of a whole class of operations of the mind. If the word Law is to be retained, Principium Contradictionis would be better translated, not Law of Contradiction, but Law of Contradictory Propositions; were it not for the consideration, that the principle of Excluded Middle is also a law of contradictory propositions.

The Law of Contradiction, according to Sir W. Hamilton, is the "principle of all logical negation." * I do not see how it can be the principle of any negation except the denial that a thing is the contradictory of itself. That a sight is not a taste is a negation, and it must be a very narrow use of the term which refuses it the title of a logical negation. But there is no contradiction between a sight and a taste. That blue is not green, involves no logical contradiction. We could believe that a green

* Lectures, iii. 82.

thing may be blue, as easily as we believe that a round thing may be blue, if experience did not teach us the incompatibility of the former attributes, and the compatibility of the latter. The negative judgment, that a man is not a horse, may indeed be said to be grounded on the Principle of Contradiction, inasmuch as the opposite assertion, that a man is a horse, is in certain of its parts contradictory, though in others only false. The word man is understood as signifying (in precise logical language, connoting) among other properties, that of having exactly two legs — the word horse, that of having four; and in respect of this particular part of the meaning of the terms, the subject and the predicate are contradictory, the one affirming and the other denying the extra number of legs. But suppose the subject and predicate of the judgment to be names of classes constituted by positive attributes without negative, as mathematician and moralist, or merchant and philosopher. An affirmation uniting them may then be false, but cannot possibly be self-contradictory. The Law of Contradiction cannot be the ground on which it is asserted that a mathematician is not a moralist, for the two Concepts are only different, not contradictory, nor even repugnant.

Others have said, that the Law or Doctrine of Contradiction is the principle of Negative Reasoning. But the obvious truth is, that it is the principle of all Reasoning, so far as reasoning can be regarded apart from objective truth or falsehood. For, abstractedly from that consideration, the only meaning of validity in reasoning is that it neither involves a contradiction, nor infers anything the denial of which would not contradict the premises. Valid reasoning, from the point of view of merely Formal Logic, is a negative conception; it means, reasoning which is not self-destructive; which cannot be discovered to be worthless from its own data. It would be absurd to suppose that the validity of the reasoning process itself, either affirmative or negative, could be proved from the Doctrine of Contradiction; for though a given syllogism may be proved valid by showing that the falsity of the conclusion, combined with the truth of one premise, would contradict the truth of the other, this can only be done by another syllogism, so that the validity of Reasoning would be taken for granted in the attempt to prove it. The Law of Contradiction is a principle of reasoning in the same sense, and in the same sense only, as the Law of Identity is. It is the generalization of a mental act which is of continual occurrence, and which cannot be dispensed with in reasoning. As we require the liberty of substituting for a given assertion, the same assertion in different words, so we require the liberty of substituting, for any assertion, the denial of its contradictory. The affirmation of the one and the denial of the other are logical equivalents, which it is allowable and indispensable to make use of as mutually convertible.

The third " Fundamental Law " is the law or principle of Excluded Middle (*principium Exclusi Medii vel Tertii*), of which the purport is, that of two directly contradictory propositions, one or the other must be true. I am now expressing the axiom in my own language, for the tortuous phraseology* by which our author evades recognizing the ideas of truth and falsity, having already been sufficiently exemplified, may here be disregarded.

* Lectures, iii. 83.

This axiom is the other half of the doctrine of Contradictory Propositions. By the law of Contradiction, contradictory propositions cannot both be true; by the law of Excluded Middle, they cannot both be false. Or, to state the meaning in other language, by the law of Contradiction a proposition cannot be both true and false; by the law of Excluded Middle it must be either true or false — there is no third possibility.

Sir W. Hamilton says that this law is "the principle of disjunctive judgments."* By disjunctive judgments, logicians have always meant, judgments in this form: Either this is true or that is true. The law of Excluded Middle cannot be the principle of any disjunctive judgment but those in which the subject of both the members is the same, and one of the predicates a simple negation of the other: as, A is either B or not B. That indeed rests on the principle of Excluded Middle, or rather, is the very formula of that principle. It is here to be remarked that Sir W. Hamilton, after Krug, but by a very unaccountable departure from the common usage of logicians, confines the name of Disjunctive Judgments to those in which all the alternative propositions have the same subject: "D is either B, or C, or A."† This is not only an arbitrary change in the meaning of words, but renders the classification of propositions incomplete, leaving two kinds of disjunctive propositions (Either B, C, or D, is A, and Either A is B or C is D) unrecognized and without a name. But even in our author's restricted sense of the word Disjunctive, I cannot see how the Law of Excluded Middle can be said to be the principle of *all* disjunctive judgments. The judgment

* Lectures, iii. 84. † Ibid. p. 239.

that A is either B or not B, is warranted and its truth certified by the Law of Excluded Middle: but the judgment that A is either B or C, both B and C being positive, requires some other voucher than the law that one or other of two contradictories must be true. Thus, "X is either a man or a brute," is not a judgment grounded on the principle of Excluded Middle, since brute is not a bare negation of man, but includes the positive attribute of being an animal, which X may possibly not be.

It might be said, with more plausibility, that the Law of Excluded Middle is the principle of Disjunctive Reasoning. Thus, in the last example, "X is either a man or a brute" may be a conclusion from two premises, that X is an animal, and that every animal is either a man or a brute: the latter of which is a disjunctive judgment grounded on the Law of Excluded Middle. But it is not the fact that all disjunctive conclusions are inferred from premises of this nature. Having been told that A has lost a son, I conclude that either B, C, or D (A having no other sons) is dead: what kind of reasoning is this? Disjunctive, surely: it has a disjunctive premise, and leads to a disjunctive conclusion. But the disjunctive premise (Every son of A is either B, C, or D) does not rest on the Law of Excluded Middle, or on any necessity of thought; it rests on my knowledge of the individual fact.

The third Law, however, like the two others, is one of the principles of all reasonings, being the generalization of a process which is liable to be required in all of them. As the Doctrine of Contradiction authorizes us to substitute for the assertion of either of two contradictory propositions, the denial of the other, so the doctrine of Excluded Middle empowers us to substitute for the denial of either of two contradictory propositions, the assertion of the other. Thus all the three principles which our author terms the Fundamental Laws of Thought, are universal postulates of Reasoning; and as such, are entitled to the conspicuous position which our author assigns to them in Logic: though it is evident that they ought not to be placed at the very beginning of the subject, but at the earliest, in its Second Part, the theory of Judgments, or Propositions: since they essentially involve the ideas of Truth and Falsity, which are attributes only of judgments, not of names, or concepts.

It is another question altogether, what we ought to think of these three principles, considered not as general expressions of legitimate intellectual processes, but as themselves speculative truths. Sir W. Hamilton considers them to be such in a very universal sense indeed, since he thinks we are bound to regard them as true beyond the sphere of either real or imaginable phænomenal experience — to be true of Things in Themselves — of Noumena. "Whatever," he says,[*] "violates the laws, whether of Identity, of Contradiction, or of Excluded Middle, we feel to be absolutely impossible, not only in thought, but in existence. Thus we cannot attribute even to Omnipotence the power of making a thing different from itself, of making a thing at once to be and not to be, of making a thing neither to be nor not to be. These three laws thus determine to us the sphere of possibility and of impossibility: and this not merely in thought but in reality, not only logically but metaphysically." And in another place:[†] "If the true charac-

---

[*] Lectures, iii. 98.   [†] Ibid. iv. 65.

ter of objective validity be universality, the laws of Logic are really of that character, for those laws constrain us by their own authority, to regard them as the universal laws not only of human thought, but of universal reason." A few pages before, our author took pains to impress upon us that we were not to regard these laws as necessities of thought, but as general precepts "which we are able to violate:" but they now appear to be necessities of thought and something more.

I readily admit that these three general propositions are universally true of all phænomena. I also admit that if there are any inherent necessities of thought, these are such. (I express myself in this qualified manner, because whoever is aware how artificial, modifiable, the creatures of circumstances, and alterable by circumstances, most of the supposed necessities of thought are (though real necessities to a given person at a given time), will hesitate to affirm of any such necessities that they are an original part of our mental constitution.) Whether the three so-called Fundamental Laws are laws of our thoughts by the native structure of the mind, or merely because we perceive them to be universally true of observed phænomena, I will not positively decide: but they are laws of our thoughts now, and invincibly so. They may or may not be capable of alteration by experience, but the conditions of our existence deny to us the experience which would be required to alter them. Any assertion, therefore, which conflicts with one of these laws — any proposition, for instance, which asserts a contradiction, though it were on a subject wholly removed from the sphere of our experience, is to us unbelievable. The belief in such a proposition is, in the present constitution of nature, impossible as a mental fact.

But Sir W. Hamilton goes beyond this: he thinks that the obstacle to belief does not lie solely in an incapacity of our believing faculty, but in objective incapacities of existence; that the "Fundamental Laws of Thought" are laws of Existence too, and may be known to be true not only of Phænomena but also of Noumena. Of this, however, as of all else relating to Noumena, the verdict of philosophy, I apprehend, must be that we are entirely ignorant. The distinction itself is but an idle one: for since Noumena, if they exist, are wholly unknowable by us except phænomenally, through their effects on us; and since all attributes which exist for us, even in our fancy, are but phænomena, there is nothing for us either to affirm or deny of a Noumenon except phænomenal attributes: existence itself, as we conceive it, being merely the power of producing phænomena. Now, in respect to phænomenal attributes, no one denies the three "Fundamental Laws" to be universally true. Since then they are laws of all Phænomena, and since Existence has to us no meaning but one which has relation to Phænomena, we are quite safe in looking upon them as laws of Existence. This is sufficient for those who hold the doctrine of the Relativity of human knowledge. But Sir W. Hamilton, as has been seen, does not hold that doctrine, though he holds a verbal truism which he chooses to call by the same name. His opinion is, that we do know something more than phænomena: that we know the Primary Qualities of Bodies as existing in the Noumena, in the things themselves, and not as mere powers of affecting us. Sir W. Hamilton, therefore, needs another kind of argument to establish the doctrine that the Laws of Identity, Contradiction, and Excluded Middle, are laws of all existence: and here we have it : *

"To deny the universal application of the three laws, is, in fact, to subvert the reality of thought; and as this subversion is itself an act of thought, it in fact annihilates itself. When, for example, I say that A is, and then say that A is not, by the second assertion I sublate or take away what, by the first assertion, I posited or laid down; thought, in the one case, undoing by negation what, in the other, it had by affirmation done." This proves only that a contradiction is unthinkable, not that it is impossible in point of fact. But what follows goes more directly to the mark. "But when it is asserted that A existing and A non-existing are at once true, what does this imply? It implies that negation and affirmation correspond to nothing out of the mind, — that there is no agreement, no disagreement between thought and its objects; and this is tantamount to saying that truth and falsehood are merely empty sounds. For if we only think by affirmation and negation, and if these are only as they are exclusive of each other, it follows, that unless existence and non-existence be opposed objectively in the same manner as affirmation and negation are opposed subjectively, all our thought is a mere illusion. Thus it is, that those who would assert the possibility of contradictions being at once true, in fact annihilate the possibility of truth itself, and the whole significance of thought."

Of this favorite style of argument with our author

* Lectures, iii. 99, 100.

we have already had many specimens, and have said so much about them, that we can afford to be brief in the present instance. Assuming it to be true that "to deny the universal application of the three laws" as laws of existence "is to subvert the reality of thought:" is anything added to the force of this consideration by saying that "this subversion is itself an act of thought"? If the reality of thought *can* be subverted, is there any peculiar enormity in doing it by means of thought itself? In what other way can we imagine it to be done? And if it were true that thought is an invalid process, what better proof of this could be given than that we could, by thinking, arrive at the conclusion that our thoughts are not to be trusted? Sir W. Hamilton always seems to suppose that the imaginary sceptic, who doubts the validity of thought altogether, is obliged to claim a greater validity for his subversive thoughts than he allows to the thoughts they subvert. But it is enough for him to claim the same validity, so that all opinions are thrown into equal uncertainty.* Sir W. Hamilton, of all men, ought to know this, for when he is himself on the sceptical side of any question, as when speaking of the Absolute, or anything else which he deems inaccessible to the human faculties, this is the very line of argument he employs. He proves the invalidity, as regards those subjects, of the thinking process, by showing that it lands us in contradictions.†

* The principal extant interpreter of the ancient Scepticism, Sextus Empiricus, expressly defines as its essence and scope, τὸ παντὶ λόγῳ λόγον ἴσον ἀντικεῖσθαι. (Pyrrh. Hypot.) It is, indeed, impossible to conceive Scepticism otherwise. Anything more would not be Scepticism, but Negative Dogmatism.

† "If I," says our author (Appendix to Lectures, i. 402), "have done anything meritorious in philosophy, it is in the attempt to explain the phæ-

But it is entirely inadmissible that to suppose that a law of thought need not necessarily be a law of existence, invalidates the thinking process. If, indeed, there were any law necessitating us to think a relation between *phænomena* which does not in fact exist between the phænomena, then certainly the thinking process would be proved invalid, because we should be compelled by it to think true something which would really be false. But if the mind is incapable of thinking anything respecting Noumena except the Phænomena which it considers as proceeding from them, and to which it can appeal to test its thoughts; and if we are under no necessity of thinking these otherwise than in conformity to what they really are; we may refuse to believe that our generalizations from the Phænomenal attributes of Noumena can be applied to Noumena in any other aspect, without in the least invalidating the operation of thought

nomena of these contradictions, in showing that they arise only when intelligence transcends the limits to which its legitimate exercise is restricted." "In generating its Antinomies, Kant's Reason transcended its limits, violated its laws. . . . Reason is only self-contradictory when driven beyond its legitimate bounds." (Appendix to Lectures, ii. 543.) "It is only when transcending that sphere, when founding on its illegitimate as on its legitimate exercise, that it affords a contradictory result. . . . The dogmatic assertion of necessity — of Fatalism, and the dogmatic assertion of Liberty, are the counter and equally inconceivable conclusions from reliance on the illegitimate and one-sided." (Appendix to Lectures, i. 403.) To the same effect Mr. Mansel, throughout his "Limits of Religious Thought."

In one of the Appendices to the Lectures on Metaphysics (ii. 527, 528), Sir W. Hamilton makes out a long list of contradictions or antinomies (of which we shall have something to say hereafter) involved, as he thinks, in the attempt to conceive the Infinite, and which he considers as evidence that the notion is beyond the reach of the human faculties. Yet he will not allow that the fact of leading to contradictions, which he habitually urges as an argument against the validity of some thought, would be admissible as an argument against Thought in general, if it could be brought home to it. At least he will not allow it in this place: for in his theory of the veracity of Consciousness he does. (Lectures, i. 277.)

in regard to anything to which thought is applicable. We may say to Sir W. Hamilton what he says himself in another case : * "I only say that thought is limited; but, within its limits, I do not deny, I do not subvert, its truth." As he elsewhere observes, translating from Esser,† truth consists "solely in the correspondence of our thoughts with their objects." If the only real objects of thought, even when we are nominally speaking of Noumena, are Phænomena, our thoughts are true when they are made to correspond with Phænomena: and, the possibility of this being denied by no one, the thinking process is valid whether our laws of thought are laws of absolute existence or not.

* Lectures, iii. 100.   † Ibid. p. 107; see also iv. 61.

CHAPTER XXII.

OF SIR WILLIAM HAMILTON'S SUPPOSED IMPROVEMENTS IN FORMAL LOGIC.

OF all Sir W. Hamilton's philosophical achievements, there is none, except perhaps his "Philosophy of the Conditioned," on account of which so much merit has been claimed for him, as the additions and corrections which he is supposed to have contributed to the doctrine of the Syllogism. These may be summed up in two principal theories, with their numerous corollaries and applications; the recognition of two kinds of Syllogism, Syllogisms in Extension and Syllogisms in Comprehension; and the doctrine of the Quantification of the Predicate. To the former of these, Sir W. Hamilton ascribed great importance. According to him, all previous logicians, "with the doubtful exception of Aristotle," "have altogether overlooked the reasoning in Comprehension"—"have marvellously overlooked one, and that the simplest and most natural of these descriptions of reasoning,—the reasoning in the quantity of comprehension:" and he claims, in directing attention to it, to have "relieved a radical defect and vital inconsistency in the present logical system."[*] For the other theory, that of the Quantification of the Predicate, still loftier claims are advanced both by himself and by others. Mr. Baynes, with an enthusiasm natural

[*] Lectures, iii. 297, 304, 378. Appendix, iv. 250.

and not ungraceful in a pupil, concludes his Essay on the subject (which still remains the clearest exposition of his master's doctrine) with the following words :* " We cannot, however, close without expressing the true joy we feel (though, were the feeling less strong, we might shrink from the intrusion) that in our own country, and in our time, this discovery has been made. We rejoice to know, that one has at length arisen, able to recognize and complete the plan of the mighty builder, Aristotle, — to lay the top-stone on that fabric, the foundations of which were laid more than two thousand years ago, by the master-hand of the Stagirite, which, after the labors of many generations of workmen, who have from time to time built up one part here and taken down another there — remains substantially as he left it; but which, when finished, shall be seen to be an edifice of wondrous beauty, harmony, and completeness."

Previous to discussing these additions to the Syllogistic Theory, it is necessary to revert to a doctrine which has been briefly stated in a former chapter, but did not then receive all the elucidation it requires, and which has a most important bearing on both of Sir W. Hamilton's supposed discoveries. This is, that all Judgments (except where both the terms are proper names) are really judgments in Comprehension; though it is customary, and the natural tendency of the mind, to express most of them in terms of Extension. In other words, we never really predicate anything but attributes, though, in the

---

* " An Essay on the New Analytic of Logical Forms, being that which gained the prize proposed by Sir William Hamilton in the year 1846 for the best exposition of the new Doctrine propounded in his Lectures. With an Historical Appendix. By Thomas Spencer Baynes, Translator of the Port Royal Logic." (p. 80.)

usage of language, we commonly predicate them by means of words which are names of concrete objects.

When, for example, I say, The sky is blue, my meaning, and my whole meaning, is, that the sky has that particular color. I am not thinking of the class blue, as regards extension, at all. I am not caring, nor necessarily knowing, what blue things there are, or if there is any blue thing except the sky. I am thinking only of the sensation of blue, and am judging that the sky produces this sensation in my sensitive faculty; or (to express the meaning in technical language) that the quality answering to the sensation of blue, or the power of exciting the sensation of blue, is an attribute of the sky. When again I say, All oxen ruminate, I have nothing to do with the predicate, considered in extension. I may know, or be ignorant, that there are other ruminating animals besides oxen. Whether I do or do not know it, it does not, unless by mere accident, pass through my mind. In judging that oxen ruminate, I do not, unless accidentally, think under the notion ruminate (to borrow Sir W. Hamilton's phraseology), any other notion than that of an ox. The Comprehension of the predicate — the attribute or set of attributes signified by it — are all that I have in my mind; and the relation of this attribute or these attributes to the subject, is the entire matter of the judgment.

In one of the examples above given, the predicate is an adjective, and in the other a verb, which, in a logical point of view, is classed with adjectives; but its being a noun substantive makes no difference. For reasons easily shown, a substantive is more strongly associated with the ideas of the concrete objects denoted by it, than an adjective or a verb is. But when we predicate a substantive — when we say, Philip is a man, or A dolphin is a fish — do the words man and fish signify anything to us but the bundles of attributes connoted by them? Do the propositions mean anything except that Philip has the human attributes, and a dolphin the piscine ones? Assuredly not. Any notion of a multitude of other men, among whom Philip is ranked, or of a variety of fishes besides dolphins, is foreign to the proposition. The proposition does not decide whether there is this additional quantity or no. It affirms the attributes of its own particular subject, and of no other.

Passing now from the predicate to the subject, we shall find that the subject also, if a general term or notion, is always construed in Comprehension, that is, by the attributes which constitute it, and has no other meaning in thought. When I judge that all oxen ruminate, what do I mean by all oxen? I have no image in my mind of all oxen. I do not, nor ever shall, know all of them, and I am not thinking even of all those I do know. " All oxen," in my thoughts, does not mean particular animals — it means the objects, whatever they may be, that have the attributes by which oxen are recognized, and which compose the notion of an ox. Wherever these attributes shall be found, there, as I judge, the attribute of ruminating will be found also: that is the entire purport of the judgment. Its meaning is a meaning in attributes, and nothing else. It supposes subjects, but merely as all attributes suppose them.

But there is another mode of interpreting the same proposition, by considering it as part of the statement of a classification and mental co-ordination of the objects which exist in nature. The proposition is then looked upon as an assertion respecting given objects; affirming what other individual objects they are classed among by the general scheme of human language. Thus interpreted, the proposition "all oxen ruminate" may be read as follows: If all creatures that ruminate were collected in a vast plain, and I were required to search the world and point out all oxen, they would all be found among the crowd on that plain, and none anywhere else. Moreover, this would have been the case in all past time, and will at any future, while the present order of nature lasts. This is the proposition "All oxen ruminate" interpreted in Extension. Will any one say that a process of thought like this passes in the mind of whoever makes the affirmation? It is a point of view in which the proposition may be regarded; it is one of the aspects of the fact asserted in the proposition. But it is not the aspect in which the proposition presents it to the mind.

It will, however, very naturally be objected — If the meaning in our mind is that the bovine attributes are always accompanied by the attribute of ruminating, why do we, except for the purposes of abstract logic or metaphysics, never say this, but always say "All oxen ruminate"? The reason is, that we have no other convenient and compact mode of speaking. Most attributes, and nearly all large "bundles of attributes," have no names of their own. We can only name them by a circumlocution. We are accustomed to speak of attributes not by names given to themselves, but by means of the names which they give to the objects they are attributes of. We do not talk of the phænomena which accompany piscinity; we talk of the phænomena of fishes. We do not frame a definition of piscinity, but a definition of a fish. The definition, however, of a fish is exactly the same which definition of piscinity would be; it is an enumeration of the same attributes. Language is constructed upon the principle of naming concrete objects first: it does not always name abstractions at all, and when it does, the names are almost always derived from those of concrete objects. The reasons are obvious. Objects — even classes of objects — being conceivable by a much less effort of abstraction than attributes, are in the necessary order of things conceived and named earlier, and remain always more familiar to the mind: attributes, even when they come to be conceived, cannot be conceived in a detached state, but are always (as may be said by an adaptation of the Hamiltonian phraseology) thought through objects of some sort. Consequently all familiar propositions are expressed in the language which denotes objects, and not in that which denotes attributes. Nor is this all. What is primarily important to us in our sensations and impressions, is their permanent groups. In our particular and passing sensations (unless in cases of exceptional intensity) the important thing to us is, not the sensation itself, but to what group it belongs; what concrete object, what Permanent Possibility of Sensation, it indicates the presence of. The mind consequently hurries on from the sensible impressions that proceed from an outward object, to the object itself, and its subsequent thoughts revolve round that. It is on the concrete object indicated, that the expectation of future sensations depends; and the concrete object, consequently, in most cases, exclusively engages our thoughts, and stimulates us to mark it by a name. The name, to answer its purpose, must remind ourselves, and inform others, of the sensations we or they have to expect: that is, it must connote an attribute, or set of attributes. And men did not at first name attributes in any other than this indirect manner. They gave no direct names to attributes, because they did not conceive attributes as having any separate existence. As they began by naming only concrete objects, so the first names by which they expressed even the results of abstraction, were not names of attributes in the abstract, regarded apart from their objects, but names of concrete objects signifying the presence of the attributes. Men talked of blue, or of blue things, before they talked of blueness. Even when they did talk of blueness, it was originally not as the attribute, but as an imaginary cause of the attribute, which cause they figured to themselves as itself a concrete thing, residing in the object.

It thus appears that though all judgments consist in ascribing attributes, the original and natural mode of expressing them was by general names denoting concrete objects, and only connoting attributes; and by the structure of language this remains the only concise mode, and the only one which, addressing itself to familiar associations, conveys the meaning at once, to minds not exercised in metaphysical abstraction. But this does not alter the obvious truth, that concrete objects are only known by attributes, are only distinguished by attributes, and that the concrete names by which we speak of them mean nothing but attributes, or "bundles of attributes." Our representation in thought of a concrete object, is but a representation of attributes, and our concept of a class of concrete objects is but a certain portion of those attributes, not, indeed, separately conceived, or imaged, but exclusively attended to. There is therefore nothing in our mind when we affirm a general proposition, but attributes, and their coexistence or repugnance : and the position is made out, that all judgments, expressed by means of general terms, are judgments in Comprehension, though always, unless for some special purpose, expressed in Extension.

If this be the true doctrine of Judgments, what is meant by saying that there are two sorts of judgment, one in Extension, the other in Comprehension, and two kinds of reasoning corresponding to these, one of which, that in Comprehension, had been overlooked by all logicians, except possibly Aristotle, up to the time of Sir W. Hamilton? All our ordinary judgments are in Comprehension only, Extension not being thought of. But we may, if we please, make the Extension of our general terms an express object of thought, and this may be called thinking in Extension, though it is rather thinking about Extension. When I judge that all oxen ruminate, I have nothing in my thoughts but the attributes and their coexistence. But when, by reflection, I perceive what the proposition implies, I remark, that other things may ruminate besides oxen ; and that the unknown multitude of things which ruminate form a mass, with which the unknown multitude of things having the attributes of oxen is either identical, or is wholly comprised in it. Which of these two is the truth I may not know, and if I did, took no notice of it when I assented to the proposition "all oxen ruminate." But I perceive, on consideration, that one or other of them must be true. Though I had not this in my mind when I affirmed that all oxen ruminate, I can have it now; I can make the concrete objects denoted by each of the two names an object of thought, as a collective though indefinite aggregate; in other words, I can make the Extension of the names (or notions) an object of direct consciousness. When I do this, I perceive that this operation introduces no new fact, but is only a different mode of contemplating the very fact which I had previously expressed by the words "all oxen ruminate." The fact is the same, but the mode of contemplating it is different; the mental operation, the act of thought, is not only a distinct act, but an act of a different kind.

There is thus, in all propositions (save those in which both terms are Proper, that is, insignificant, names) a judgment concerning attributes (called by Sir W. Hamilton a judgment in comprehension), which we make as a matter of course, and a possible judgment in or concerning Extension, which we may make, and which will be true if the former is true. Nevertheless (as has just been shown), the conditions of primitive thought, and subsequent convenience, cause us generally to enunciate our propositions in terms appropriate to the derivative judgment which we seldom make, rather than to the primitive judgment which we always make. And this explains why, though the meaning of all propositions in which general terms are used is in Comprehension, writers on logic always explain the rules of the Syllogism in reference to Extension alone. It is because the framers of the rules did not concern themselves with propositions or reasonings as they exist in thought, but only as they are expressed in language. And in this they were justified. For the syllogism is not the form in which we necessarily reason, but a test of reasoning; a form into which we may translate any reasoning, with the effect of exposing all the points at which any unwarranted inference can have got in. According to this view of the Syllogism — for the justification of which I must refer to the Second Book of my System of Logic — the syllogistic theory is only concerned with providing forms suitable to test the validity of inferences; and it was not necessary that the forms in which reasoning was directed to be written, should be those in which it is carried on in thought, so long as they are practically equivalent, that is, so long as the propositions in words are always true or false according as the judgments in thought are so. The propositions in Extension, being, in this sense, exactly equivalent to the judgments in Comprehension, served quite as well to ground forms of ratiocination upon; and as the validity of the forms was more easily and conveniently shown through the concrete conception of comparing classes of objects, than through the abstract one of recognizing coexistence of attributes, logicians were perfectly justified in taking the course which, in any case, the established forms of language would doubtless have forced upon them. They are thus deserving of no blame, though their mode of proceeding has been attended with some practical mischief, by diverting the attention of thinkers from what really constitutes the meaning of Propositions. It has also been one of the causes of the prejudice so general in the last three centuries, against the syllogistic theory. For, a doctrine which defined one of the two great processes of the discovery of truth as consisting in the operation of placing objects in a class and then finding them there, can never, I think, have really satisfied any competent thinker, however he may have acquiesced in it for want of a better. There must always have been a dormant sense of discontent, an obscure feeling that this was a description of the reasoning process by one of its accidents, though an inseparable accident.

Sir W. Hamilton distinguishes two kinds of Syllogism, Extensive and Comprehensive. "For while* every syllogism infers that the part of a part is a part of the whole, it does this either in the quantity of Extension — the Predicate of the two notions compared in the Question and Conclusion being the greatest whole, and the Subject the smallest part; or in the counter quantity of Comprehension, the subject of these two notions being the greatest whole, and the Predicate the smallest part." He acknowledges, however, that both syllogisms are identically the same argument: "every syllogism in the one quantity being convertible into a syllogism absolutely equivalent in the other quantity." And what is the difference in form and language between the two syllogisms? According to our author, it is merely a difference in the order of the premises. The following,†

"Every morally responsible agent is a free agent;
"Man is a morally responsible agent;
"Therefore, man is a free agent,"

is, according to him, a syllogism in Extension. Transpose the premises, and write it thus, ‡

"Man is a responsible agent;
"But a responsible agent is a free agent;
"Therefore, man is a free agent,"

and we have, according to him, a syllogism in Compre-

---

* Lectures, iii. 286, 287.   † Ibid. p. 270.   ‡ Ibid. p. 273.

hension. Far, however, from constituting two kinds of reasoning, this does not even supply us with two different forms of it. He himself says elsewhere,* that "the transposition of the propositions of a syllogism affords no modifications of form yielding more than a superficial character." And even this superficial difference he with his own hands abolishes, saying,† that any syllogism whatever "can be perspicuously expressed not only by the normal, but by any of the five consecutions of its propositions which deviate from the regular order," and that "a syllogism in Comprehension is equally susceptible of a transposition of its propositions as a syllogism in Extension." So that the slight distinction of form which he seemed at first to contend for, does not exist; a Syllogism in Comprehension, and the corresponding Syllogism in Extension, are word for word the same. Instead of "every syllogism in the one quantity" being "convertible into a syllogism absolutely equivalent in the other quantity," every syllogism is already a syllogism in both quantities. ‡

* Lectures, iii. 399.   † Ibid. pp. 397, 398.

‡ It is curious to observe with what facility Sir W. Hamilton drives two conflicting opinions together in a team. The passages quoted in the text are destructive of any notion of a different order of the premises in a Syllogism of Extension and in one of Comprehension. Yet this notion maintains full possession of our author's mind. We have found him accusing all logical writers of overlooking Reasoning in Comprehension; but he thinks that they exceptionally recognized it in the case of the Sorites, and that in that case, by a contrary error, they "altogether overlooked the possibility of a Reasoning in Extension" (Lectures, iii. 379–384), solely because, in the Sorites, they inverted the usual order of the premises. On a similar foundation stands his charge against the Fourth Figure, of being "a monster undeserving of toleration," because instead of keeping to one of the two quantities, Extension and Comprehension, it reasons (he says) across from one of them to the other. This is merely because the Fourth Figure, while it draws the same conclusion which might have been drawn in the First, reverses the order of the premises. (Lectures, iii. 425–428.)

The distinction, therefore, is not between two kinds, or even between two forms, of syllogism, but between two modes of construing the meaning of the same syllogism. And what are these two modes? Sir W. Hamilton says, that they are distinguished by a difference in the meaning of the copula. "In* the one process, that, to wit, in extension, the copula *is*, means *is contained under*, whereas in the other, it means *comprehends in*. Thus, the proposition *God is merciful*, viewed as in the one quantity, signifies *God is contained under merciful*, that is, the notion *God* is contained under the notion *merciful;* viewed as in the other, means, *God comprehends merciful*, that is, the notion God *comprehends in it* the notion *merciful*."

I cannot admit this to be a true analysis of the meaning of the proposition, either in Extension or in Comprehension. The statement that God is merciful I construe as an affirmation not concerning the notion God, but the Being God. Interpreted in Comprehension I hold it to mean, that this Being has the attribute signified by the word merciful, or in our author's language, comprehended in the concept. Interpreted in Extension I render it thus: The Being, God, is either the only being, or one of the beings, forming the class merciful, or in other words, possessing the attribute mercifulness. Thus stated, who can doubt which of the two is the original and natural judgment, and which is a derivative and artificial mode of restating it? The difference between them is slight, but real, and consists in this, that the second construction introduces the idea of other possible merciful beings, an idea not suggested by the first construc-

* Lectures, iii. 274.

tion. This suggestion gives rise to the idea of a *class* merciful, and of God as a member of that class: notions which are not present to the mind at all when it simply assents to the proposition that God is merciful. To make a distinction between Reasoning in Extension and in Comprehension, when the same syllogism serves for both, could only be admissible if we employed the same words having sometimes in our mind the meaning in Extension, sometimes that in Comprehension: but in reality all reasoning is thought solely in Comprehension, except when we, for a technical purpose, perform a second act of thought upon the Extension — which in general we do not, and have no need to, consider.

Nor is this the only objection to Sir W. Hamilton's doctrine. There is another, less obvious, but equally fatal. The statement in Comprehension is, that A has the attributes comprehended in B. The statement in Extension is, that A belongs to the class of things which have the attributes comprehended in B. These statements are either, as I affirm them to be, one and the same assertion in slightly different words, or they are different assertions. If they are the same assertion, there is but one judgment, which is both in Extension and in Comprehension, and but one kind of reasoning, which is in both. But supposing them, for the sake of argument, to be two different assertions, the judgment respecting Extension is a corollary from that in Comprehension, expressing an artificial point of view in which we may regard the natural judgment. Now, on this supposition, that the judgment respecting Extension is not the same, but an additional judgment, it is, like all other judgments, a judgment in Comprehension. "A is part of class B" must be interpreted thus: The phænomenon A possesses, or the concept A comprehends, the attribute of being included in the class B. So that, while every judgment in Comprehension warrants, by way of immediate inference, a corresponding judgment respecting Extension, this very judgment respecting Extension is itself but a particular kind of judgment in Comprehension. Even, therefore, on the untenable doctrine that there are two different judgments in the case, the distinction between judgments in Extension and judgments in Comprehension is not sustainable; and the supposed addition to the theory of the Syllogism is a mere excrescence and incumbrance on it.

How great the incumbrance is, all are able to judge, who follow our author through the details of the syllogistic logic. He not only finds it necessary to expound and demonstrate every one of the doctrines twice over, as adapted to Extension and to Comprehension, but struggles to express all the fundamental principles in a manner combining both points of view; and is thereby compelled either to state those principles in terms too wide and abstract for easy apprehension, in order that what is laid down respecting wholes and their parts may be applicable to both kinds of wholes (in Extension and in Comprehension), or else to embarrass the learner with the necessity of carrying on two trains of thought at once, in the attempt to apprehend a single principle. I need not dwell on the additional error, of considering the relation of whole and parts as the foundation of the Syllogism in both aspects. To the point of view of Extension that relation is applicable. In every affirmative proposition, if true, the object or class of objects denoted by the subject is a part (when it is not the whole) of the class of objects denoted by the predicate. But no similar relation exists between the two " bundles of attributes " comprehended in the subject and in the predicate, except in the case of Analytical Judgments, that is, of merely verbal propositions. In Synthetical Judgments, that is, in all propositions which convey information about anything except the meaning of words, the relation between the two sets of attributes is not a relation of Whole and Part, but a relation of Coexistence.

I now pass to the doctrine of the Quantification of the Predicate; examining it by the light of the same principles which we have applied to the distinction between the supposed two kinds of Reasoning.

It will be desirable to state in Sir W. Hamilton's own words, as first published in 1846, the claims he prefers in behalf of this doctrine, and the important consequences to which he considers it to lead.*

"The self-evident truth, — That we can only rationally deal with what we already understand, determines the simple logical postulate, — *To state explicitly what is thought implicitly.* From the consistent application of this postulate, on which Logic ever insists, but which Logicians have never fairly obeyed, it follows : — that, logically, we ought to take into account the *quantity*, always understood in thought, but usually, and for manifest reasons, elided in its expression, not only of the *subject*, but also of the *predicate* of a judgment. This being done, and the necessity of doing it will be proved against Aristotle and his repeaters, we obtain, *inter alia*, the ensuing results :

---

* Discussions, Appendix ii. pp. 650, 651.

" 1°. That the *preindesignate terms* of a proposition, whether subject or predicate, are never, on that account, thought as *indefinite* (or indeterminate) in quantity. The only indefinite, is *particular*, as opposed to *definite*, quantity; and this last, as it is either of an extensive *maximum* undivided, or of an extensive *minimum* indivisible, constitutes quantity *universal* (general) and quantity *singular* (individual). In fact, *definite* and *indefinite* are the only quantities of which we ought to hear in Logic; for it is only as indefinite that particular, it is only as definite that individual and general, quantities have any (and the same) logical avail.

" 2°. The revocation of the *two terms of a proposition* to their *true relation;* a proposition being always an *equation* of its subject and its predicate.

" 3°. The consequent reduction of the *Conversion of Propositions* from three species to *one* — that of Simple Conversion.

" 4°. The reduction of all the *General Laws of Categorical Syllogisms* to a *Single Canon.*

" 5°. The evolution from that *one canon* of all the Species and varieties of Syllogism.

" 6°. The *abrogation* of all the *Special Laws of Syllogism.*

" 7°. A demonstration of the *exclusive possibility of Three Syllogistic Figures;* and (on new grounds) the scientific and final *abolition of the Fourth.*

" 8°. A manifestation that *Figure* is an *unessential variation* in syllogistic form; and the consequent *absurdity of Reducing* the syllogisms of the other figures to the first.

" 9°. An enouncement of *one Organic Principle* for each *Figure.*

"10°. A determination of the true *number* of the legitimate *Moods*, with

"11°. Their *amplification* in number (*thirty-six*);

"12°. Their numerical *equality* under all the figures; and

"13°. Their *relative equivalence*, or virtual identity, throughout every schematic difference.

"14°. That, in the *second* and *third* figures, the extremes holding both the same relation to the middle term, there *is not*, as in the first, *an opposition and subordination between a term major and a term minor mutually containing and contained, in the counter wholes of Extension and Comprehension.*

"15°. Consequently, in the *second* and *third* figures, there is *no determinate major and minor premise*, and there are *two indifferent conclusions;* whereas, in the *first*, the *premises* are *determinate*, and there is a *single proximate conclusion*.

"16°. That the *third*, as the figure in which *Comprehension* is predominant, is more appropriate to *Induction*.

"17°. That the *second*, as the figure in which *Extension* is predominant, is more appropriate to *Deduction*.

"18°. That the *first*, as the figure in which *Comprehension* and *Extension* are in equilibrium, is common to *Induction* and *Deduction* indifferently."

The doctrine which leads to all these consequences, or rather, which necessitates all these changes of expression (for they are no more), is that the Predicate is always quantified in thought; that we always think it either as signifying the whole, or as signifying only a part, of the objects included in its Extension. "In reality and in thought, every quantity is necessarily either all, or some, or none."[*] The proposition, All A is B, must mean, in thought, either All A is all B, or All A is some B. When I judge that all oxen ruminate, it must not only be true, but I must mean, either that All ox is all ruminating, or that All ox is some ruminating. Logic, therefore, postulates to express in words what is already in the thoughts, and to write all other propositions in one or other of these forms: which makes it necessary that all the rules for reasoning should be altered, at least in expression, and grounded on the relation of exact equality between the terms.

But if, as I have endeavored to show, the predicate B is present in thought only in respect of its Comprehension; if it be an error to suppose that it is thought of as an aggregate of objects at all; still less is it thought of as an aggregate with a determinate quantity, as some or all. I repeat the appeal which I have already made to every reader's consciousness: Does he, when he judges that all oxen ruminate, advert even in the minutest degree to the question whether there is anything else which ruminates? Is this consideration at all in his thoughts, any more than any other consideration foreign to the immediate subject? One person may know that there are other ruminating animals, another may think that there are none, a third may be without any opinion on the subject; but if they all know what is meant by ruminat-

---

[*] Discussions, Appendix ii. p. 601. But the whole meaning of this assertion, as available for our author's purpose, is destroyed by the statement which he is presently obliged to make, that "the Indesignate is thought, either precisely, as whole or as part, *or vaguely, as the one or the other, unknown which, but the worse always presumed.*" The concession, though fatal to himself, is short of the truth; for the Indesignate is not necessarily thought either as a whole, or as part, or as "unknown which:" it is often not thought in any relation of quantity at all.

ing, they all, when they judge that every ox ruminates, mean exactly the same thing. The mental process they go through, as far as that one judgment is concerned, is precisely identical; though some of them may go on further, and add other judgments to it.*

The fact, that the proposition "Every A is B" only means Every A is *some* B, far from being always present in thought, is not at first seized without some difficulty by the tyro in logic. It requires a certain effort of thought to perceive that when we say, All As are Bs, we only identify A with a part of the class B. When the learner is first told that the proposition All As are Bs can

* Not only we do not (unless exceptionally for some special purpose) quantify the predicate in thought, but we do not even quantify the subject, in the sense which Sir W. Hamilton's theory requires. Even in a universal proposition, we do not think of the subject as an aggregate whole, but as its several parts: we do not judge that all A is B, but that all As are Bs, which is a different thing. That what is true of the whole must be true of any part, only holds good when the whole means the parts themselves, and not when it means the aggregate of them. All A, is a very different notion from Each A. What is true of A only as a whole, forms no element of a judgment concerning its parts — even concerning all its parts. Sir W. Hamilton thinks that the relation of quantity in extension which the class A bears to the class B, is always present in my thoughts when I predicate B of A. This relation of quantity, however, does not belong to individual As, but specifically and solely to A as a whole, and as a whole I am not thinking of it. When I am predicating B of all As severally, I am not adverting to any property or relation which belongs to A as their aggregate. Accordingly we do not say, all ox ruminates, but all oxen ruminate. The distinction is of little importance when A is only coextensive with part of B; for if A altogether is but a part, still more must this be true of any particular A, and it is indifferent whether we say all A is some B, or Each of the As is some B. But it is quite another matter when the assertion is that all A is all B. This, if true at all, is true *only* of A considered as a whole; and expresses a relation between the two classes as totals, not between either of them and its parts. Now, to affirm that when we judge every A to be a B, we always, and necessarily, recognize in thought a fact which is not true of every, or even of any A, but only of the aggregate composed of all As, seems to me as baseless a fancy as ever implanted itself in the intellect of an eminent thinker.

only be converted in the form "Some Bs are As," I apprehend that this strikes him as a new idea; and that the truth of the statement is not quite obvious to him, until verified by a particular example, in which he already knows that the simple converse would be false, such as, All men are animals, therefore all animals are men. So far is it from being true that the proposition, All As are Bs, is spontaneously quantified in thought as All A is some B.

The pretension, therefore, of the doctrine of a Quantified Predicate, to be a more correct representation and analysis of the reasoning process than the common doctrine of the Syllogism, I hold to be psychologically false. And this is fatal to the doctrine, if we admit Sir W. Hamilton's theory that Logic is the science of the laws according to which we *must* think in order that our thought may be valid. But according to the very different view I myself take of Formal Logic, this doctrine might still be a valuable addition to it; since, in my view, the Syllogistic theory altogether is not an analysis of the reasoning process, but only furnishes a test of the validity of reasonings by supplying forms of expression into which all reasonings may be translated if valid, and which, if they are invalid, will detect the hidden flaw. In this point of view it might well be, that a form which always exhibited the quantity of the predicate might be an improvement on the common form. And I am not disposed to deny that for occasional use, and for purposes of illustration, it is so. The exposition of the theory of the syllogism is made clearer, by pointing out that All As are B only implies that all A is some B, while No As are B excludes A from the whole of B. This, in fact, is taught to all who learn logic in the common way, by what is called the doctrine of Suppositio; or (in the many books which leave this doctrine out) by the theory of Conversion, and the syllogistic rules against Undistributed Middle, and against proceeding *à non distributo ad distributum*. There is no harm, and some little good, in giving to these essential doctrines the more explicit expression demanded for them by Sir W. Hamilton. But to obtain any advantage from it, we must be content with quantifying such propositions as, in their unquantified form, are really asserted and used. To foist in any others, overlays and confuses, instead of illuminating, the theory. "All A is some B" is admissible, because it is the quantification really implied in All As are B; but "All A is all B" is inadmissible, because it is not the equivalent of any single proposition capable of being asserted in an unquantified form. As all reasoning, except in the process of teaching Logic, will always be carried on in the forms which men use in real life; and as the only purpose of providing other forms, is to supply a test for those which are really used; it is essential that the forms provided should be forms into which the propositions expressed in common language can be translated — that every proposition in logical form, should be the exact equivalent of some proposition in the common form. Now, there is no proposition capable of being expressed in the ordinary form, which is equivalent to the proposition, All A is all B. That form of expression combines the import of two propositions in common language, expressive of two separate judgments, All As are Bs, and all Bs are As.

If this had not been denied, I should have deemed it

too obvious to require either proof or illustration. But Sir W. Hamilton does deny it, and therefore some enforcement of it is indispensable. When we make an assertion in the cramped and unnatural form, All man is all rational, can anything seem more evident than that to cover the whole ground occupied by this statement, two judgments are required; namely, first, that every man has the attribute reason; and secondly, that nothing which is not man has that attribute, or (which is the same thing) that every rational creature has the attributes of man? How is it possible to make only one judgment, out of an assertion divisible into two parts, one of which may be unknown and the other known, one unthought of and the other thought of, one false and the other true?*

Unless Sir W. Hamilton was prepared to maintain that whenever the universal converse of a universal affirmative proposition would be true, we cannot know the one without knowing the other, it is in vain for him to contend that a form which asserts both of them at once is only one proposition. If in judging that "All equilateral triangles are equiangular," we judge that all

* The only answer I can imagine to this is, that having the two concepts Man and Rational, and being engaged in actually comparing them with each other, we *must* perceive and judge whether the one is merely a part of the other, or a whole coinciding with it. But this answer it is not competent to Sir W. Hamilton, or any other Conceptualist, to make. An adversary of Sir W. Hamilton might make it. I have myself said, and have offered as a *reductio ad absurdum* of his analysis of Reasoning, that if we have two concepts and compare them, we cannot but perceive any relation of whole and part which exists between them. Sir W. Hamilton, however, is precluded from making this reply; for all Reasoning, even to the longest process in Mathematics, consists, according to him, in discovering this relation of whole and part by circuitous means, when direct comparison does not disclose it. From his point of view, therefore, the argument is not tenable; and from mine it has no pertinence, since I do not admit that Reasoning is a comparison of Concepts at all.

equilateral triangles are all equiangular, in what condition of judgment is the mind of the tyro to whom it has just been proved that all equilateral triangles are equiangular, but who does not yet know the proof of the converse proposition that all equiangular triangles are equilateral? If "All equilateral triangles are all equiangular" is only one judgment, what is the proposition that all equilateral triangles are equiangular? Is it half a judgment?*

---

* Sir W. Hamilton goes the length of asserting (Appendix to Lectures, iv. 292, *et seqq.*) that to a person who knows all trilateral figures to be triangular, the proposition "all triangles are trilateral" must, if expressed as understood, be written "all triangles are all trilateral:" as if every proposition which I affirm respecting a subject, must include all I know about it.

That the proposition All A is B is not a single judgment, but compounded of two, has already been urged against Sir W. Hamilton by Mr. De Morgan, and we are in possession of Sir W. Hamilton's answer (Discussions, Appendix ii. pp. 687, 688). Unhappily Mr. De Morgan (by an oversight not usual with that able thinker) gave Sir W. Hamilton an apparent triumph, by mistaking the two judgments which the pretended single proposition is composed of. He appears to have said, that the proposition "All Xs are all Ys," is compounded of the propositions, "All Xs are some Ys," and "Some Xs are all Ys." Sir W. Hamilton replies, that these two propositions are (in his own peculiar language) incompossible, inasmuch as we cannot think X both as some Y, that is, a part of Y, and as the whole. The argument is little better than a quibble, because other people do not (though Sir W. Hamilton does) mean by some, *some only*; they mean *some at least*; and if the first of Mr. De Morgan's two propositions identifies X with only some of Y, the second superadds the remainder. But in reality the two judgments which go to the composition of "All A is all B," are not judgments with quantified predicates at all. They are, All A is B, and all B is A. The one ascribes the attributes of B to every A, the other the attributes of A to every B. Judgments more distinct and independent of one another do not exist.

According to Sir W. Hamilton (Appendix to Lectures, iv. 259) "ordinary language quantifies the Predicate as often as this determination becomes of the smallest import." And he cites such instances as "Virtue is the *only* nobility;" "Of animals man alone is rational," and the like. The truth is, that ordinary language quantifies the predicate in the rare cases in which it is quantified in thought, and in no others. And even then the quantified

This is not the only case in which Sir W. Hamilton insists upon wrapping up two different assertions in one form of words, and demands that they shall be considered one assertion. He strenuously contends that the form "Some A is B," or (in its quantified form) "Some A is some B," ought in logical propriety to be used and understood in the sense of "some and *some only*."[*] No shadow of justification is shown for thus deviating from the practice of all writers on logic, and of all who think and speak with any approach to precision, and adopting into logic a mere *sous-entendu* of common conversation in its most unprecise form. If I say to any one, "I saw some of your children to-day," he might be justified in inferring that I did not see them all, not because the words mean it, but because, if I had seen them all, it is most likely that I should have said so: though even this cannot be presumed unless it is presupposed that I must have known whether the children I saw were all or not. But to carry this colloquial mode of interpreting a statement into Logic, is something novel. If Some A is B is to be understood of some *only*, it is a double judgment, compounded of the propositions, Some As are Bs, and some As are not Bs. If quantified in our author's manner, the propositions would run thus: Some A is some B, and some (other)

proposition is an abbreviated expression of two judgments. The German logician Scheibler, to whom our author refers in a foot-note (Ibid. p. 261), could have set him right here.

Propositions in Extension have absolutely no meaning but what they derive from Comprehension. The Logic of the quantified predicate takes the Comprehension out of them, and leaves them a *caput mortuum*.

[*] See, among many other places, Discussions, Appendix ii. pp. 600, 601, where he says, "Every quantity is necessarily either *all*, or *none*, or *some*; of these the third is formally *exclusive* of the other two."

IMPROVEMENTS IN FORMAL LOGIC. 211

A is not any B. If two statements, one of which affirms and the other denies a different predicate of a different subject, are not two distinct judgments, it is impossible to say what are so. One of the great uses of discipline in Formal Logic, is to make us aware when something which claims to be a single proposition, really consists of several, which, not being necessarily involved one in another, require to be separated, and considered each by itself, before we admit the compound assertion. This separation may be called, with reason, stating explicitly in words what is implicitly in thought. But it is a new postulate of Logic to state *i*mplicitly in words what is *ex*plicitly in thought, and I do not think that Logic is at all enriched by the acquisition.

With these compound propositions falls the whole pretension of the quantified mode of expression to yield legitimate inferences which are not recognized by the old Logic. Whatever can be proved from "All A is all B," can be proved in the old form from one or both of its elements, All As are Bs, and all Bs are As. Whatever can be proved from "Some, and only some, A is some (or all) B," can be proved in the old form from its elements, Some As are Bs, Some As are not Bs, and (in the case last mentioned) All Bs are As. If we choose to alter the forms of all our propositions, the forms of our syllogisms naturally require alteration too; and there may be a greater number of forms in which quantified conclusions can be drawn from quantified premises, than in which unquantified conclusions can be drawn from unquantified premises. But there is not a single instance, nor is it possible in the nature of things that there should be an instance, in which a conclusion that is provable from quantified premises, could not be proved from the same premises unquantified, if we set forth all those which are really involved. If there could be such an instance, the quantified Syllogism would be a real addition to the theory of Logic: if not, not.

As I have already once remarked, it does not follow, because the quantified Syllogism is not a true expression of what is in thought, that writing the predicate with a quantification may not be a real help to the *art* of Logic. Though not a correct analysis of the reasoning process, it may, in some cases, enable us more readily to see whether the conclusion really follows from the premises. But without rejecting it as an available help for this purpose, I must observe that its use in this capacity appears to me extremely limited: for two reasons. First; the problem is, to test the validity of a reasoning as expressed in the language in which men ordinarily reason. We do this by taking the propositions as they are, and measuring the extent of the assertions made in the two premises and in the conclusion respectively, so as to ascertain whether the former are broad enough to cover and include the latter. This it requires some practice to do, but the task is not avoided by quantifying the predicate: on the contrary, it must have been actually performed before the predicate can be correctly quantified; so that by quantifying it in expression, no trouble is saved. My second reason is, that after the predicate has been quantified, it is often equally or more difficult to follow the consecution of the thought through the symbols, than as expressed in ordinary language. Take one of the common cases of invalid inference, a syllogism in the first figure with the major premise particular, such as this:

Some Ms are Ps
All Ss are Ms
Therefore all Ss are Ps;

the inference fails, because the Ms which are identified with Ss may not be the same Ms which are Ps, but other Ms. Let us now quantify the predicates thus:

Some Ms are some Ps
All Ss are some Ms
Therefore all Ss are some Ps:

is the invalidity of the inference at all clearer? Does it require less exertion of thought to perceive that "some Ms" may not mean the same *some* in both premises, than it did to recognize the equivalent truth as to M in the minor, and "some M" in the major premise? On the contrary, the quantified form is the more plausibly misleading of the two, since the middle term, though really ambiguous, is, in that form, verbally the same, which in the unquantified form it is not.

The general result of these considerations is, that the utility of the new forms is by no means such as to compensate for the great additional complication which they introduce into the syllogistic theory; a complication which would make it at the same time difficult to learn or remember, and intolerably tiresome both in the learning and in the using. The sole purpose of any syllogistic forms is to afford an available test for the process of drawing inferences in the common language of life, from premises in the same common language; and the ordinary forms of Syllogism effect this purpose completely. The new forms do not, in any appreciable degree, facilitate the process, while they are chargeable, in a far greater degree than the common forms, with diverting the mind from the true meaning of propositions (the ascription of attributes to objects considered severally), and concentrating it upon the highly artificial, and generally unimportant, consideration of the relation of extent between classes of objects, considered not severally, but as collective wholes. The new forms have thus no practical advantage which can countervail the objection of their entire psychological irrelevancy; and the invention and acquisition of them have little value, except as one among many other feats of mental gymnastic, by which students of the science may exercise and invigorate their faculties. They should, in short, be dealt with as Sir W. Hamilton deals with Mr. De Morgan's forms of "numerically definite" Syllogism, viz., "taken into account by Logic as authentic forms, but then relegated as of little use in practice, and cumbering the science with a superfluous mass of words."*

* Appendix to Lectures, iv. 355.

CHAPTER XXIII.

OF SOME MINOR PECULIARITIES OF DOCTRINE IN SIR WILLIAM HAMILTON'S VIEW OF FORMAL LOGIC.

THE two theories examined in the preceding chapter are the only important novelties which Sir W. Hamilton has introduced into the Science or Art of Logic. But he has here and there departed from the common doctrine of logicians on subordinate points. Some of these deviations deserve notice from their connection with some principal part of our author's doctrine, others chiefly as throwing light on the character of his mind. The one to which I shall first advert is of the former class.

I. Almost all writers on the Syllogistic Logic have directed attention to the fact, that though we cannot, while observing the forms of Logic, draw a false conclusion from true premises, we may draw a true one from false premises: in other words, the falsity of the premises does not prove the falsity of the conclusion; nor does the truth of the conclusion prove the truth of the premises. The warning is needed; for it is by no means unusual to mistake a refutation of the reasons from which a doctrine has been deduced, for a disproof of the doctrine itself; and there is no error of thought more common than the acceptance of premises because they lead to a conclusion already assented to as true. Not only is this caution useful, but it is relevant to Logic, even in the restricted point of view of Formal Logic. When it is affirmed that Formal Logic has nothing to do with Material Truth, all that ought to be meant, is that in Logic we are not to consider whether the conclusion supposed to be proved is true in fact. But we are to consider whether it is true conditionally, true if the premises are true: that question is the specific business of Formal Logic: if Formal Logic does not teach us that, there is nothing for it to teach. The theorem, that in a valid Syllogism the falsity of the premises does not prove the falsity of the conclusion, is as germane to Logic as that the truth of the premises proves the truth of the conclusion. We have therefore reason to be surprised at finding Sir W. Hamilton delivering himself as follows: *—

"Logic does not warrant the truth of its premises, except in so far as these may be the formal conclusions of anterior reasonings; it only warrants (on the hypothesis that the premises are truly assumed) the truth of the inference. In this view the conclusion may, as a separate proposition, be true; but if this truth be not a necessary consequence from the premises, it is a false conclusion, that is, in fact, no conclusion at all. Now, on this point there is a doctrine prevalent among logicians, which is not only erroneous, but if admitted, is subversive of the distinction of Logic as a purely formal science. The doctrine in question is in its result this,— that if the conclusion of a syllogism be true, the premises may be either true or false, but that if the conclusion be false, one or both of its premises must be false: in other words, that it is possible to infer true from false, but not false from true. As an example of this I have given the following syllogism: —

* Lectures, iii. 450, 451.

Aristotle is a Roman ;
A Roman is a European ;
Therefore, Aristotle is a European.

The inference, in so far as expressed, is true ; but I would remark, that the whole inference which the premises necessitate, and which the conclusion, therefore, virtually contains, is not true, — is false. For the premises of the preceding syllogism gave not only the conclusion, *Aristotle is a European*, but also the conclusion, *Aristotle is not a Greek;* for it not merely follows from the premises, that Aristotle is conceived under the universal notion of which the concept *Roman* forms a particular sphere, but likewise that he is conceived as excluded from all the other particular spheres which are contained under that universal notion. The consideration of the truth of the premise, *Aristotle is a Roman*, is, however, more properly to be regarded as extralogical ; but if so, then the consideration of the conclusion, *Aristotle is a European*, on any other view than as a mere formal inference from certain hypothetical antecedents, is likewise extralogical. Logic is only concerned with the formal truth, — the technical validity, — of its syllogisms, and anything beyond the legitimacy of the consequence it draws from certain hypothetical antecedents, it does not profess to vindicate. Logical truth and falsehood are thus contained in the correctness and incorrectness of logical inference ; and it was, therefore, with no impropriety that we made a true or correct, and a false or incorrect, syllogism convertible expressions."

The statement that a true proposition may be correctly inferred from false premises, or in other words, that a true opinion may be supported by false reasons, is one of which we could hardly have expected to find the truth disputed, whatever might be said of the connection of Logic with it. So unlooked-for a paradox required to be defended by the strongest arguments: who, then, would expect such shabby, not arguments, but hints of arguments, as the author presents us with? He stops short in the middle of the first, as if afraid that it would break down if relied upon, and hurries to the second, which is still more incapable of bearing weight. "The consideration of the conclusion, *Aristotle is a European*, in any other view than as a mere formal inference from certain hypothetical antecedents, is extralogical." Nobody proposes to consider it as anything but a formal inference from certain hypothetical antecedents. The gist of the whole question is that it is such an inference, and consequently that a proposition really true, may be a formal inference from premises wholly or partially false: in other words, the falsity of the conclusion does not follow from the falsity of the premises. It is as much the business of the theory of "formal inference" to show what conclusions are not formally legitimate, as what are. It is not the business of Formal Logic to determine what is actually true, but it is, to tell what does or does not follow from what. In the first unfinished part of his argument, Sir W. Hamilton makes a faint attempt to show that the conclusion, Aristotle is a European, is not true. He admits it to be true as far as expressed, but says that it virtually contains something which is false, namely, that Aristotle is not a Greek. By what analysis can he find this in the proposition, Aristotle is a European? He does not pretend that it is in the proposition considered in itself, but only in the proposition as inferred from "Aristotle is a Roman."

But it is a strange doctrine that a proposition is true or false not according to what it asserts, but according to the mode in which the belief of it has been arrived at. It is a very irrational mode of speaking to say that a proposition, besides its obvious meaning, contains a meaning which the words do not convey, which in the mouths of other people it does not bear, but which is so essential a part of it as by its falsity to make the proposition false which otherwise would be true. Suppose that the register of a man's birth having been destroyed, some one, to whom the date is of importance, proves it by a false entry in the parish books: would that make the man not to have been born on the day he was born on? But let us concede this point, however unreasonable, and admit that the proposition Aristotle is a European, when inferred from the premise that he is a Roman, includes that premise as part of its own meaning. Does it therefore contain an implication that he is not a Greek? Suppose that I have never heard of Greeks; or that, having heard of them, I suppose a Greek to be a kind of Roman, or a Roman a kind of Greek. Will this ignorance or misapprehension on my part prevent me from concluding, that if a Roman is a European and Aristotle a Roman, Aristotle must be a European; or will it make the inference illegitimate, or the conclusion false? One sentence in our quotation from Sir W. Hamilton is a singular illustration of the length he will go to support a favorite thesis. "The premises," he says, "of the syllogism gave not only the conclusion, Aristotle is a European, but also the conclusion, Aristotle is not a Greek." Let us try:—

    Aristotle is a Roman;
    A Roman is a European;
    Therefore, Aristotle is not a Greek.

This is Formal Logic. This is the philosopher who is so rigidly bent upon excluding from Logic all consideration of what is true or false *vi materiæ*. What shadow of connection is there, unless it be *vi materiæ*, between this conclusion and those premises? Nothing can explain this aberration in a thinker of Sir W. Hamilton's acuteness, except his dogged determination in no shape to recognize belief as an element of judgment, or truth as in any way concerned in Pure Logic.

Sir W. Hamilton has a salvo for all this, though it is one which would not occur to everybody. According to him there are two kinds of truth, or rather the word truth has two meanings, so that it is possible for a proposition to be true although it is false. There is Formal Truth, and Real Truth.* Real Truth is "the harmony between a thought and its matter." Formal Truth is of two kinds, Logical, and Mathematical. Logical Truth is "the harmony or agreement of our thoughts with themselves as thoughts, in other words, the correspondence of thought with the universal laws of thinking." And Mathematical Truth is some other harmony of thought, in which truth of fact is equally dispensed with. In another place, he says† that if the consequent is correctly "evolved out of" the antecedent, the conclusion out of the premises, this is "Logical or Formal or Subjective truth: and an inference may be subjectively or formally true, which is objectively or really false." To support his denial of the common doctrine, he has to alter the meaning of words, and make false in the new meaning what cannot be denied to be true in the old. But I object *in toto* to such an abuse of terms as

---

* Lectures, iv. 64–68.   † Ibid. ii. 343.

affirming a false proposition to be true, because it is in such a relation to another false proposition, that if that false proposition had been true it would have been true likewise. There is no fitness in the word truth, to express this mere relation of consecution between false propositions. No qualification by adjectives, whether "logical," or "formal," or "subjective," will make this assertion anything but a solecism in language, claiming to be the correction of a philosophical doctrine.

The whole theory of the difference between Formal and Real truth is treated as it deserves, in a passage from one of Sir W. Hamilton's favorite authorities, Esser, which he quotes, and, strange to say, quotes with approbation.

"One party of philosophers," says Esser,* "defining truth in general, the absolute harmony of our thoughts and cognitions, — divide truth into a formal or logical, and into a material or metaphysical, according as that harmony is in consonance with the laws of formal thought, or, over and above, with the laws of real knowledge. The criterion of formal truth they place in the principles of Contradiction and of Sufficient Reason, enouncing that what is non-contradictory and consequent is formally true. This criterion, which is positive and immediate of formal truth (inasmuch as what is non-contradictory and consequent can always be thought as possible), they style a negative and mediate criterion of material truth: as what is self-contradictory and logically inconsequent is in reality impossible; at the same time, what is not self-contradictory and not logically inconsequent, is not, however, to be regarded as having an actual

* Lectures, iii. 106, 107.

existence. But here the foundation is treacherous; the notion of truth is false. When we speak of truth, we are not satisfied with knowing that a thought harmonizes with a certain system of thoughts and cognitions; but, over and above, we require to be assured that what we think is real, and is as we think it to be. Are we satisfied on this point, we then regard our thoughts as true; whereas, if we are not satisfied of this, we deem them false, how well soever they may quadrate with any theory or system. It is not, therefore, in any absolute harmony of mere thought, that truth consists, but solely in the correspondence of our thoughts with their objects. The distinction of formal and material truth is thus not only unsound in itself, but opposed to the notion of truth universally held, and embodied in all languages. But if this distinction be inept, the title of Logic, as a positive standard of truth, must be denied; it can only be a negative criterion, being conversant with thoughts and not with things, with the possibility and not with the actuality of existence."

After all the experience we have had of the facility with which Sir W. Hamilton forgets in one part of his speculations what he has thought in another, it remains scarcely credible that he indorses, in his third volume, this emphatic protest against the distinction which he draws, and the opinion which he maintains, in his second and fourth. "Two opposite doctrines," he says,* "have sprung up, which, on opposite sides, have overlooked the true relations of Logic;" and one of these is the doctrine (the "inaccuracy" our author styles it) which Esser, in this passage, protests against. And he there-

* Lectures, iii. 106.

upon quotes Esser's condemnation of his (Sir W. Hamilton's) own doctrine. Truly, if arguments *ad hominem* were sufficient, a controversialist who undertakes to refute Sir W. Hamilton would have an easy task.

II. I have already noticed one unacknowledged departure by our author from the usage of Logicians as regards the sense of the word Disjunctive; confining Disjunctive judgments to those in which all the alternative propositions have the same subject: A is either B or C, or D. This limitation excludes two other forms of the assertion of an alternative: that in which the propositions have different subjects but the same predicate, " Either A, or B, or C, is D ; " and that in which they have different subjects and different predicates, " Either A is B, or C is D." The former is exemplified in such judgments as these, Either Brown or Smith did this act; Either John or Thomas is dead. The latter in such as these: Either the witness has told a falsehood, or the prisoner has committed a murder; Either Macbeth has killed all Macduff's children, or Macduff has children who were not there present. While arbitrarily excluding both these kinds of assertion from the class and denomination in which they had always been placed, our author does not assign to them any other; so that the effect is not a mere innovation in language, but a hiatus in his logical system; these two kinds of judgment having no place, name, or recognition in it. I have now to point out a second deviation from the received doctrine of logicians in connection with the same subject. In respect to the class of judgments to which he restricts the name of Disjunctive, those in which two or more predicates are disjunctively affirmed of the same subject, he takes for granted through the whole of his exposition,* that when we say, A is either B or C, we imply that it cannot be both: that we may as legitimately argue, A is either B or C, but it is B, therefore it is not C, as we may argue, A is either B or C, but it is not B, therefore it is C. This is what enables him to affirm, as he does, that the principle of Disjunctive Judgments is the Law of Excluded Middle. The predicates are supposed to be either explicitly or implicitly contradictory, so that one or other of them must be true of the subject, but both of them cannot. I conceive this to be both an incompleteness in his theory, and a positive error in fact. An incompleteness, because we may judge, and legitimately judge, that a thing is either this or that, though aware that it may possibly be both. Sir W. Hamilton is so severe on the ordinary Logic for omitting, as he thinks, some valid forms of thought, that it was peculiarly incumbent on him not to commit a similar oversight in his own exposition of the science. But Sir W. Hamilton does not merely leave unrecognized those disjunctive judgments in which the alternative predicates are mutually compatible; he assumes that the disjunctive form of assertion denies their compatibility, which it assuredly does not. If we assert that a man who has acted in some particular way, must be either a knave or a fool, we by no means assert, or intend to assert, that he cannot be both. Very important consequences may sometimes be drawn from our knowledge that one or other of two perfectly compatible suppositions must be true. Suppose such an argument as this. To make an entirely unselfish use of despotic power a man must be either a saint or a

* Lectures, iii. 326, *et seqq.*

philosopher: but saints and philosophers are rare; therefore those are rare, who make an entirely unselfish use of despotic power. The conclusion follows from the premises, and is of great practical importance. But does the disjunctive premise necessarily imply, or must it be construed as supposing, that the same person cannot be both a saint and a philosopher! Such a construction would be ridiculous.*

There is a great quantity of intricate and obscure speculation in our author's Lectures and their Appendices, relating to Disjunctive and Hypothetical Propositions. But, much as he had thought on the subject, the simple idea never seems to have occurred to him, that every Disjunctive judgment is compounded of two or more Hypothetical ones. "Either A is B, or C is D," means, If A is not B, C is D; and if C is not D, A is B. This is obvious enough to most people; but if Sir W. Hamilton had thought of it, he probably would have denied it: its admission would not have been in keeping with the disposition he shows in so many places, to consider as one judgment all that it is possible to assert in one formula. Again, though he takes much pains to determine what is the real import of an Hypothetical Judgment, the thought never occurs to him that it is a judgment concerning judgments. (If A is B, C is D, means, The judgment C is D follows as a consequence from the judgment A is B.) Not seeing this, Sir W. Hamilton tacitly adopts the assertion of Krug, that the conversion of an hypothetical syllogism into a categorical "is not always possible." †

* Mr. Mansel does not fall into this mistake (Prolegomena Logica, p. 221).
† Lectures, iii. 342.

III. The next of Sir W. Hamilton's minor innovations in Logic has reference to the Sorites. It is scarcely necessary to say, that a Sorites is an argument in the form, A is B, B is C, C is D, D is E, therefore A is E: an abridged expression for a series of syllogisms, but not requiring to be decomposed into them in order to make its conclusiveness visible. Sir W. Hamilton accuses all writers on Logic of having overlooked the possibility of a Sorites in the Second or Third Figure.* By this he does not mean, one in which the ultimate syllogism, which sums up the argument, is in the second or third figure, for this all logicians have admitted. For example, to the Sorites given above, there might be added the proposition, No F is E; in which case, the ultimate syllogism would be, A is E, but no F is E, therefore A is not an F: a syllogism in the second figure. Or there might be added, at the opposite end of the series, A is G; when the ultimate syllogism would be in the third figure; A is E, but A is G, therefore some G is an E. These are real Sorites, real chain arguments, and they conclude in the second and third figures: we may call them, if we please, Sorites in the second and in the third figure, the truth being that they are Sorites in which one of the steps is in the second or third figure, all the others being in the first. And every one who understands the laws of the second and third figures (or even the general laws of the Syllogism) can see that no more than one step in either of them is admissible in a Sorites, and that it must either be the first or the last. About this, however, Logicians have always been agreed. These are not the kinds of Sorites

* Lectures, iii. 342. Appendix to Lectures, iv. 395.

which Sir W. Hamilton contends for. By a Sorites in the second or third figure, he means one in which all the steps are in the second, or all in the third, figure (a thing impossible in a real Sorites), and in which, accordingly, instead of a succession of middle terms establishing a connection between the two extremes, there is but one middle term altogether. His paradigm in the second figure would be, No B is A, No C is A, No D is A, No E is A, All F is A, therefore no B, or C, or D, or E, is F. In the third figure, it would be, A is B, A is C, A is D, A is E, A is F, therefore some B, and C, and D, and E, are F. One would have thought that anybody who had the smallest notion of the meaning of a Sorites, must have seen that either of these is not a Sorites at all. It is not a chain argument. It does not ascend to a conclusion by a series of steps, each introducing a new premise. It does not deduce one conclusion from a succession of premises, all necessary to its establishment. It draws as many different conclusions as there are syllogisms, each conclusion depending only on the two premises of one syllogism. That no B is F, follows from No B is A, and All F is A; not from those premises combined with No C is A, No D is A, No E is A. That some B is F, follows from A is B and A is F; and would be proved, though all the other premises of the pretended Sorites were rejected. If Sir W. Hamilton had found in any other writer such a misuse of logical language as he is here guilty of, he would have roundly accused him of total ignorance of logical writers. Since it cannot be imputed to any such cause in himself, I can only ascribe it to the passion which appears to have seized him, in the later years of his life, for finding more and more new discoveries to be made in Syllogistic Logic. If he had transported his ardor for originality into the other departments of the science, in which there was so great an unexhausted field for discovery, he might have enlarged the bounds of philosophy to a much greater extent, than I am afraid he will now be found to have done.

IV. I next turn to a singular misapplication of logical language, in which Sir W. Hamilton departs from all good authorities, and misses one of the most important distinctions drawn by the Aristotelian logic. I refer to his use of the word Contrary. He confounds contrariety with simple incompatibility. " Opposition of Notions," he says,* " is twofold : 1°. *Immediate* or *Contradictory Opposition*, called likewise *Repugnance* (τὸ ἀντιφατικῶς ἀντικεῖσθαι, ἀντίφασις, *oppositio immediata* sive *contradictoria, repugnancia*) ; and 2°. *Mediate* or *Contrary Opposition* (τὸ ἐναντίως ἀντικεῖσθαι, ἐναντιότης, *oppositio media* vel *contraria*). The former emerges, when one concept abolishes (*tollit*) directly or by simple negation, what another establishes, *ponit;* the latter, when one concept does this not directly or by simple negation, but through the affirmation of something else."

The exemplification and illustration of this † is not of our author's devising, but is a citation from Krug, who had preceded him in the error. " To speak now of the distinction of Contradictory and Contrary Opposition, or of Contradiction and Contrariety ; of these the former, Contradiction, is exemplified in the opposites, — *yellow, not yellow; walking, not walking*. Here each notion is directly, immediately, and absolutely, repugnant to the other, — they are reciprocal negatives. This

---

* Lectures, iii. 213, 214. † Ibid. pp. 214, 215.

opposition is, therefore, properly called that of *Contradiction* or of *Repugnance;* and the opposing notions themselves are *contradictory* or *repugnant* notions, in a single word, *contradictories.* The latter, or Contrary Opposition, is exemplified in the opposites, *yellow, blue, red,* &c., *walking, standing, lying,* &c."

It can hardly have been imagined by Krug or Sir W. Hamilton, that this is the meaning of Contrariety in common discourse, or that any one ever speaks of yellow or blue as the contrary of red, or even as the opposite of it. The very phrase, "*the* contrary," testifies that a thing cannot have more contraries than one. Black is regarded as the contrary of white, but no other contrariety is recognized among colors at all. Sir W. Hamilton, versed as he was in the literature of logic, can hardly have fancied that the world of logicians, any more than the common world, was on his side. In the language of logicians, as in that of life, a thing has only one contrary — its extreme opposite; the thing farthest removed from it in the same class. Black is the contrary of white, but neither of them is the contrary of red. Infinitely great is the contrary of infinitely small, but is not the contrary of finite. It is the more strange that Krug and Sir W. Hamilton should have misunderstood or rejected this, as the definition they ignore is the foundation of the distinction between Contradictory and Contrary Propositions, in the famous Parallelogram of Opposition. The contrary proposition to All A is B, is No A is B, its extreme opposite; the assertion most widely differing from it that can be made; denying, not it merely, but a great deal more. Its contradictory is merely, Some A is not B. Sir W. Hamilton could not have imagined the distinction between these negative propositions to be, that the one denies by simple negation, the other through the affirmation of something else.

That the teachers of the Syllogistic Logic have taken this view, and not Sir W. Hamilton's, of the meaning of Contrariety, might be shown by any number of quotations. I have only looked up the authorities nearest at hand. I begin with Aristotle : Τὰ γὰρ πλεῖστον ἀλλήλων διεστηκότα τῶν ἐν τῷ αὐτῷ γένει, ἐναντία ὁρίζονται.*

Aristotle again : Τὰ γὰρ ἐναντία, τῶν πλεῖστον διαφερόντων περὶ τὸ αὐτό.†

Aristotle ἐν τῷ δεκάτῳ τῆς θεολογικῆς πραγματείας, as cited by Ammonius Hermiæ : ‡ Επεὶ δὲ διαφέρειν ἐνδέχεται ἀλλήλων τὰ διαφέροντα πλεῖον καὶ ἔλαττον, ἔστι τις, καὶ μεγίστη διαφορά, καὶ ταύτην λέγω ἐναντίωσιν.

Ammonius himself thereon : Ἡ τῶν ἐναντίων διαφορὰ μεγίστη τῶν ἄλλων, καὶ οὐδὲν ἔχουσα ἐξωτέρω αὐτῆς δυνάμενον πεσεῖν.

My next extract shall be from a well-known treatise, which Sir W. Hamilton particularly recommended to his pupils : Burgersdyk's Institutiones Logicæ.

"Oppositorum species sunt quinque : Disparata, contraria, relativé opposita, privative opposita, et contradictoria.

"Disparata sunt, quorum unum pluribus opponitur, eodem modo. Sic homo et equus, album et cæruleum, sunt disparata : quia homo non equo solum, sed etiam cani, leoni, cæterisque bestiarum speciebus, et album, non solum cæruleo, sed etiam rubro, viridi, cæterisque

---

* Categoriæ, cap. 6.   † Περὶ Ἑρμηνείας, cap. 14.

‡ Ammonii Hermiæ in Aristotelis de Interpretatione Librum Commentarius, ed. Aldi, pp. 175, 176.

coloribus mediis, opponitur *eodem modo*, hoc est, eodem oppositorum genere. . . *.

"Contraria sunt duo absolute, quæ sub eodem genere plurimum distant." *

This passage informs us, not only that what Sir W. Hamilton terms Contraries were not so called by the Aristotelian logicians, but also what they were called. They were called Disparates; a term employed by Sir W. Hamilton, but in a totally different meaning.†

The next is from one of the ablest, and, though in a comparatively small compass, one of the completest in essentials, of all the expositions I have seen of Logic from the purely Aristotelian point of view: *Manuductio ad Logicam*, by the Père Du Trieu, of Douai.‡

"Contraria sunt, quæ posita sub eodem genere maxime a se invicem distant, eidem subjecto susceptivo vicissim insunt, a quo se mutuo expellunt, nisi alterum insit a natura; ut, *album*, et *nigrum*.

"In hac definitione continentur quatuor conditiones, sive leges contrariorum.

"Prima, ut sint sub eodem genere. . . .

"Secunda conditio contrariorum est ut sub illo eodem genere maxime distent, id est *precise* repugnent. . . . Hinc excluduntur disparata."

The next is from Saunderson's Logicæ Artis Compendium, one of the best known elementary treatises on Logic by British authors.§

"Oppositio Contraria est inter terminos contrarios. Sunt autem ea contraria quæ posita sub eodem genere

---

* Burgersdicii Institutiones Logicæ, lib. 1. cap. 22; Theorema 1.
† Lectures, iii. 224.   ‡ Pars Tertia, cap. iii. art. 1.
§ Pars Prima, cap. 15.

maxime inter se distant, et vim habent expellendi se vicissim ex eodem subjecto susceptibili."

Crackanthorp : * "Contraria sunt Opposita quorum unum alteri sic opponitur ut nulli alteri aut æque aut magis opponatur. Sic Albedo Nigredini, Homini Brutum, Rationale Irrationali contrarium est. Nam nihil est quod æque Albedini opponitur atque Nigredo, et sic in reliquis." On the other hand, "Disparata sunt Opposita quorum unum uni sic opponitur, ut alteri vel æque vel magis opponatur. Sic Liberalitas et Avaritia disparata sunt. Nam Avaritia magis opponitur Prodigalitati quam Liberalitati. Sic Albedo et Rubedo disparata sunt, quia Albedo æque opponitur Viriditati atque Rubedini, et magis Nigredini quam ambobus. Nam plus inter se semper distant extrema, quam vel media inter se, vel medium ab alterutro extremo."

Brererwood : † "Contraria a Dialecticis ita definiri solent: Sunt Opposita quæ sub eodem genere posita maxime a se invicem distant, et eodem subjecto susceptibili vicissim insunt, a quo se mutuo expellunt, nisi alterum insit a natura. . . . Sed quoniam hæc definitio (quamvis sit præcipue in Dialecticorum scholis authoritans) laborat et tædio, et summa difficultate, placet ex Aristotele faciliorem adducere, et breviorem : "*Contraria sunt quæ sub eodem genere posita, maxime distant.*"

Samuel Smith : ‡ "Contraria sunt quæ sub eodem genere posita, maxime a se invicem distant, et eidem susceptibili vicissim insunt, a quo se mutuo expellunt, nisi alterum eorum insit a natura. Ad Contraria igitur

* Logica, cap. 20.
† Tractatus Quidam Logici de Prædicabilibus et Prædicamentis. Tractatus Decimus, de Post-Prædicamentis, Sect. 5 et 6.
‡ Aditus ad Logicam (Oxoniæ, 1656), lib. 1. cap. 14.

tria requiruntur: primo ut sint sub eodem genere, scilicet Qualitatis: nam solarum qualitatum est contrarietas; secundo, ut maxime a se invicem distent in natura positiva, id est, ut ambo extrema sint positiva."

Wallis: * "Contraria definiri solent, quæ sub eodem genere maxime distant. Ut calidum et frigidum, album et nigrum: quæ contrariæ qualitatis dici solent."

Even Aldrich, right for once, may be added to the list of Oxford authorities.† "Contraria sub eodem genere maxime distant. Non maxime distant *omnium;* magis enim distant quæ nec idem genus summum habent, magis Contradictoria: sed maxime eorum quæ in genere conveniunt."

Keckermann ‡ does not employ this, but another definition of Contraries; not, however, Sir W. Hamilton's; and all his examples of Contraries are taken from Extreme Opposites.

Casparus Bartholinus: § "Contraria sunt, quæ sub eodem genere maxime distant, eidemque subjecto susceptibili a quo se mutuo expellunt, vicissim insunt, nisi alterum insit a natura."

Du Hamel: ‖ "Oppositio contraria est inter duo extrema positiva, quæ sub eodem genere posita maxime distant, et ab eodem subjecto sese expellunt."

Grammatica Rationis, sive Institutiónes Logicæ: ¶ "Contraria adversa sunt accidentia, posita sub eodem

* Institutio Logicæ, lib. i. cap. 16.
† Artis Logicæ Compendium, Quæstionum Logicarum Determinatio, quæst. 19.
‡ Systema Logicæ.
§ Enchiridion Logicæ (Lipsiæ, 1618) lib. i. cap. 23.
‖ Philosophia vetus et nova ad usum scholæ accommodata (Amstelodami, 1700), p. 197.
¶ Oxonii, 1673.

genere, quæ maxime distant, et se mutuo pellunt ab eodem subjecto in quo vicissim insunt."

Familiar as Sir W. Hamilton was with the whole series of writers on Logic, he cannot have overlooked, and can hardly have forgotten, such passages as these. I have not had the fortune to meet with a single passage, from a single Aristotelian writer, who can be cited in his support. I presume, therefore, that he intentionally made (or adopted from Krug) a change in the meaning of a scientific term, the inverse of that which it is the proper office and common tendency of science to make. Instead of giving a more determinate signification to a name vaguely used, by binding it down to express a precise specific distinction, he laid hold of a name which already denoted a definite species, and applied it to the entire genus, which stood in no need of a name; leaving the particular species unnamed. But if he knowingly took this very unscientific liberty with a scientific term, diverting it from both its scientific and its popular meaning, — leaving the scientific vocabulary, never too rich, with one expression the fewer, and an important scientific distinction without a name, — he at least should not have done so without informing the reader. He should not have led the unsuspecting learner to believe that this was the received use of the term. Remark, too, that he embezzles not only the English word, but its Greek and Latin equivalents, exactly as if he agreed with the writers of the Greek and Latin treatises, and was only explaining their meaning.

V. One of the charges brought by Sir W. Hamilton against the common mode of stating the doctrine of the Syllogism, is that it does not obviate the objection often made to the syllogism of being a *petitio principii*, grounded on the admitted truth, that it can assert nothing in the conclusion which has not already been asserted in the premises. This objection, our author says,* "stands hitherto unrefuted, if not unrefutable." But he entertains the odd idea, that it can be got rid of by merely writing the propositions in a different order, putting the conclusion first. One might almost imagine that a little irony had been intended here. Putting the conclusion first, certainly makes it impossible any longer to say that the syllogism asserts in the conclusion what has *already* been asserted in the premises; and if any one is of opinion that the logical relation between premises and a conclusion depends on the order in which they are pronounced, such an objector, I must allow, is from this time silenced. But our author can have meditated very little on the meaning of the objection of *petitio principii* against the Syllogism, when he thought that such a device as this would remove it. The difficulty, which that objection expresses, lies in a region far below the depth to which such logic reaches; and he was quite right in regarding the objection as unrefuted. Nor is its refutation, I conceive, possible, on any theory but that which considers the Syllogism not as a process of Inference, but as the mere interpretation of the record of a previous process; the major premise as simply a formula for making particular inferences; and the conclusions of ratiocination as not inferences from the formula, but inferences drawn according to the formula. This theory, and the grounds of it, having been very fully stated in another work, need not be further noticed here.

* Appendix to Lectures, iv. 401, and Appendix to Discussions, p. 652.

CHAPTER XXIV.

OF SOME NATURAL PREJUDICES COUNTENANCED BY SIR WILLIAM HAMILTON, AND SOME FALLACIES WHICH HE CONSIDERS INSOLUBLE.

WE have concluded our review of Sir W. Hamilton as a teacher of Logic; but there remain to be noticed a few points, not strictly belonging either to Logic or to Psychology, but rather to what is inappropriately termed the Philosophia Prima. It would be more properly called *ultima*, since it consists of the widest generalizations respecting the laws of Existence and Activity; generalizations which by an unfortunate, though at first inevitable mistake, men fancied that they could reach *uno saltu*, and therefore placed them at the beginning of science, though, if they were ever legitimate, they could only be so as its tardy and final result. Every physical science, up to the time of Bacon, consisted mainly of such first principles as these: The ways of Nature are perfect: Nature abhors a vacuum: *Natura non habet saltum:* Nothing can come out of nothing: Like can only be produced by like: Things always move towards their own place: Things can only be moved by something which is itself moving; and so forth. And the Baconian revolution was far indeed from expelling such doctrines from philosophy. On the contrary, the Cartesian movement, which went on for a full century simultaneously with the Baconian, threw up many more of these imaginary axioms concerning things in general, which took a deep root in Continental philosophy, found their way into English, and are by no means, even now, discredited as they deserve to be. Most of these were fully believed, by the philosophers who maintained them, to be intuitively evident truths — revelations of Nature in the depths of human consciousness, and recognizable by the light of reason alone: while all the time they were merely bad generalizations of the vulgarest outward experience; rough interpretations of the appearances most familiar to sense, and which therefore had grown into the strongest associations in thought; never tested by the conditions of legitimate induction, not only because those conditions were still unknown, but because these wretched first attempts at generalization were deemed to have a higher than inductive origin, and were erected into general laws from which the order of the universe might be deduced, and to which every scientific theory for the explanation of phænomena must be required to conform. It is a material point in the estimation of a philosopher and of his doctrines, whether he has taken his side for or against this mode of philosophizing; whether he has countenanced any of these spurious axioms by his adhesion. Sir W. Hamilton cannot be acquitted of having done so, in more than one instance.

In treating of the problem of Causality, Sir W. Hamilton had occasion to argue, that we ought not to postulate a special mental law in order to explain the belief that everything must have a cause, since that belief is sufficiently accounted for by the "Law of the Conditioned," which makes it impossible for us to conceive an absolute commencement of anything. I do not mean to return to the discussion of this theory of Causality; but let us ask ourselves why we are interdicted from assuming a special law, in order to account for that which is already sufficiently accounted for by a general one. The real ground of the prohibition is what our author terms the Law of Parcimony: a principle identical with the famous maxim of the Nominalists, known as Occam's Razor — *Entia non sunt multiplicanda præter necessitatem;* understanding by Entia, not merely substances but also Powers. Sir W. Hamilton, instead of resting it on this logical injunction, grounds it on an ontological theory. His reason is, "Nature never works by more and more complex instruments than are necessary." * He cites,† with approbation, the maxims of Aristotle, "that God and Nature never operate without effect (οὐδὲν μάτην, οὐδὲν ἐλλειπῶς, ποιοῦσι); they never operate superfluously (μηδὲν περίεργον — περιττῶς — ἀργῶς); but always through one rather than through a plurality of means (καθ' ἕν, μᾶλλον ἢ κατὰ πολλά):" thus borrowing a general theory of the very kind which Bacon exploded, to support a rule which can stand perfectly well without it. Have *we* authority to declare that there is anything which God and Nature never do? Do we know all Nature's combinations? Were we called into counsel in fixing its limits? By what canons of induction has this theory ever been tried? By what observation has it been verified? We know well that Nature, in many of its operations, works by means which are of a complexity so extreme, as to be an almost insuperable obstacle to our investigations. On what evidence do we presume to say that this complexity was necessary, and that the effect

---

* Appendix to Discussions, p. 622.   † Ibid. p. 629.

could not have been produced in a simpler manner? If we look into the meaning of words, of what kind is the necessity which is supposed to be binding on God and Nature — the pressure they are unable to escape from? Is there any necessity in Nature which Nature did not make? or if not, what did? What is this power superior to Nature and its author, and to which Nature is compelled to adapt itself?

There is one supposition under which this doctrine has an intelligible meaning — the hypothesis of the Two Principles. If the universe was moulded into its present form by a Being who did not make it wholly, and who was impeded by an obstacle which he could only partially overcome — whether that obstacle was a rival intelligence, or, as Plato thought, an inherent incapacity in Matter; it is on that supposition admissible, that the Demiourgos may have always worked by the simplest possible means; the simplest, namely, which were permitted by the opposition of the conflicting Power, or the intractableness of the material. This is, in fact, the doctrine of Leibnitz's Théodicée; his famous theory, that a world, made by God, must be the best of all possible worlds, that is, the best world which could be made under the conditions by which, as it would appear, Providence was restricted. This doctrine, commonly called Optimism, is really Manicheism, or, to call it by a more proper name, Sabæism. The word "possible" assumes the existence of hinderances insurmountable by the divine power, and Leibnitz was only wrong in calling a power limited by obstacles by the name Omnipotence: for it is almost too obvious to be worth stating, that real Omnipotence could have effected its ends totally without means, or could have made any means sufficient. This Sabæan theory is the only one by which the assertion, that Nature always works by the simplest means, can be made consistent with known fact. Even so, it remains wholly unproved; and, were it proved, would be but a speculative truth of Theology, incapable of affording any practical guidance. We could never be justified in rejecting an hypothesis for being too complicated; it being beyond our power to set limits to the complication of the means that might possibly be necessary, to evade the obstacles which Ahriman or Matter may have perversely thrown in the Creator's way.

The "Law of Parcimony" needs no such support; it rests on no assumption respecting the ways or proceedings of Nature. It is a purely logical precept; a case of the broad practical principle, not to believe anything of which there is no evidence. When we have no direct knowledge of the matter of fact, and no reason for believing it except that it would account for another matter of fact, all reason for admitting it is at an end when the fact requiring explanation can be explained from known causes. The assumption of a superfluous cause, is a belief without evidence; as if we were to suppose that a man who was killed by falling over a precipice, must have taken poison as well. The same principle which forbids the assumption of a superfluous fact, forbids that of a superfluous law. When Newton had shown that the same theorem would express the conditions of the planetary motions and the conditions of the fall of bodies to the earth, it would have been illogical to recognize two distinct laws of nature, one for heavenly and the other for earthly attraction; since both these laws, when stripped of the circumstances ascertained to be irrelevant to the effect, would have had to be expressed in the very same words. The reduction of each of the two generalizations to the expression of only those circumstances which influence the result, reduces both of them to the same proposition; and to decline to do so, would be to make an assumption of difference between the cases, for which none of the observations afforded the smallest ground. The rule of Parcimony, therefore, whether applied to facts or to theories, implies no theory concerning the propensities or proceedings of Nature. If Nature's ways and inclinations were the reverse of what they are supposed to be, it would have been as illegitimate as it is now, to assume a fact of Nature without any evidence for it, or to consider the same property as two different properties, because found in two different kinds of objects.

In another place,* Sir W. Hamilton says that the Law of Parcimony, which he terms "the most important maxim in regulation of philosophical procedure when it is necessary to resort to an hypothesis," has "never, perhaps, been adequately expressed;" and he proposes the following expression for it: "Neither *more* nor *more onerous* causes are to be assumed, than are necessary to account for the phænomena." This conception of some causes as "more onerous" to the general scheme of things than others, is a distinction greatly requiring what our author says it has never yet had — to be "articulately expressed." He does not, however, articulate it in general terms, but only in its application to the particular question of Causality. From this we may collect, — 1st. That a "posi-

* Appendix to Discussions, pp. 628–631.

tive power" is a more onerous hypothesis than a "negative impotence." 2d. That a special hypothesis, which serves to explain only one phænomenon, is more onerous than a general one which will explain many. 3d. That the explanation of an effect by a cause of which the very existence is hypothetical, is more onerous than its hypothetical explanation by a cause otherwise known to exist. The last two of these three canons are but particular cases of the general rule, that we should not assume an hypothetical cause of a phænomenon which admits of being accounted for by a cause of which there is other evidence.* The remaining canon, that we should prefer the hypothesis of an incapacity to that of a power, is, I apprehend, only valid when its infringement would be a violation of one of the other two rules.

The time-honored, but gratuitous, assumption respecting Nature, on which I have now commented, is not the only generality of the pre-Baconian type which Sir W. Hamilton has countenanced. He gives his sanction to the old doctrine that "a thing can act only where it is." The dictum appears in this direct form in one of the very latest of his writings, the notes for an intended memoir of Professor Dugald Stewart.† He has so much faith in it as to make it the foundation of two of his favorite theories. One is, that ‡ "the thing perceived, and the

---

* This is what Newton meant by a *vera causa*, in his celebrated maxim, "Causas rerum naturalium non plures admitti debere quam quæ *et veræ sint*, et earum phænomenis explicandis sufficiant." It is singular that Sir W. Hamilton does not seem to have understood, that by *veræ causæ* Newton meant agencies the existence of which was otherwise authenticated: for he says (foot-note to Reid, p. 236), "In their plain meaning, the words *et veræ sint* are redundant; or what follows is redundant, and the whole rule a barren truism."

† Appendix to Lectures, ii. 522. ‡ Ibid.

percipient organ, must meet in place, must be contiguous. The consequence of this doctrine is a complete simplification of the theory of perception, and a return to the most ancient speculation on the point. All sensible cognition is, in a certain acceptation, reduced to Touch, and this is the very conclusion maintained by the venerable authority of Democritus. According to this doctrine, it is erroneous to affirm that we are percipient of distant objects." Conformably to this, we have seen him not only maintaining, in opposition to Reid, that we do not see the sun — that we see only an image of it in our eye — but also, that we directly perceive Extension, whether by sight or touch, only in our own bodily organs; thus preferring the *à priori* axiom, that a thing can only act where it is, to the authority of those "natural beliefs" which he, in other cases, so strenuously asserts against impugners, and so often affirms that we ought either to accept as a whole, or never appeal to at all.

The other theory which our author maintains on the authority of the same dictum, is that the mind acts directly throughout the whole body, and not through the brain only. "There is * no good ground to suppose that the mind is situate solely in the brain, or exclusively in any part of the body. On the contrary, the supposition that it is really present wherever we are conscious that it acts, — in a word, the Peripatetic aphorism, The soul is all in the whole, and all in every part, — is more philosophical, and consequently more probable, than any other opinion. . . . Even if we admit that the nervous system is the part to which it is proximately united, still the

* Lectures, ii. 127, 128.

nervous system is itself universally ramified throughout the body; and we have no more right to deny that the mind feels at the finger-points, as consciousness assures us, than to assert that it thinks exclusively in the brain." Sir W. Hamilton should at least have shown how this hypothesis can be reconciled with the fact, that a slight pressure on the nerve at a place intermediate between the finger and the brain, takes away the mind's power of feeling in the finger, while at any point above the ligature the feeling is the same as before. I shall not here inquire how much is positively proved by this experiment, or with what hypotheses it is inconsistent: my object is to show the amount of evidence which Sir W. Hamilton will disregard, rather than admit that one thing can act directly upon another without immediate contact.* What he would have thought of the application of his doctrine to the solar system, he has not told us; but it commits him to the opinion, that gravitation acts through an intervening medium, which he must postulate, first, as existing, and secondly, as possessed of inscrutable properties; in palpable repugnance to his own Law of Parcimony, and to all the canons grounded thereon. Descartes postulated his vortices in obedience to the same axiom.

What, however, is the worth of this doctrine, that things can only act upon one another by direct contact? Mr. Carlyle says, "a thing can only act where it is; with all my heart; only where is it?" In one sense of the word, a thing *is* wherever its action is: its power is

* In the Lectures, I mean; for, in the Dissertations on Reid (p. 861), the doctrine, that we feel in the toe, and not in a *sensorium commune*, is at least so far retracted, that the possibility of the opposite theory is explicitly acknowledged.

there, though not its corporeal presence. But to say that a thing can only act where its power is, would be the idlest of mere identical propositions. And where is the warrant for asserting that a thing cannot act when it is not locally contiguous to the thing it acts upon? Shall we be told that such action is inconceivable? Even if it was, this, according to Sir W. Hamilton's philosophy, is no evidence of impossibility. But that it is conceivable, is shown by every fairy tale, as well as by every religion. Then, again, what is the meaning of contiguity? According to the best physical knowledge we possess, things are never actually contiguous: what we term contact between particles, only means that they are in the degree of proximity at which their mutual repulsions are in equilibrium with their attractions. If so, instead of never, things always act on one another at some, though it may be a very small, distance. The belief that a thing can only act where it is, is a common case of inseparable, though not ultimately indissoluble, association. It is an unconscious generalization, of the roughest possible description, from the most familiar cases of the mutual action of bodies, superficially considered. The temporary difficulty found in apprehending any action of body upon body unlike what people were accustomed to, created a Natural Prejudice, which was long a serious impediment to the reception of the Newtonian theory; but it was hoped that the final triumph of that theory had extinguished it; that all educated persons were now aware that action at a distance is intrinsically quite as credible as action in contact, and that there is no reason, apart from specific experience, to regard the one as in any respect less probable than the other. That Sir W. Hamilton should be an instance to the contrary, is an example of the obstinate vitality of these *idola tribûs*, and shows that we are never safe against the rejuvenescence of the most superannuated error, if in throwing it off we have not reformed the bad habit of thought, the wrong and unscientific tendency of the intellect, from which the error took its rise.*

Though but remotely connected with the preceding considerations, yet as belonging in common with them to the subject of Fallacies, I will notice in this place the curious partiality which our author shows to a particular group of sophisms, the Eleatic arguments for the impossibility of motion. He believed these arguments, though leading to a false conclusion, to be irrefutable; as Brown thought concerning Berkeley's argument against the existence of matter — that as a mere play of reasoning it was unanswerable, while it was impossible for the human mind to admit the conclusion; forgetting that if this were so it would be a *reductio ad absurdum* of the reasoning faculty. There is no philosopher to whom, I imagine, Sir W. Hamilton would have less liked to be

* In the course of his speculations, our author comes across a fact which is positively irreconcilable with his axiom; the fact of repulsion. This brings him to a dead stand. He knows not whether to advance or recede. Repulsion, he says (Dissertations on Reid, p. 852) "remains, as apparently an *actio in distans*, even when forced upon us as a fact, still inconceivable as a possibility." He is soon afterwards obliged to confess that the same is true of attraction: "As attraction and repulsion seem equally *actiones in distans*, it is not more difficult to realize to ourselves the action of the one, than the action of the other." Action from distance being "a fact," though inconceivable, this fact would seem to require of him the retractation of his axiom; yet he does not retract it. I need hardly remark that attraction and repulsion are not inconceivable; except indeed in another of the numerous senses of that equivocal word; that in which it is used when our author tells us that all ultimate facts are inconceivable, meaning only that they are inexplicable.

assimilated, than Brown; and he would probably have defended himself against the imputation, by saying that the Eleatic arguments do not prove motion to be impossible, but only to be inconceivable by us. Yet if a fact which we see and feel every minute of our lives, is not conceivable by us, what is? Our author does not enter at any length into the question, but expresses his opinion on several occasions incidentally. "It is," he says,* "on the inability of the mind to conceive either the ultimate indivisibility, or the endless divisibility of space and time, that the arguments of the Eleatic Zeno against the possibility of motion are founded; arguments which at least show, that motion, however certain as a fact, cannot be conceived possible, as it involves a contradiction." We have been told in very emphatic terms by Sir W. Hamilton, that the Law of Contradiction is binding not on our conceptions merely, but on Things. If, then, motion involves a contradiction, how is it possible? and if it is possible, and a fact, as we know it to be, how can it involve a contradiction? The appearance of contradiction must necessarily be fallacious, even were we unable to point out the fallacy. Our author, apparently, has attempted to resolve it, and failed. He calls the argument † "an exposition of the contradictions involved in our notion of motion," and says that its "fallacy has not yet been detected." And again,‡ "The Eleatic Zeno's demonstration of the impossibility of motion is not more insoluble than could be framed a proof that the Present has no reality; for however certain we may be of both, we can positively think neither." It must,

---

* Lectures, ii. 373. To the same effect, iv. 71.
† Foot-note to Reid, p. 102. ‡ Appendix to Discussions, p. 606.

one would suppose, be a great difficulty, which could appear insoluble to Sir W. Hamilton. The "demonstration," at all events, cannot yet have been refuted, and superhuman ingenuity must be needed to refute it. Yet the fallacy in it has been pointed out again and again; and the contradictions which Sir W. Hamilton regards it as an exposure of, do not exist.

Zeno's reasonings against motion, as handed down by Aristotle, consist of four arguments, which are stated and criticised with considerable prolixity by Bayle. Several of these are substantially the same argument in different forms, and if we examine the two most plausible of them it will suffice. The first is the ingenious fallacy of Achilles and the Tortoise. If Achilles starts a thousand yards behind the tortoise, and runs a hundred times as fast, still, while Achilles runs those thousand yards, the tortoise will have got on ten; while Achilles runs those ten, the tortoise will have run a tenth of a yard; and as this process may be continued to infinity, Achilles will never overtake the tortoise. In our author's opinion, this argument is logically correct, and evolves a contradiction in our idea of motion. But it is neither logically correct, nor evolves a contradiction in anything. It assumes, of course, the infinite divisibility of space. But we have no need to entangle ourselves in the metaphysical discussion whether this assumption is warrantable. Let it be granted or not, the argument always remains a fallacy. For it assumes that to pass through an infinitely divisible space, requires an infinite time. But the infinite divisibility of space means the infinite divisibility of *finite* space; and it is only infinite space which cannot be passed over in less than infinite time. What the argument proves is, that to pass over the infinitely divisible space, requires an infinitely divisible time: but an infinitely divisible time may itself be finite; the smallest finite time is infinitely divisible; the argument, therefore, is consistent with the tortoise's being overtaken in the smallest finite time. It is a sophism of the type Ignoratio Elenchi, or, as Archbishop Whately terms it, Irrelevant Conclusion; an argument which proves a different proposition from that which it pretends to prove, the difference of meaning being disguised by similarity of language.

The other plausible form of Zeno's argument is at first sight more favorable to Sir W. Hamilton's theory, being a real attempt to prove that the fact of motion involves impossible conditions. The usual mode of stating it is this. If a body moves, it must move either in the place where it is or in the place where it is not: but either of these is impossible: therefore it cannot move. First of all, this argument, even if we were unable to refute it, does not exhibit any contradiction in our "notion" of motion. We do not conceive a body as moving either in the place where it is, or in the place where it is not, but from the former to the latter: in other words, we conceive the body as in the one place and in the other at successive instants. Where is the "contradiction" between being in one place at this moment, and in another at the next? As for the fallacy itself, it is strange that when everybody sees the answer to it, a practised logician should have any difficulty in putting that answer into logical forms. It is not necessary that motion should be *in* a place. An object must be in a place; but motion is not an object—it is a change: and that a change of place should be either in the old place or in the new, is a real contradiction in terms. To put the thing in another way: Place may be understood in two senses: it may either be a divisible, or an indivisible part of space. If it be a divisible part, as a room, or a street, it is true that in that sense, every motion is in a place, that is, within a limited portion of space: but in this meaning of the term the dilemma breaks down, for the body really moves in the place where it is; the room, the field, or the house. If, on the contrary, we are to understand by Place an indivisible minimum of space, the proposition that motion must be in a place is evidently false; for motion cannot be *in* that which has no parts; it can only be *to* or *from* it.

A parallel sophism might easily be invented, turning upon Time instead of Space. It might be said that sunset is impossible, since if it be possible, it must take place either while the sun is still up, or after it is down. The answer is obvious: it is just the change from one to the other which is sunset. And so it is the change from one position in space to another which is motion. The parallelism between the two cases was evidently seen by Sir W. Hamilton, and the sophism was too hard for him in both: and this is what he must have meant by saying that we cannot "positively think" the Present. That he should have missed the solution of the fallacy is strange enough: but, as a matter of fact, the assertion that we have no positive perception, on the one hand, of Motion, on the other, of present time, deserves notice as one of the most curious deliverances of so earnest an assertor of "our natural beliefs."

These paralogisms are only part of a long list of puzzles concerning infinity, which, though by no means hard to clear up, appear to our author insoluble. I append in a note the entire list.* Many of them are resolved by the observations already made, their difficulty being merely that of separating the two ideas of Infinite and Infinitely Divisible. To our author's thinking, infinite divisibility and the Finite contradict one another. But even allowing (which, as was seen in a former chapter, I do not) that infinite divisibility is inconceivable, it does not therefore involve a contradiction. The remaining puzzles mostly result from inability to conceive that one infinity can be greater or less than another: a conception familiar to all mathematicians. Our author refuses to consider that a space or a time which is infinite in one direction and bounded in another, is necessarily

---

* "Contradictions proving the Psychological Theory of the Conditioned.

"1. Finite cannot comprehend, contain, the Infinite. — Yet an inch or minute, say, are finites, and are divisible *ad infinitum*, that is, their terminated division incogitable.

"2. Infinite cannot be terminated or begun. — Yet eternity *ab ante* ends *now*; and eternity *a post* begins *now*. So apply to Space.

"3. There cannot be two infinite maxima. — Yet eternity *ab ante* and *a post* are two infinite maxima of time.

"4. Infinite maximum if cut in two, the halves cannot be each infinite, for nothing can be greater than infinite, and thus they could not be parts; nor finite, for thus two finite halves would make an infinite whole.

"5. What contains infinite quantities (extensions, protensions, intensions) cannot be passed through, — come to an end. An inch, a minute, a degree contains these; *ergo*, &c. Take a minute. This contains an infinitude of protended quantities, which must follow one after another; but an infinite series of successive protensions can, *ex termino*, never be ended; *ergo*, &c.

"6. An infinite maximum cannot but be all-inclusive. Time *ab ante* and *a post* infinite and exclusive of each other; *ergo*, &c.

"7. An infinite number of quantities must make up either an infinite or a finite whole. I. The former. — But an inch, a minute, a degree, contain each an infinite number of quantities; therefore an inch, a minute, a degree, are each infinite wholes; which is absurd. II. The latter. — An infinite number of quantities would thus make up a finite quantity, which is equally absurd.

less than a space or a time which is infinite in every direction. The space between two parallels, or between two diverging lines or surfaces, extends to infinity, but it is necessarily less than entire space, being a part of it. Not only is one infinity greater than another, but one infinity may be infinitely greater than another. Mathematicians habitually assume this, and reason from it; and the results always coming out true, the assumption is justified. But mathematicians, I must admit, seldom know exactly what they are about when they do this. As the results always prove right, they know empirically that the process cannot be wrong — that the premises must be true in a sense; but in what sense, it is beyond the ingenuity of most of them to understand.

"8. If we take a finite quantity (as an inch, a minute, a degree), it would appear equally that there are, and that there are not, an equal number of quantities between these and a greatest, and between these and a least.

"9. An absolutely quickest motion is that which passes from one point to another in space in a minimum of time. But a quickest motion from one point to another, say a mile distance, and from one to another, say a million million of miles, is thought the same; which is absurd.

"10. A wheel turned with quickest motion; if a spoke be prolonged, it will, therefore, be moved by a motion quicker than the quickest. The same may be shown using the rim and the nave.

"11. Contradictory are Boscovich Points, which occupy space, and are unextended. Dynamism, therefore, inconceivable. *E contra*,

"12. Atomism also inconceivable; for this supposes atoms, — minima extended but indivisible.

"13. A quantity, say a foot, has an infinity of parts. Any part of this quantity, say an inch, has also an infinity. But one infinity is not larger than another. Therefore an inch is equal to a foot.

"14. If two divaricating lines are produced *ad infinitum* from a point where they form an acute angle, like a pyramid, the base will be infinite, and, at the same time, not infinite; 1°. Because terminated by two points; and, 2°. Because shorter than the sides; 3°. Base could not be drawn, because sides infinitely long.

"15. An atom, as existent, must be able to be turned round. But if turned round, it must have a right and left hand, &c., and these its signs [sides?] must change their place: therefore be extended." (Appendix to Lectures, ii. 527–529.)

The doctrine long remained a part of that mathematical mysticism, so mercilessly shown up by Berkeley in his "Analyst," and "Defence of Freethinking in Mathematics." To clear it up required a philosophical mathematician — one who should be both a mathematician and a metaphysician; and it found one. To complete Sir W. Hamilton's discomfiture, this philosophic mathematician is his old antagonist Mr. De Morgan, whom he described as too much of a mathematician to be anything of a philosopher.* Mr. De Morgan, however, has proved himself, as far as this subject is concerned, a far better metaphysician than Sir W. Hamilton. He has let the light of reason into all the logical obscurities and paradoxes of the infinitesimal calculus. By merely following out, more thoroughly than had been done before, the rational conception of infinitesimal division, as synonymous with division into as many and as small parts as we choose, Mr. De Morgan, in his Algebra, has fully explained and justified the conception of successive orders of differentials, each of them infinitely less than the differential of the preceding, and infinitely greater than that of the succeeding order. Whoever is acquainted with this masterly specimen of analysis, will find his way through Sir W. Hamilton's series of riddles respecting Infinity, without ever being at a loss for their solution. I shall therefore trouble the reader no further with them in this place.

* Appendix to Discussions, p. 707.

CHAPTER XXV.

SIR WILLIAM HAMILTON'S THEORY OF PLEASURE AND PAIN.

I HAVE now concluded my remarks on the principal department of Sir W. Hamilton's psychology, that which relates to the Cognitive Faculties. The remaining two of the three portions into which he divides the subject, are the Feelings, and what he terms the Conative Faculties, meaning those which tend to Action. On the Conative Faculties, however, he barely touches, in the concluding part of his last lecture; and of the Feelings he does not treat at any length. What he propounds on the subject, chiefly consists of a general theory of Pleasure and Pain. Not a theory of what they are in themselves, for he is not so much the dupe of words as to suppose that they are anything but what we feel them to be. The speculation with which he has presented us, does not relate to their essence, but to the causes they depend on; "the * general conditions which determine the existence of Pleasure and Pain . . . the fundamental law by which these phænomena are governed in all their manifestations."

The inquiry is scientifically legitimate, and of great interest; but we must not be very confident that it is a practicable one, or can lead to any positive result. It is quite possible that in seeking for the law of pleasure and

* Lectures, ii. 434.

pain, like Bacon in seeking for the laws of the sensible properties of bodies, we may be looking for unity of cause, where there is a plurality, perhaps a multitude, of different causes. Such attempts, however, even if unsuccessful, are far from being entirely useless. They often lead to a more careful study of the phænomenon in some of its aspects, and to the discovery of relations between them, not previously understood, which, though not adequate to the formation of a universal theory of the phænomenon, afford a clearer insight into some of its forms and varieties. This merit must be allowed to Sir W. Hamilton's theory, in common with several others which preceded it on the same subject. But, regarded as a theorem of the universal conditions which are present whenever pleasure (or pain) is present, and absent whenever it is absent, the doctrine will hardly bear investigation. The simplest and most familiar cases are exactly those which obstinately refuse to be reduced within it.

I shall, as usual, state Sir W. Hamilton's theory in his own words, though in the present case it is a questionable advantage, the terms being so general and abstract that they are scarcely capable of being understood, apart from the illustrations. "Pleasure," he says,[*] "is a reflex of the spontaneous and unimpeded exertion of a power, of whose energy we are conscious. Pain, a reflex of the overstrained or repressed exertion of such a power." By a "reflex" he has shortly before said that [†] he means merely a "concomitant;" but I think it will appear that he means at least an effect. At all events, these are what he regards as the ultimate conditions of pleasure

[*] Lectures, ii. 440.   [†] Ibid. p. 436.

and pain, the most general expression of the circumstances in which they occur.

This theory was of course suggested by the pleasures and pains of intellectual or physical exertion, or, as it is otherwise termed, exercise. These are the phænomena which principally afford to it such foundation of fact, and such plausibility in speculation, as it possesses. As we all know, moderate exertion, either of body or mind, is pleasurable; a greater amount is painful, except when set in motion by an impulse which renders it, in our author's meaning of the word, "spontaneous:" and a felt impediment to any kind of active exertion, when there is an impulse towards it, is painful. It at first appears as if Sir W. Hamilton had overlooked the pains and pleasures in which the mind and body are passive, as in most of the organic, and a large proportion of the emotional pleasures and pains. He claims, however, to include all these in his formula. The "powers" and "energies" whose free action he holds to be the condition of pleasure, and their impeded or overstrained action, of pain, include our passive susceptibilities as well as our active energies. Accordingly he suggests a correction of his own language, saying that "occupation" or "exercise" would perhaps be fitter expressions than "energy."*
"The term *energy*,† which is equivalent to *act, activity*, or *operation*, is here used to comprehend also all the mixed states of action and passion of which we are conscious; for, inasmuch as we are conscious of any modification of mind, there is necessarily more than a mere passivity of the subject; consciousness itself implying at least a reaction" (what has become of his doctrine that

---

* Lectures, ii. note to p. 435, and p. 466. † Ibid. p. 435.

to be conscious of a feeling is only another phrase for having the feeling?) "Be this, however, as it may, the nouns *energy, act, activity, operation*, with the correspondent verbs, are to be understood to denote, indifferently and in general, all the processes of our higher and our lower life of which we are conscious."

Understanding the theory in this enlarged sense, let us test it by application to one of the simplest of our organic feelings, the pleasure of a sweet taste. This pleasure, according to the theory, arises from the free exercise, without either restraint or excess, of one of our powers or capacities: what capacity shall we call it? That of tasting sweetness? This will not do; for if the capacity of having the sensation of sweet is called into play in any degree, great or small, the effect is a sweet taste, which is a pleasure. Besides, instead of a sweet taste, let us suppose an acrid taste. In this taste the capacity exercised is that of tasting acridity. But the result of the exercise of this capacity, neither repressed nor overstrained, which therefore, according to the theory, should be a pleasure, is an acrid taste, which is a pain. It must, therefore, be meant that the capacity which when freely exercised causes pleasure, and when repressed or overstrained, pain, is some more general capacity than that of sweet or acrid taste — say the power of taste in the abstract: that the power of taste, the organic action of the gustatory nerves, by its spontaneous exercise, yields pleasure, and by its repression, or its strained exercise, produces pain. The theory thus entirely turns upon what is meant by spontaneous; as is shown still more clearly by our author's comments. "It has been stated," he observes in a recapitulation of his doctrine,* "that a feeling of pleasure is experienced, when any power is consciously exercised in a suitable manner; that is, when we are neither, on the one hand, conscious of any restraint upon the energy which it is disposed spontaneously to put forth, nor, on the other, conscious of any effort in it to put forth an amount of energy greater either in degree or in continuance, than what it is disposed freely to exert. In other words, we feel positive pleasure, in proportion as our powers are exercised, but not over-exercised; we feel positive pain, in proportion as they are compelled either not to operate, or to operate too much. All pleasure, thus, arises from the free play of our faculties and capacities; all pain from their compulsory repression or compulsory activity."

All, therefore, depends upon what is meant by "free" or "spontaneous," and what by "compulsory," activity. The difference cannot be that which the words suggest, the presence or absence of will. It cannot be meant, that pleasure accompanies the process when wholly involuntary, and that pain begins when a voluntary element enters into the exercise of the sensitive faculty. There is nothing voluntary in the agonies of the rack, or of an excruciating bodily disease: while, in the case of a pleasure, the exercise of will, in the only mode in which it can be exercised on a feeling, namely by voluntarily attending to it, instead of converting it from a pleasure into a pain, often greatly heightens the pleasure. This doctrine, therefore, would be absurd, nor is Sir W. Hamilton chargeable with it. What he means by "spontaneous" as applied to the exercise of our capacities of feeling, we gather from the following passage,† and others similar to it.

* Lectures, ii. 477.   † Ibid. p. 441.

THEORY OF PLEASURE AND PAIN. 259

"Every power, all conditions being supplied, and all impediments being removed, tends, of its proper nature and without effort, to put forth a certain determinate maximum, intensive and protensive, of free energy. This determinate maximum of free energy, it, therefore, exerts spontaneously: if a less amount than this be actually put forth, a certain quantity of tendency has been forcibly repressed: whereas, if a greater than this has been actually exerted, a certain amount of nisus has been forcibly stimulated in the power. The term *spontaneously*, therefore, provides that the exertion of the power has not been constrained beyond the proper limit, — the natural maximum, to which, if left to itself, it freely springs. Again, in regard to the term *unimpeded*, — this stipulates that the conditions requisite to allow this spring have been supplied, and that all impediments to it have been removed. This postulates, of course, the presence of an object."

The spontaneous and unimpeded exercise of a capacity means, therefore, it would appear, the exercise which takes place when "all conditions" are "supplied," and "all impediments removed." Let us apply this to a particular case. I taste, at different instants, two different objects; an orange, and rhubarb. In both cases, all conditions are supplied; the object is present, and in contact with my organs: and in both cases, all impediments are removed to the unstrained and natural action of the object upon my gustatory organs. Yet the result is in one case a pleasure, in the other a sensation of nauseousness. On Sir W. Hamilton's theory, it ought, in both cases, to have been pleasure: for in neither does anything interfere with the free action of my sense of taste.

Sir W. Hamilton can scarcely have overlooked this objection, and the answer which he may be supposed to make, is that in the case of the rhubarb, the object itself was of a nature to disturb the gustative faculty, and exact from it a greater degree of action (or a less, for I would not undertake to say which) than is exacted by the orange. But where is the proof of this? and what, even, does the assertion mean? A greater degree of what action? Of the action of tasting? If so, a pain should differ from a pleasure only by being more (or perhaps less) intense. Is the action that is meant, some occult process in the organ? But what ground is there for affirming that there is more action of any kind, on the part of the organ or the sense of taste, in a disagreeable savor than in an agreeable one? It is perhaps true that more than a certain quantity of action is always painful: every sensation, intensified beyond a certain degree, may become a pain. But the converse proposition, that wherever there is a pain there is an excess of action (or a deficiency, for we are offered that alternative), I know of no reason for believing. Moreover, if admitted, it would seem to involve the consequence, that in every case of pain, a less or a greater degree of the cause which produces it is pleasurable.

Our author is more than half aware that his theory does not fit the passive organic feelings; for he says,[*] "When it is required of us to explain particularly and in detail, why the rose, for example, produces this sensation of smell, assafœtida that other, and so forth, and to say in what peculiar action does the perfect or pleasurable, and the imperfect or painful, activity of an organ

[*] Lectures, ii. 495.

consist, we must at once profess our ignorance." He lays the responsibility of the failure, not upon his theory, but upon the general inexplicability of ultimate facts. "But it is the same with all our attempts at explaining any of the ultimate phænomena of creation. In general, we may account for much; in detail, we can rarely account for anything: for we soon remount to facts which lie beyond our powers of analysis and observation."

This appears to me a great misconception, on our author's part, of what may rightfully be demanded from a theorist. He is not entitled to frame a theory from one class of phænomena, extend it to another class which it does not fit, and excuse himself by saying that if we cannot make it fit, it is because ultimate facts are inexplicable. Newton did not proceed in this manner with the theory of gravitation. He made it an absolute condition of adopting the theory, that it should fit; and when, owing to incorrect data, he could not make it fit perfectly, he abandoned the speculation for many years. If the smell of a rose and the smell of assafœtida are ultimate facts, be it so; but in that case, it is useless setting up a theory to explain them. If we do propound a theory, we are bound to prove all it asserts: and this, in the present case, is, that in smelling a rose the organ is in "perfect" activity, but when smelling assafœtida, in "imperfect," which is either greater or less than perfect. It is not philosophical to assert this, and fall back upon the incomprehensibility of the subject as a dispensation from proving it. What is a hinderance to proving a theory, ought to be a hinderance to affirming it.

What meaning, in fact, can be attached to perfect and imperfect activity, as the phrases are here used? Perfection or imperfection is treated as a question of quantity: activity is called perfect when there is exactly the right quantity, imperfect when there is either more or less. But what is the test of right or wrong quantity, except the pleasure or pain attending it? The theory amounts to this, that pleasure or pain is felt, according as the activity is of the amount fitted to produce the one or the other. In this futile mode of explaining the phænomena our author had been preceded by Aristotle, one of the greatest of recorded thinkers, but who must have been more than human if, in the state of knowledge and scientific cultivation in his time, he had avoided slips which hardly any one, even now, is able completely to guard against. Aristotle's theory, which, as understood by our author, differs little from his own, is presented by Sir W. Hamilton in the following words:[*] "When a sense, for example, is in perfect health, and it is presented with a suitable object of the most perfect kind, there is elicited the most perfect energy, which, at every instant of its continuance, is accompanied with pleasure. The same holds good with the function of Imagination, Thought, &c. Pleasure is the concomitant in every case where powers and objects are in themselves perfect, and between which there subsists a suitable relation." The conditions whereon, upon this showing, pleasure depends, are the healthiness of the sense, and the perfection of the object presented to it. (This is simply making the fact its own theory.) When is a sense in perfect health, and its object perfect? The function of a sense is two-

[*] Lectures, ii. 452.

fold; as a source of cognition, and of feeling. If the perfection meant be in the function of cognition, the doctrine that pleasure depends on this is manifestly erroneous: according to Sir W. Hamilton, it is even the reverse of the truth, for he holds that the knowledge given by an act of sense, and the feeling accompanying it, are in an inverse proportion to one another. Remains the supposition that the perfection of which Aristotle spoke, was perfection not in respect of cognition, but of feeling. It cannot, however, consist in acuteness of feeling, for our acutest feelings are pains. What then constitutes it? Pleasurableness of feeling: and the theory only tells us, that pleasure is the result of a pleasurable state of the sense, and a pleasure-giving quality in the object presented to it. Aristotle and Sir W. Hamilton did not, certainly, state the doctrine to themselves in this manner; but they reduced it to this, by affirming pleasure or pain to depend on the perfect or imperfect action of the sense, when there was no criterion of imperfect or perfect action except that it produced pain or pleasure.

The theory of our author, considered as a *resumé* of the universal conditions of pleasure and pain, being so manifestly inadequate, this is not the place for sifting out the detached fragments of valuable thought which are disseminated through it. Such stray truths may be gleaned from every excursion through the phænomena of human nature by a person of ability. What Sir W. Hamilton says of the different classes of mental pleasures and pains, though brief, is very suggestive of thought. To make a proper use of the hints he throws out towards an explanation of the pleasures derived from sublimity and beauty, would require much study, and a wide survey of the subject, as well as of the speculations of other thinkers regarding it. The question has no direct connection with any other of those discussed in the present volume, and but a slight one with Sir W. Hamilton's merits as a philosopher; since the brevity with which he treats it, gives ground for believing that he had not bestowed on it the amount of thought which would enable his opinion to claim the rank of a philosophic theory.

CHAPTER XXVI.

OF THE FREEDOM OF THE WILL.

THE last of the three classes of mental phænomena, that of Conation, in other words, of Desire and Will, is barely commenced upon in the last pages of Sir W. Hamilton's last lecture: whether it be that in the many years during which he taught the class, he never got beyond this point, or that his teaching in the concluding part of the course was purely oral, and has not been preserved. Nor has he, in any of his writings, treated *ex professo* of this subject; though doubtless he would have done so, had his health permitted him to complete the Dissertations on Reid. We consequently know little of what his sentiments were on any of the topics comprised in this branch of Pyschology, except the *vexata quæstio* of the Freedom of the Will; on which he could not help giving indications, in various parts of his works, both of his opinion and of the reasons on which he grounded it. The doctrine of Free-will was indeed so fundamental with him, that it may be regarded as the central idea of his system — the determining cause of most of his philosophical opinions; and, in a peculiar manner, of the two which are most completely emanations from his own mind, the Law of the Conditioned, and his singular theory of Causation. He breaks ground on the subject at the very opening of his Lectures, in his introductory remarks on the utility of the study of Metaphysics. He puts in a claim for metaphysics, grounded on the freewill doctrine, of being the only medium "through which our unassisted reason can ascend to the knowledge of a God."* He supports this position by a line of argument which, I think, must be startling to the majority of believers.

"The Deity," he says, "is not an object of immediate contemplation; as existing and in himself, he is beyond our reach; we can know him only mediately through his works, and are only warranted in assuming his existence as a certain kind of cause necessary to account for a certain state of things, of whose reality our faculties are supposed to inform us. The affirmation of a God being thus a regressive inference, from the existence of a special class of effects to the existence of a special character of cause, it is evident, that the whole argument hinges on the fact, — Does a state of things really exist, such as is only possible through the agency of a Divine Cause? For if it can be shown that such a state of things does not really exist, then, our inference to the kind of cause requisite to account for it, is necessarily null.

"This being understood, I now proceed to show you that the class of phænomena which requires that kind of cause we denominate a Deity, is exclusively given in the phænomena of mind, — that the phænomena of matter, taken by themselves (you will observe the qualification, taken by themselves), so far from warranting any inference to the existence of a God, would, on the contrary, ground even an argument to his negation; that the study of the external world, taken with, and insubordination to, that of the internal, not only loses its atheistic

* Lectures, i. 25, *et seqq.*

tendency, but, under such subservience, may be rendered conducive to the great conclusion from which, if left to itself, it would dissuade us."

The reasoning by which he thinks that he establishes this position, runs as follows: A God is only an inference from Nature; a cause assumed, as necessary to account for phænomena. Now, fate or necessity, without a God, might account for the phænomena of matter. It is only as man is a free intelligence, that to account for his existence requires the hypothesis of a Creator who is a free intelligence. If our feeling of liberty is an illusion, if our intelligence is only a result of material organization, we are entitled to conclude that in the universe also, the phænomena of intelligence and design are, in the last analysis, the products of brute necessity. Existence in itself being unknown to us, we can only infer its character from the particular order presented to us within the sphere of our experience, which in the case under consideration means observation of our own minds. If, therefore, our intelligence is produced and bounded by a blind fate, the like may be concluded to be true of the Divine Intelligence. If, on the contrary, intelligence in man is a free power, independent of matter, we may legitimately conclude the same thing of the intelligence manifested in the universe. Again, there is properly no God at all unless there is a moral Governor of the world. "Now,* it is self-evident, in the first place, that if there be no moral world, there can be no moral governor of such a world; and in the second, that we have, and can have, no ground on which to believe in the reality of a moral world, except in so far as we

* Lectures, i. 32, 33.

ourselves are moral agents. . . . But in what does the character of man as a moral agent consist? Man is a moral agent only as he is accountable for his actions,— in other words, as he is the object of praise or blame; and this he is, only inasmuch as he has prescribed to him a rule of duty, and as he is able to act, or not to act, in conformity with its precepts. The possibility of morality thus depends on the possibility of liberty; for if man be not a free agent, he is not the author of his actions, and has, therefore, no responsibility, — no moral personality at all." *

Fully to develop all the just criticisms which might be made on this single thesis, would require a long chapter. In the first place, the practice of bribing the pupil to accept a metaphysical dogma, by the promise or threat that it affords the only valid argument for a foregone conclusion — however transcendently important that conclusion may be thought to be — is not only repugnant to all the rules of philosophizing, but a grave offence against the morality of philosophic inquiry. The eager attempts of almost every metaphysical writer to create a religious prejudice in favor of the theory he patronizes, are a very serious grievance in philosophy. If I could permit myself, even by way of retort, to follow so bad an example, I might warn the defenders of religion, of the danger of sacrificing, in turn, every one of its evidences to some other. It has been remarked, with truth, that there is not one of the received arguments in support either of natural religion or of revelation, a formal condemnation of which might not be extracted from the writings of sincerely religious

---

* See also a passage in the essay on the Study of Mathematics, Discussions, pp. 307, 308.

thinkers. I am far from imputing this to them as matter of blame: the rejection of what they deem bad arguments in a good cause must always be honorable to them, when led to it by honestly following the promptings of their reason, and not by an egotistic preference for their own special modes of proof. But, looking at the question as one of prudence, it would be wise in them, whatever else they give up, not to part company with the Design argument. For, in the first place, it is the best; and besides, it is by far the most persuasive. It would be difficult to find a stronger argument in favor of Theism, than that the eye must have been made by one who sees, and the ear by one who hears. If, after this, it pleases Sir W. Hamilton or any other person to say that unless we believe in free-will, the Being who by hypothesis made the ear and the eye is no God; or that to regard the goodness of God as the result of a necessity, which from the very meaning of a First Cause, can only be a necessity of his own nature, a love of Good which is part of himself and inseparable from him, is denying him to be a moral being; there is really nothing left for us but, with equal positiveness, to aver the contrary; for the two parties will never be able to agree about the meaning of terms.

This is but one specimen among many, of the bad logic which pervades Sir W. Hamilton's attempt to show that Theism depends on the reception of his favorite doctrine. He proceeds, throughout, on the assumption that the falsely called Doctrine of Necessity * is the

---

* Both Sir W. Hamilton and Mr. Mansel sometimes call it by the fairer name of Determinism. But both of them, when they come to close quar-

same thing with Materialism. He treats those opinions as precisely equivalent.* Yet no two doctrines can be more distinct. Reid, an enemy of both, affirms that Necessity, "far from being a direct inference," can "receive no support from" Materialism.† It may be true, nevertheless, that Materialists are always or generally Necessitarians; and it is not denied that many Necessitarians are Materialists: but nearly all the theologians of the Reformation, beginning with Luther, and the entire series of Calvinistic divines represented by Jonathan Edwards, are proofs that the most sincere Spiritualists may consistently hold the doctrine of so-called Necessity. Of such Spiritualists there is an illustrious example in Leibnitz, to say nothing of Condillac ‡ or Brown. They believe man to be a spiritual being, not dependent on Matter, but yet, in respect of his actions as in all other respects, subject to the law of Causation: his volitions not being self-caused, but determined by spiritual antecedents (*e. g.*, desires, associations of ideas, &c., all of which are spiritual if the mind is spiritual) in such sort that when the antecedents are the same, the volitions will always be the same. But to confound Necessity

ters with the doctrine, in general call it either Necessity, or, less excusably, Fatalism. The truth is, that the assailants of the doctrine cannot do without the associations engendered by the double meaning of the word Necessity, which, in this application, signifies only invariability, but in its common employment, compulsion. Vide System of Logic, Book vi. chap. 2.

* "The atheist who holds *matter or necessity* to be the original principle of all that is." (Lectures, i. 26, 37.) "Those who do not allow that mind is matter—who hold that there is in man a principle of action superior to the determinations of a physical necessity, a brute or blind fate." (Ibid. p. 133.) And the entire argument in page 31 of the same volume.

† Reid's Works, Hamilton's edition, p. 635.

‡ That Condillac was a Spiritualist, is shown by the chapter on the Soul, which stands as the first chapter of his Art de Penser.

with Materialism, though an historical and psychological error, is indispensable to Sir W. Hamilton's argument, which depends for all its plausibility on the picture he draws of a God subject to a "brute necessity" of a purely material character. For if the necessity predicated of human actions is not a material, but a spiritual necessity; if the assertion that the virtuous man is virtuous necessarily, only means that he is so because he dreads a departure from virtue more than he dreads any personal consequence; there is nothing absurd or invidious in taking a similar view of the Deity, and believing that he is necessitated to will what is good, by the love of good and detestation of evil which are in his own nature.

There is also at the root of our author's argument another logical error — that of inferring that whatever is given by observation and analysis as a law of human intelligence, must be supposed to be an absolute law extending to the Divine. He says, truly, that the Divine Intelligence is but an assumption, to account for the phænomena of the universe; and that we can only be warranted in referring the origin of those phænomena to an Intelligence, by analogy to the effects of human intellect. But can this analogy be carried up to complete identity in conditions and modes of action between the human and the Divine intelligence? Does Sir W. Hamilton draw this inference in any other case? On the contrary, he holds us bound to believe that the Deity, whether as Will or as Intelligence, is Absolute — unrestricted by any conditions; though, as such, neither knowable nor conceivable by us. And though I do not acknowledge the obligation of believing what can neither be known nor conceived, as little can it be admitted that the Divine Will cannot be free unless ours is so; any more than that the Divine Intelligence cannot know the truths of geometry by direct intuition, because we are obliged to mount laboriously up to them through the twelve books of Euclid.

So much for Sir W. Hamilton's attempt to prove that one who disbelieves free-will has no business to believe in a God. Let us now consider his view of the doctrine itself, and of the evidence for it.

His view of the controversy is peculiar, but harmonizes with his Philosophy of the Conditioned, which seems indeed to have been principally suggested to him by the supposed requirements of this question. He is of opinion that Free-will and Necessity are both inconceivable. Free-will, because it supposes volitions to originate without cause; because it affirms an absolute commencement, which, as we are aware, our author deems it impossible for the human mind to conceive. On the other hand, the mind is equally unable to conceive an infinite regress; a chain of causation going back to all eternity. Both the one and the other theory thus involve difficulties insurmountable by the human faculties. But, as Sir W. Hamilton has so often told us, the inconceivability of a thing by us, is no proof that it is objectively impossible by the laws of the universe; on the contrary, it often happens that both sides of an alternative are alike incomprehensible to us, while from their nature we are certain that the one or the other must be true. Such an alternative, according to Sir W. Hamilton, exists between the conflicting doctrines of Free-will and Necessity. By the law of Excluded Middle, one or other of them must be true; and inconceivability, as common to both, not operating more against one than against the other, does not operate against either. The balance, therefore, must turn in favor of the side for which there is positive evidence. In favor of Free-will we have the distinct testimony of consciousness; perhaps directly, though of this he speaks with some appearance of doubt;* but at all events, indirectly, freedom being implied in the consciousness of moral responsibility. As there is no corresponding evidence in favor of the other theory, the Free-will doctrine must prevail. "How † the will can possibly be free must remain to us, under the present limitation of our faculties, wholly incomprehensible. We cannot conceive absolute commencement; we cannot, therefore, conceive a free volition. But as little can we conceive the alternative on which liberty is denied, on which necessity is affirmed. And in favor of our moral nature, the fact that we are free is given us in the consciousness of an uncompromising law of Duty, in the consciousness of our moral accountability; and this fact of liberty cannot be redargued on the ground that it is incomprehensible, for the doctrine of the Conditioned proves, against the necessitarian, that something may, nay, must, be true, of which the mind is wholly unable to construe to itself the possibility, whilst it shows that the objection of incomprehensibility applies no less to the doctrine of fatalism than to the doctrine of moral freedom."

The inconceivability of the Free-will doctrine is maintained by our author, not only on the general ground just stated, of our incapacity to conceive an absolute

* Foot-notes to Reid, pp. 599, 602, 624.   † Lectures, ii. 412, 413.

commencement, but on the further and special ground, that the will is determined by motives. In rewriting the preceding passage for the Appendix to his " Discussions," he made the following addition to it : * " A determination by motives cannot, to our understanding, escape from necessitation. Nay, were we even to admit as true, what we cannot think as possible, still the doctrine of a motiveless volition would be only casualism; and the free acts of an indifferent, are, morally and rationally, as worthless as the pre-ordered passions of a determined will.† *How*, therefore, I repeat, moral liberty is possible in man or God, we are utterly unable speculatively to understand. But . . . the scheme of freedom is not more inconceivable than the scheme of necessity. For whilst fatalism is a recoil from the more obtrusive inconceivability of an *absolute* commencement, on the fact of which commencement the doctrine of liberty proceeds, the fatalist is shown to overlook the equal, but less obtrusive, inconceivability of an *infinite* non-commencement, on the assertion of which non-commencement his own doctrine of necessity must ultimately rest." It rests on no such thing, if he believes in a First Cause, which a Necessitarian may. What is more, even if he does not believe in a First Cause, he makes no "assertion of non-

---

* Appendix to Discussions, pp. 624, 625.

† To the same effect in another passage: " That, though inconceivable, a motiveless volition would, if conceived, be conceived as morally worthless, only shows our impotence more clearly." (Appendix to Discussions, pp. 614, 615.) And in a foot-note to Reid (p. 602), "Is the person an *original undetermined* cause of the determination of his will? If he be not, then he is not a *free agent*, and the scheme of Necessity is admitted. If he be, in the first place, it is impossible to *conceive* the possibility of this; and, in the second, if the fact, though inconceivable, be allowed, it is impossible to see how a cause, undetermined by any motive, can be a rational, moral, and accountable cause."

commencement;" he only declines to make an assertion of commencement; a distinction of which Sir W. Hamilton, of all men, ought to recognize the importance. But to resume the quotation: "As equally unthinkable, the two counter, the two one-sided, schemes are thus theoretically balanced. But, practically, our consciousness of the moral law, which, without a moral liberty in man, would be a mendacious imperative, gives a decisive preponderance to the doctrine of freedom over the doctrine of fate. We are free in act, if we are accountable for our actions."

Sir W. Hamilton is of opinion that both sides are alike unsuccessful in repelling each other's attacks. The arguments against both are, he thinks, to the human faculties, irrefutable. "The champions[*] of the opposite doctrines are at once resistless in assault and impotent in defence. Each is hewn down, and appears to die under the home thrusts of his adversary; but each again recovers life from the very death of his antagonist, and, to borrow a simile, both are like the heroes in Valhalla, ready in a moment to amuse themselves anew in the same bloodless and interminable conflict. The doctrine of Moral Liberty cannot be made conceivable, for we can only conceive the determined and the relative. As already stated, all that can be done is to show, 1°. That, for the *fact* of Liberty, we have immediately or mediately, the evidence of Consciousness; and 2°. That there are among the phænomena of mind, many facts which we *must* admit as actual, but of whose possibility we are wholly unable to form any notion. I may merely observe that the fact of *Motion* can be shown to be im-

---

[*] Foot-note on Reid, p. 602.

possible, on grounds not less strong than those on which it is attempted to disprove the fact of Liberty." These "grounds no less strong" are the mere paralogisms which we examined in a recent chapter, and with regard to which our author showed so surprising a deficiency in the acuteness and subtlety to be expected from the general quality of his mind.

Conformably to these views, Sir W. Hamilton, in his foot-notes on Reid, promptly puts an extinguisher on several of that philosopher's arguments against the doctrine of so-called Necessity. When Reid affirms that Motives are not causes — that they may influence to action, but do not act, Sir W. Hamilton observes,* "If Motives influence to action, they must co-operate in producing a certain effect upon the agent; and the determination to act, and to act in a certain manner, is that effect. They are thus, on Reid's own view, in this relation, *causes*, and *efficient* causes. It is of no consequence in the argument whether motives be said to determine a man to act, or to influence (that is, to determine) him to determine himself to act." † This is one of the neatest specimens in our author's writings of a fallacy cut clean through by a single stroke.

Again, when Reid says that acts are often done without any motive, or when there is no motive for preferring the means used, rather than others by which the same end might have been attained, Sir W. Hamilton asks,‡ "Can we conceive any act of which there was not a sufficient cause or concourse of causes why the man per-

---

* Foot-note on Reid, p. 608.
† To the same effect see Discussions, Appendix on Causality, p. 614.
‡ Foot-note on Reid, p. 609.

formed it and no other? If not, call this cause, or these concauses, the *motive*, and there is no longer a dispute."

Reid asks, "Is there no such thing as wilfulness, caprice, or obstinacy among mankind?" Sir W. Hamilton, *e contra:* * "But are not these all tendencies, and fatal tendencies, to act or not to act? By contradistinguishing such tendencies from motives strictly so called, or rational impulses, we do not advance a single step towards rendering liberty comprehensible."

According to Reid, the determination is made by the man, and not by the motive. "But," asks Sir W. Hamilton,† "was the *man* determined by no motive to that determination? Was his specific volition to this or to that without a cause? On the supposition that the sum of influences (motives, dispositions, and tendencies) to volition A, is equal to 12, and the sum of influences to counter-volition B equal to 8 — can we conceive that the determination of volition A should not be necessary? — We can only conceive the volition B to be determined by supposing that the man *creates* (calls from non-existence into existence) a certain supplement of influences. But this creation as actual, or in itself, is inconceivable, and even to conceive the possibility of this inconceivable act, we must suppose some cause by which the man is determined to exert it. We thus, in *thought*, never escape determination and necessity. It will be observed that I do not consider this inability to the *notion*, any disproof of the *fact* of Free-will." Nor is it: but if, as our author so strongly inculcates, "every ‡ effort to bring the fact of liberty within the compass of our conceptions only results in the substitution in its place of some more

---

* Foot-note to Reid, p. 610.   † Ibid. p. 611.   ‡ Lectures, i. 34.

or less disguised form of necessity," it is a strong indication that some form of necessity is the opinion naturally suggested by our collective experience of life.*

Sir W. Hamilton having thus, as is often the case (and it is one of the best things he does), saved his opponents the trouble of answering his friends, his doctrine is left resting exclusively on the supports which he has himself provided for it. In examining them, let us place ourselves, in the first instance, completely at his point of view, and concede to him the coequal inconceivability of the conflicting hypotheses, an uncaused commencement, and an infinite regress. But this choice of inconceivabilities is not offered to us in the case of volitions only. We are held, as he not only admits but contends, to the same alternative in all cases of causation whatsoever. But we find our way out of the difficulty, in other cases, in quite a different manner. In the case of every other kind of fact, we do not elect the hypothesis that the event took place without a cause: we accept the other supposition, that of a regress, not indeed to infinity, but either generally into the region of the Unknowable, or back to a Universal Cause, regarding which, as we are only concerned with it in relation to what it preceded, and not as itself preceded by anything, we can afford to make a plain avowal of our ignorance.

Now, what is the reason, which, in the case of all

---

* So difficult is it to escape from this fact, that Sir W. Hamilton himself says (Lectures, i. 188), "Voluntary conation is a faculty which can only be determined to energy through a pain or pleasure — through an estimate of the relative worth of objects." If I am determined to prefer innocence to the satisfaction of a particular desire, through an estimate of the relative worth of innocence and of the gratification, can this estimate, while unchanged, leave me at liberty to choose the gratification in preference to innocence?

things within the range of our knowledge except volitions, makes us choose this side of the alternative? Why do we, without scruple, register all of them as depending on causes, by which (to use our author's language) they are determined necessarily, though, in believing this, we, according to Sir W. Hamilton, believe as utter an inconceivability as if we supposed them to take place without a cause? Apparently it is because the causation hypothesis, inconceivable as he may think it, possesses the advantage of having experience on its side. And how, or by what evidence, does experience testify to it? Not by disclosing any *nexus* between the cause and the effect, any Sufficient Reason in the cause itself why the effect should follow it. No philosopher now makes this supposition, and Sir W. Hamilton positively disclaims it What experience makes known, is the fact of an invariable sequence between every event and some special combination of antecedent conditions, in such sort that wherever and whenever that union of antecedents exists, the event does not fail to occur. Any *must* in the case, any necessity, other than the unconditional universality of the fact, we know nothing of. Still, this à posteriori "does," though not confirmed by an à priori "must," decides our choice between the two inconceivables, and leads us to the belief that every event within the phænomenal universe, except human volitions, is determined to take place by a cause. Now, the so-called Necessitarians demand the application of the same rule of judgment to our volitions. They maintain that there is the same evidence for it. They affirm, as a truth of experience, that volitions do, in point of fact, follow determinate moral antecedents with the same uniformity, and (when we have sufficient knowledge of the circumstances) with the same certainty, as physical effects follow their physical causes. These moral antecedents are desires, aversions, habits, and dispositions, combined with outward circumstances suited to call those internal incentives into action. All these again are effects of causes, those of them which are mental being consequences of education, and of other moral and physical influences. This is what Necessitarians affirm : and they court every possible mode in which its truth can be verified. They test it by each person's observation of his own volitions. They test it by each person's observation of the voluntary actions of those with whom he comes into contact; and by the power which every one has of foreseeing actions, with a degree of exactness proportioned to his previous experience and knowledge of the agents, and with a certainty often quite equal to that with which we predict the commonest physical events. They test it further, by the statistical results of the observation of human beings acting in numbers sufficient to eliminate the influences which operate only on a few, and which on a large scale neutralize one another, leaving the total result about the same as if the volitions of the whole mass had been affected by such only of the determining causes as were common to them all. In cases of this description the results are as uniform, and may be as accurately foretold, as in any physical inquiries in which the effect depends upon a multiplicity of causes. The cases in which volitions seem too uncertain to admit of being confidently predicted, are those in which our knowledge of the influences antecedently in operation is so incomplete, that with equally imperfect data there would be the same uncertainty in the predictions of the astronomer and the chemist. On these grounds it is contended, that our choice between the conflicting inconceivables should be the same in the case of volitions as of all other phænomena; we must reject equally in both cases the hypothesis of spontaneousness, and consider them all as caused. A volition is a moral effect, which follows the corresponding moral causes as certainly and invariably as physical effects follow their physical causes. Whether it *must* do so, I acknowledge myself to be entirely ignorant, be the phænomenon moral or physical; and I condemn, accordingly, the word Necessity as applied to either case. All I know is, that it always *does*.

This argument from experience Sir W. Hamilton passes unnoticed, but urges, on the opposite side of the question, the argument from Consciousness. We are conscious, he affirms, either of our freedom, or at all events (it is odd that, on his theory, there should be any doubt) of something which implies freedom. If this is true, our internal consciousness tells us one thing, and the whole outward experience of the human race tells another. This is surely a very unfortunate predicament we are in, and a sore trial to the puzzled metaphysician. Philosophy is far from having so easy a business before her as our author thinks: the arbiter Consciousness is by no means invoked to turn the scale between two equally balanced difficulties; on the contrary, she has to sit in judgment between herself and a complete Induction from experience. Consciousness, it will probably be said, is the best evidence; and so it would be, if we were always certain what is Consciousness. But while there are so many varying testimonies respecting this; when Sir W.

Hamilton can himself say,* "many philosophers have attempted to establish, on the principles of common sense, propositions which are not original data of consciousness, while the original data of consciousness from which these propositions were derived, and to which they owed all their necessity and truth, these same philosophers were (strange to say) not disposed to admit;" when M. Cousin and nearly all Germany find the Infinite and the Absolute in Consciousness, Sir W. Hamilton thinking them utterly repugnant to it; when philosophers, for many generations, fancied that they had Abstract Ideas — that they could conceive a triangle which was neither equilateral, isosceles, nor scalene,† which Sir W. Hamilton and all other people now consider to be simply absurd; with all these conflicting opinions respecting the things to which Consciousness testifies, what is the perplexed inquirer to think? Does all philosophy end, as in our author's opinion Hume believed it to do, in a persistent contradiction between one of our mental faculties and another? We shall find there is a solution, which relieves the human mind from this embarrassment:

---

* Dissertations on Reid, p. 749.

† "Does it not require," says Locke (Essay on the Human Understanding, Book iv. chap 7, sect. 9), "some pains and skill to form the general idea of a triangle (which yet is none of the most abstract, comprehensive, and difficult)? for it must be neither oblique nor rectangle, neither equilateral, equicrural, nor scalene; but all and none of these at once. In effect, it is something imperfect, that cannot exist; an idea wherein some parts of several different and inconsistent ideas are put together." Yet this union of contradictory elements such a philosopher as Locke was able to fancy that he conceived. I scarcely know a more striking example of the tendency of the human mind to believe that things can exist separately because they can be separately named; a tendency strong enough, in this case, to make a mind like Locke's believe itself to be conscious of that which by the laws of mind cannot be a subject of consciousness to any one.

namely, that the question to which experience says yes, and that to which consciousness says no, are different questions.

Let us cross-examine the alleged testimony of consciousness. And, first, it is left in some uncertainty by Sir W. Hamilton whether Consciousness makes only one deliverance on the subject, or two; whether we are conscious only of moral responsibility, in which free-will is implied, or are directly conscious of free-will. In his Lectures, Sir W. Hamilton speaks only of the first. In the notes on Reid, which were written subsequently, he seems to affirm both, but the latter of the two in a doubtful and hesitating manner: so difficult, in reality, does he find it to ascertain with certainty what it is that Consciousness certifies. But as there are many who maintain, with a confidence far greater than his, that we are directly conscious of free-will,* it is necessary to examine that question.

To be conscious of free-will, must mean, to be conscious, before I have decided, that I am able to decide either way. Exception may be taken *in limine* to the use of the word consciousness in such an application. Consciousness tells me what I do or feel. But what I

---

* Mr. Mansel, among others, makes the assertion in the broadest form it is capable of, saying, "In every act of volition, I am fully conscious that I can at this moment act in either of two ways, and that, all the antecedent phænomena being precisely the same, I may determine one way to-day and another way to-morrow." (Prolegomena Logica, p. 152.) Yes, though the antecedent phænomena remain the same; but not if my judgment of the antecedent phænomena remains the same. If my conduct changes, either the external inducements or my estimate of them must have changed.

Mr. Mansel (as I have already observed) goes so far as to maintain that our immediate intuition of Power is given us by the ego producing its own volitions, not by its volitions producing bodily movements (pp. 139, 140, and 151).

am *able* to do, is not a subject of consciousness. Consciousness is not prophetic; we are conscious of what is, not of what will or can be. We never know that we are able to do a thing, except from having done it, or something equal and similar to it. We should not know that we were capable of action at all, if we had never acted. Having acted, we know, as far as that experience reaches, how we are able to act; and this knowledge, when it has become familiar, is often confounded with, and called by the name of, consciousness. But it does not derive any increase of authority from being misnamed; its truth is not supreme over, but depends on, experience. If our so-called consciousness of what we are able to do is not borne out by experience, it is a delusion. It has no title to credence but as an interpretation of experience, and if it is a false interpretation, it must give way.

But this conviction, whether termed consciousness or only belief, that our will is free — what is it? Of what are we convinced? I am told, that whether I decide to do or to abstain, I feel that I could have decided the other way. I ask my consciousness what I do feel, and I find, indeed, that I feel (or am convinced) that I could have chosen the other course *if I had preferred it;* but not that I could have chosen one course while I preferred the other. When I say preferred, I of course include with the thing itself, all that accompanies it. I know that I can, because I know that I often do, elect to do one thing, when I should have preferred another in itself, apart from its consequences, or from a moral law which it violates. And this preference for a thing in itself, abstractedly from its accompaniments, is often loosely described as preference for the thing. It is this unprecise mode of speech which makes it not seem absurd to say that I act in opposition to my preference; that I do one thing when I would rather do another; that my conscience prevails over my desires — as if conscience were not itself a desire — the desire to do right. Take any alternative: say, to murder or not to murder. I am told, that if I elect to murder, I am conscious that I could have elected to abstain: but am I conscious that I could have abstained if my aversion to the crime, and my dread of its consequences, had been weaker than the temptation? If I elect to abstain: in what sense am I conscious that I could have elected to commit the crime? Only if I had desired to commit it with a desire stronger than my horror of murder; not with one less strong. When we think of ourselves hypothetically as having acted otherwise than we did, we always suppose a difference in the antecedents: we picture ourselves as having known something that we did not know, or not known something that we did know; which is a difference in the external motives; or as having desired something, or disliked something, more or less than we did; which is a difference in the internal motives.

I therefore dispute altogether that we are conscious of being able to act in opposition to the strongest present desire or aversion. The difference between a bad and a good man is not that the latter acts in opposition to his strongest desires; it is that his desire to do right, and his aversion to doing wrong, are strong enough to overcome, and in the case of perfect virtue, to silence, any other desire or aversion which may conflict with them. It is because this state of mind is possible to human nature, that human beings are capable of moral government: and moral education consists in subjecting them to the discipline which has most tendency to bring them into this state. The object of moral education is to educate the will: but the will can only be educated through the desires and aversions; by eradicating or weakening such of them as are likeliest to lead to evil; exalting to the highest pitch the desire of right conduct and the aversion to wrong; cultivating all other desires and aversions of which the ordinary operation is auxiliary to right, while discountenancing so immoderate an indulgence of them, as might render them too powerful to be overcome by the moral sentiment, when they chance to be in opposition to it. The other requisites are, a clear intellectual standard of right and wrong, that moral desire and aversion may act in the proper places, and such general mental habits as shall prevent moral considerations from being forgotten or overlooked, in cases to which they are rightly applicable.

Rejecting, then, the figment of a direct consciousness of the freedom of the will, in other words, our ability to will in opposition to our strongest preference; it remains to consider whether, as affirmed by Sir W. Hamilton, a freedom of this kind is implied in what is called our consciousness of moral responsibility. There must be something very plausible in this opinion, since it is shared even by Necessitarians. Many of these — in particular Mr. Owen and his followers — from a recognition of the fact that volitions are effects of causes, have been led to deny human responsibility. I do not mean that they denied moral distinctions. Few persons have had a stronger sense of right and wrong, or been more devoted to the things they deemed right. What they denied was the rightfulness of inflicting punishment. A man's actions, they said, are the result of his character, and he is not the author of his own character. It is made *for* him, not *by* him. There is no justice in punishing him for what he cannot help. We should try to convince or persuade him that he had better act in a different manner; and should educate all, especially the young, in the habits and dispositions which lead to well-doing : though how this is to be effected without any use whatever of punishment as a means of education, is a question they have failed to resolve. The confusion of ideas, which makes the subjection of human volitions to the law of Causation seem inconsistent with accountability, must thus be very natural to the human mind; but this may be said of a thousand errors, and even of some merely verbal fallacies. In the present case there is more than a verbal fallacy, but verbal fallacies also contribute their part.

What is meant by moral responsibility? Responsibility means punishment. When we are said to have the feeling of being morally responsible for our actions, the idea of being punished for them is uppermost in the speaker's mind. But the feeling of liability to punishment is of two kinds. It may mean, expectation that if we act in a certain manner, punishment will actually be inflicted upon us, by our fellow-creatures or by a Supreme Power. Or it may only mean, being conscious that we shall deserve that infliction.

The first of these cannot, in any correct meaning of the term, be designated as a consciousness. If we believe that we shall be punished for doing wrong, it is because the belief has been taught to us by our parents and tutors, or by our religion, or is generally held by those who surround us, or because we have ourselves come to the conclusion by reasoning, or from the experience of life. This is not Consciousness. And, by whatever name it is called, its evidence is not dependent on any theory of the spontaneousness of volition. The punishment of guilt in another world is believed with undoubting conviction by Turkish fatalists, and by professed Christians who are not only Necessitarians, but believe that the majority of mankind were divinely predestined from all eternity to sin and to be punished for sinning. It is not, therefore, the belief that we shall be *made* accountable, which can be deemed to require or presuppose the free-will hypothesis; it is the belief that we ought so to be; that we are justly accountable; that guilt deserves punishment. It is here that the main issue is joined between the two opinions.

In discussing it, there is no need to postulate any theory respecting the nature or criterion of moral distinctions. It matters not, for this purpose, whether the right and wrong of actions depends on the consequences they tend to produce, or on an inherent quality of the actions themselves. It is indifferent whether we are utilitarians or anti-utilitarians; whether our ethics rest on intuition or on experience. It is sufficient if we believe that there is a difference between right and wrong, and a natural reason for preferring the former; that people in general, unless when they expect personal benefit from a wrong, naturally and usually prefer what they think to be right: whether because we are all dependent for what makes existence tolerable, upon the right conduct of other people, while their wrong conduct is a standing menace to our security, or for some more mystical and transcendental reason. Whatever be the cause, we are entitled to assume the fact; and its consequence is, that whoever cultivates a disposition to wrong, places his mind out of sympathy with the rest of his fellow-creatures, and if they are aware of his disposition, becomes a natural object of their active dislike. He not only forfeits the pleasure of their good will, and the benefit of their good offices, except when compassion for the human being is stronger than distaste towards the wrong-doer; but he also renders himself liable to whatever they may think it necessary to do in order to protect themselves against him; which may probably include punishment, as such, and will certainly involve much that is equivalent in its operation on himself. In this way he is certain to be made accountable, at least to his fellow-creatures, through the normal action of their natural sentiments. And it is well worth consideration, whether the practical expectation of being thus called to account, has not a great deal to do with the internal feeling of being accountable; a feeling, assuredly, which is seldom found existing in any strength in the absence of that practical expectation. It is not usually found that Oriental despots, who cannot be called to account by anybody, have much consciousness of being morally accountable. And (what is still more significant) in societies in which caste or class distinctions are really strong — a state so strange to us now, that we seldom realize it in its full force — it is a matter of daily experience that persons may show the strongest sense of moral accountability as regards their equals, who can make them accountable, and not the smallest vestige of a similar feeling towards their inferiors who cannot.

Another fact which it is of importance to keep in view, is, that the highest and strongest sense of the worth of goodness, and the odiousness of its opposite, is perfectly compatible with even the most exaggerated form of Fatalism. Suppose that there were two peculiar breeds of human beings, — one of them so constituted from the beginning, that however educated or treated, nothing could prevent them from always feeling and acting so as to be a blessing to all whom they approached; another, of such original perversity of nature that neither education nor punishment could inspire them with a feeling of duty, or prevent them from being active in evil doing. Neither of these races of human beings would have free-will; yet the former would be honored as demigods, while the latter would be regarded and treated as noxious beasts; not punished perhaps, since punishment would have no effect on them, and it might be thought wrong to indulge the mere instinct of vengeance: but kept carefully at a distance, and killed like other dangerous creatures when there was no other convenient way of being rid of them. We thus see that even under the utmost possible exaggeration of the doctrine of Necessity, the distinction between moral good and evil in conduct would not only subsist, but would stand out in a more marked manner than now, when the good and the wicked, however unlike, are still regarded as of one common nature.

But these considerations, though pertinent to the subject, do not touch the root of the difficulty. The real question is one of justice — the legitimacy of retribution, or punishment. On the theory of Necessity (we are told) man cannot help acting as he does; and it cannot be just that he should be punished for what he cannot help.

Not if the expectation of punishment enables him to help it, and is the only means by which he can be enabled to help it?

To say that he cannot help it, is true or false, according to the qualification with which the assertion is accompanied. Supposing him to be of a vicious disposition, he cannot help doing the criminal act, if he is allowed to believe that he will be able to commit it unpunished. If, on the contrary, the impression is strong in his mind that a heavy punishment will follow, he can, and in most cases, does, help it.

The question deemed to be so puzzling is, how punishment can be justified, if men's actions are determined by motives, among which motives punishment is one. A more difficult question would be, how it can be justified if they are not so determined. Punishment proceeds on the assumption that the will is governed by motives. If punishment had no power of acting on the will, it would be illegitimate, however natural might be the inclination to inflict it. Just so far as the will is supposed free, that is, capable of acting *against* motives, punishment is disappointed of its object, and deprived of its justification.

There are two ends which, on the Necessitarian theory, are sufficient to justify punishment: the benefit of the offender himself, and the protection of others. The first justifies it, because to benefit a person cannot be to do him an injury. To punish him for his own good, provided the inflictor has any proper title to constitute himself a judge, is no more unjust than to administer medicine. As far, indeed, as respects the criminal himself, the theory of punishment is, that by counterbalancing the influence of present temptations or acquired bad habits, it restores the mind to that normal preponderance of the love of right, which the best moralists and theologians consider to constitute the true definition of our freedom.* In its other aspect, punishment is a precaution taken by society in self-defence. To make this just, the only condition required is, that the end which society is attempting to enforce by punishment, should be a just one. Used as a means of aggression by society on the just rights of the individual, punishment is unjust. Used to protect the just rights of others against unjust aggression by the offender, it is just. If it is possible to have just rights, it cannot be unjust to defend them. Free-will or no free-will, it is just to punish so far as is necessary for this purpose, exactly as it is just to put a wild beast to death (without unnecessary suffering) for the same object.

Now, the primitive consciousness we are said to have, that we are accountable for our actions, and that if we violate the rule of right we shall deserve punishment, I contend is nothing else than our knowledge that punishment will be just; that by such conduct we shall place ourselves in the position in which our fellow-creatures, or the Deity, or both, will naturally, and may justly,

---

* "La liberté, complète, réelle, de l'homme, est la perfection humaine, le but à atteindre." From a paper by M. Albert Réville, in the *Revue Germanique* for September 1863, in which the question of free-will is discussed (though only parenthetically) with a good sense and philosophy seldom found in recent writings on that subject.

inflict punishment upon us. By using the word *justly*, I am not assuming, in the explanation, the thing I profess to explain. As before observed, I am entitled to postulate the reality, and the knowledge and feeling, of moral distinctions. These, it is both evident metaphysically and notorious historically, are independent of any theory concerning the will. We are supposed capable of understanding that other people have rights, and all that follows from this. The mind which possesses this idea, if capable of placing itself at the point of view of another person, must recognize it as just that others should protect themselves against any disposition on his part to infringe their rights; and he will do so the more readily, because he also has rights, and his rights continually require the same protection. This, I maintain, is our feeling of accountability, in so far as it can be separated from the prospect of being actually called to account. No one who understands the power of the principle of association, can doubt its sufficiency to create out of these elements the whole of the feeling of which we are conscious. To rebut this view of the case would require positive evidence; as, for example, if it could be proved that the feeling of accountability precedes, in the order of development, all experience of punishment. No such evidence has been produced, or is producible. Owing to the limited accessibility to observation of the mental processes of infancy, direct proof can as little be produced on the other side: but if there is any validity in Sir W. Hamilton's Law of Parcimony, we ought not to assume any mental phænomenon as an ultimate fact, which can be accounted for by other known properties of our mental nature.

I ask any one who thinks that the justice of punishment is not sufficiently vindicated by its being for the protection of just rights, how he reconciles his sense of justice to the punishment of crimes committed in obedience to a perverted conscience? Ravaillac, and Balthasar Gérard, did not regard themselves as criminals, but as heroic martyrs. If they were justly put to death, the justice of punishment has nothing to do with the state of mind of the offender, further than as this may affect the efficacy of punishment as a means to its end. It is impossible to assert the justice of punishment for crimes of fanaticism, on any other ground than its necessity for the attainment of a just end. If that is not a justification, there is no justification. All other imaginary justifications break down in their application to this case.

If, indeed, punishment is inflicted for any other reason than in order to operate on the will; if its purpose be other than that of improving the culprit himself, or securing the just rights of others against unjust violation, then, I admit, the case is totally altered. If any one thinks that there is justice in the infliction of purposeless suffering; that there is a natural affinity between the two ideas of guilt and punishment, which makes it intrinsically fitting that wherever there has been guilt, pain should be inflicted by way of retribution; I acknowledge that I can find no argument to justify punishment inflicted on this principle. As a legitimate satisfaction to feelings of indignation and resentment which are on the whole salutary and worthy of cultivation, I can in certain cases admit it; but here it is still a means to an end. The merely retributive view of punishment derives no justification from the doctrine I support. But it derives quite as little from the free-will doctrine. Suppose it true that the will of a malefactor, when he committed an offence, was free, or in other words, that he acted badly, not because he was of a bad disposition, but for no reason in particular: it is not easy to deduce from this the conclusion that it is just to punish him. That his acts were beyond the command of motives might be a good reason for keeping out of his way, or placing him under bodily restraint; but no reason for inflicting pain upon him, when that pain, by supposition, could not operate as a deterring motive.*

While the doctrine I advocate does not support the idea that punishment in mere retaliation is justifiable, it at the same time fully accounts for the general and natural sentiment of its being so. From our earliest childhood, the ideas of doing wrong and of punishment are presented to our mind together, and the intense character of the impressions causes the association between them to attain the highest degree of closeness and intimacy. Is it strange, or unlike the usual processes of the human mind, that in these circumstances we should retain the feeling, and forget the reason on which it is grounded? But why do I speak of forgetting? In most cases the reason has never, in our early education, been

* Several of Sir W. Hamilton's admissions are strong arguments against the alleged self-evident connection between free-will and accountability. We have found him affirming that a volition not determined by motives "would, if conceived, be conceived as morally worthless;" that "the free acts of an indifferent, are, morally and rationally, as worthless as the preordained passions of a determined, will;" and that "it is impossible to see how a cause, undetermined by any motive, can be a rational, moral, and accountable cause." If all this be so, there can be no intuitive perception of a necessary connection between free will and morality; it would appear, on the contrary, that we are naturally unable to recognize an act as moral, if it is, in the sense of the theory, free.

presented to the mind. The only ideas presented have been those of wrong and punishment, and an inseparable association has been created between these directly, without the help of any intervening idea. This is quite enough to make the spontaneous feelings of mankind regard punishment and a wrongdoer as naturally fitted to each other — as a conjunction appropriate in itself, independently of any consequences. Even Sir W. Hamilton recognizes as one of the common sources of error, that "the associations of thought are mistaken for the connections of existence."* If this is true anywhere, it is truest of all in the associations into which emotions enter. A strong feeling, directly excited by an object, is felt (except when contradicted by the feelings of other people) as its own sufficient justification — no more requiring the support of a reason than the fact that ginger is hot in the mouth; and it almost requires a philosopher, to recognize the need of a reason for his feelings, unless he has been under the practical necessity of justifying them to persons by whom they are not shared.

That a person holding what is called the Necessitarian doctrine should on that account *feel* that it would be unjust to punish him for his wrong actions, seems to me the veriest of chimeras. Yes, if he really "could not help" acting as he did, that is, if his *will* could not have helped it; if he was under physical constraint, or under the action of such a violent motive that no fear of punishment could have any effect; which, if capable of being ascertained, is a just ground of exemption, and is the reason why by the laws of most countries people are

* Lectures, iii. 47.

not punished for what they were compelled to do by immediate danger of death. But if the criminal was in a state capable of being operated upon by the fear of punishment, no metaphysical objection, I believe, will make him feel his punishment unjust. Neither will he feel that because his act was the consequence of motives, operating upon a certain mental disposition, it was not his own fault. For, first, it was at all events his own defect or infirmity, for which the expectation of punishment is the appropriate cure. And secondly, the word fault, so far from being inapplicable, is the specific name for the kind of defect or infirmity which he has displayed— insufficient love of right and aversion to wrong. The weakness of these feelings or their strength is in every one's mind the standard of fault or merit, of degrees of fault and degrees of merit. Whether we are judging of particular actions, or of the character of a person, we are wholly guided by the indications afforded of the energy of these influences. If the desire of right and aversion to wrong have yielded to a small temptation, we judge them to be weak, and our disapprobation is strong. If the temptation to which they have yielded is so great that even strong feelings of virtue might have succumbed to it, our moral reprobation is less intense. If, again, the moral desires and aversions have prevailed, but not over a very strong force, we hold that the action was good, but that there was little merit in it; and our estimate of the merit rises, in exact proportion to the greatness of the obstacle which the moral feeling proved strong enough to overcome.

Mr. Mansel * has furnished what he thinks a refu-

* Prolegomena Logica, Note C at the end.

tation of the Necessitarian argument, of which it is as well to take notice, the more so, perhaps, as it is directed against some remarks on the subject by the present writer in a former work :* remarks which were not intended as an argument for so-called Necessity, but only to place the nature and meaning of that ill-understood doctrine in a truer light. With this purpose in view, it was remarked that "by saying that a man's actions necessarily follow from his character, all that is really meant (for no more is meant in any case whatever of causation) is that he invariably does act in conformity to his character, and that any one who thoroughly knew his character could certainly predict how he would act in any supposable case. No more than this is contended for by any one but an Asiatic fatalist." "And no more than this," observes Mr. Mansel, "is needed to construct a system of fatalism as rigid as any Asiatic can desire."

Mr. Mansel is mistaken in thinking that the doctrine of the causation of human actions is fatalism at all, or resembles fatalism in any of its moral or intellectual effects. To call it by that name is to break down a fundamental distinction. Real fatalism is of two kinds. Pure, or Asiatic fatalism — the fatalism of the Œdipus, — holds that our actions do not depend upon our desires. Whatever our wishes may be, a superior power, or an abstract destiny, will overrule them, and compel us to act, not as we desire, but in the manner predestined. Our love of good and hatred of evil are of no efficacy, and though in themselves they may be virtuous, as far as conduct is concerned it is unavailing to cultivate them. The other kind, Modified Fatalism I will call it, holds that our

* System of Logic, Book vi. ch. 2.

actions are determined by our will, our will by our desires, and our desires by the joint influence of the motives presented to us and of our individual character; but that, our character having been made for us and not by us, we are not responsible for it, nor for the actions it leads to, and should in vain attempt to alter them. The true doctrine of the Causation of human actions maintains, in opposition to both, that not only our conduct, but our character, is in part amenable to our will; that we can, by employing the proper means, improve our character; and that if our character is such that while it remains what it is, it necessitates us to do wrong, it will be just to apply motives which will necessitate us to strive for its improvement, and so emancipate ourselves from the other necessity: in other words, we are under a moral obligation to seek the improvement of our moral character. We shall not indeed do so unless we desire our improvement, and desire it more than we dislike the means which must be employed for the purpose. But does Mr. Mansel, or any other of the free-will philosophers, think that we can will the means if we do not desire the end, or if our desire of the end is weaker than our aversion to the means?

Mr. Mansel is more rigid in his ideas of what the freewill theory requires, than one of the most eminent of the thinkers who have adopted it. According to Mr. Mansel, the belief that whoever knew perfectly our character and our circumstances could predict our actions, amounts to Asiatic fatalism. According to Kant, in his Metaphysics of Ethics, such capability of prediction is quite compatible with the freedom of the will. This seems, at first sight, to be an admission of everything which the rational supporters of the opposite theory could desire. But Kant avoids this consequence, by changing (as lawyers would say) the *venue* of free-will, from our actions generally, to the formation of our character. It is in that, he thinks, we are free, and he is almost willing to admit that while our character is what it is, our actions are necessitated by it. In drawing this distinction, the philosopher of Königsberg saves inconvenient facts at the expense of the consistency of his theory. There cannot be one theory for one kind of voluntary actions, and another theory for the other kinds. When we voluntarily exert ourselves, as it is our duty to do, for the improvement of our character, or when we act in a manner which (either consciously on our part or unconsciously) deteriorates it, these, like all other voluntary acts, presuppose that there was already something in our character, or in that combined with our circumstances, which led us to do so, and accounts for our doing so. The person, therefore, who is supposed able to predict our actions from our character as it now is, would, under the same conditions of perfect knowledge, be equally able to predict what we should do to change our character; and if this be the meaning of necessity, that part of our conduct is as necessary as all the rest. If necessity means more than this abstract possibility of being foreseen; if it means any mysterious compulsion, apart from simple invariability of sequence, I deny it as strenuously as any one. To enforce this distinction was the principal object of the remarks which Mr. Mansel has criticised. If an unessential distinction from Mr. Mansel's point of view, it is essential from mine, and of supreme importance in a practical aspect.

The free-will metaphysicians have made little endeavor to prove that we can will in opposition to our strongest desire, but have strenuously maintained that we can will when we have no strongest desire. With this view Dr. Reid formerly, and Mr. Mansel now, have thrown in the teeth of Necessitarians the famous *asinus Buridani.* If, say they, the will were solely determined by motives, the ass, between two bundles of hay exactly alike, and equally distant from him, would remain undecided until he died of hunger. From Sir W. Hamilton's notes on this chapter of Reid,* I infer that he did not countenance this argument; and it is surprising that writers of talent should have seen anything in it. I waive the objection that if it applies at all, it proves that the ass also has free will; for perhaps he has. But the ass, it is affirmed, would starve before he decided. Yes, possibly, if he remained all the time in a fixed attitude of deliberation; if he never for an instant ceased to balance one against another the rival attractions, and if they really were so exactly equal that no dwelling on them could detect any difference. But this is not the way in which things take place on our planet. From mere lassitude, if from no other cause, he would intermit the process, and cease thinking of the rival objects at all: until a moment arrived when he would be seeing or thinking of one only, and that fact, combined with the sensation of hunger, would determine him to a decision.

But the argument on which Mr. Mansel lays most stress (it is also one of Reid's) is the following: Necessitarians say that the will is governed by the strongest motive; "but I only know the strength of motives in

* Pp. 609–611.

relation to the will by the test of ultimate prevalence; so that this means no more than that the prevailing motive prevails." I have heretofore complimented Mr. Mansel on seeing farther, in some things, than his master. In the present instance I am compelled to remark, that he has not seen so far. Sir W. Hamilton was not the man to neglect an argument like this, had there been no flaw in it. The fact is that there are two. First, those who say that the will follows the strongest motive, do not mean the motive which is strongest in relation to the will, or in other words, that the will follows what it does follow. They mean the motive which is strongest in relation to pain and pleasure; since a motive, being a desire or aversion, is proportional to the pleasantness, as conceived by us, of the thing desired, or the painfulness of the thing shunned. And when what was at first a direct impulse towards pleasure, or recoil from pain, has passed into a habit or a fixed purpose, then the strength of the motive means the completeness and promptitude of the association which has been formed between an idea and an outward act. This is the first answer to Mr. Mansel. The second is, that even supposing there were no test of the strength of motives but their effect on the will, the proposition that the will follows the strongest motive would not, as Mr. Mansel supposes, be identical and unmeaning. We say, without absurdity, that if two weights are placed in opposite scales, the heavier will lift the other up; yet we mean nothing by the heavier, except the weight which will lift up the other. The proposition, nevertheless, is not unmeaning, for it signifies that in many or most cases there *is* a heavier, and that this is always the same one, not one or the other as it may happen. In like manner, even if the strongest motive meant only the motive which prevails, yet if there is a prevailing motive — if, all other antecedents being the same, the motive which prevails to-day will prevail to-morrow and every subsequent day — Sir W. Hamilton was acute enough to see that the free-will theory is not saved. I regret that I cannot, in this instance, credit Mr. Mansel with the same acuteness.

Before leaving the subject, it is worth while to remark, that not only the doctrine of Necessity, but Predestination in its coarsest form — the belief that all our actions are divinely preordained — though, in my view, inconsistent with ascribing any moral attributes whatever to the Deity, yet if combined with the belief that God works according to general laws, which have to be learned from experience, has no tendency to make us act in any respect otherwise than we should do if we thought our actions really contingent. For if God acts according to general laws, then, whatever he may have preordained, he has preordained that it shall take place through the causes on which experience shows it to be consequent; and if he has predestined that I shall attain my ends, he has predestined that I shall do so by studying and putting in practice the means which lead to their attainment. When the belief in predestination has a paralyzing effect on conduct, as is sometimes the case with Mahomedans, it is because they fancy they can infer what God has predestined, without waiting for the result. They think that either by particular signs of some sort, or from the general aspect of things, they can perceive the issue towards which God is working, and having discovered this, naturally deem useless any attempt to defeat it. Because something will certainly happen if nothing is done to prevent it, they think it will certainly happen whatever may be done to prevent it: in a word, they believe in Necessity in the only proper meaning of the term — an issue unalterable by human efforts or desires.

CHAPTER XXVII.

SIR WILLIAM HAMILTON'S OPINIONS ON THE STUDY OF MATHEMATICS.

No account of Sir W. Hamilton's philosophy could be complete, which omitted to notice his famous attack on the tendency of mathematical studies: for though there is no direct connection between this and his metaphysical opinions, it affords the most express evidence we have of those fatal *lacunæ* in the circle of his knowledge, which unfitted him for taking a comprehensive or even an accurate view of the processes of the human mind in the establishment of truth. If there is any pre-requisite which all must see to be indispensable in one who attempts to give laws to human intellect, it is a thorough acquaintance with the modes by which human intellect has proceeded, in the cases where by universal acknowledgment, grounded on subsequent direct verification, it has succeeded in ascertaining the greatest number of important and recondite truths. This requisite Sir W. Hamilton had not, in any tolerable degree, fulfilled. Even of pure mathematics he apparently knew little but the rudiments. Of mathematics as applied to investigating the laws of physical nature; of the mode in which the properties of number, extension, and figure, are made instrumental to the ascertainment of truths other than arithmetical or geometrical—it is too much to say that he had even a superficial knowledge: there is not a line in his works which shows him to have had any knowledge at all. He had no conception of what the process is. In this he differed greatly and disadvantageously from his immediate predecessor in the same school of metaphysical thought, Professor Dugald Stewart; whose works derive a great part of their value from the foundation of sound and accurate scientific knowledge laid by his mathematical and physical studies, and which his subsequent metaphysical pursuits enabled him, quite successfully to the length of his tether, to clarify and reduce to principles.

If Sir W. Hamilton had contented himself with saying of mathematics, that it is not, of itself alone, a sufficient education of the intellectual faculties; that it cultivates the mind only partially; that there are important kinds of intellectual cultivation and discipline which it does not give, and to which, therefore, if pursued to the exclusion of the studies which do give them, it is unfavorable; he would have said something, not new indeed, but true, not of mathematics alone, but of every limited and special employment of the mental faculties; of every study in which the human mind can engage, except the two or three highest, most difficult, and most imperfect, which, requiring all the faculties in their greatest attainable perfection, can never be recommended or thought of as preparatory discipline, but are themselves the chief purpose for which such preparation is required. Sir W. Hamilton, however, has asserted much more than this. He undertakes to show that the study of mathematics is not a useful intellectual discipline at all, except in one comparatively humble particular, which it has in common with some of the most despised pursuits; and that if prosecuted far, it positively unfits the mind for the useful employment of its faculties on any other object. As might be expected from an attempt to maintain such a thesis by one who, however acute on other matters, had no sufficient knowledge of the subject he was writing about, this celebrated dissertation is one of the weakest parts of his works. He ignores not only the whole of his adversary's case, but the most important part of his own; and has made a far less powerful attack on the tendencies of mathematical studies, than could easily be made by one who understood the subject. He has, in fact, missed the most considerable of the evil effects to the production of which those studies have contributed: and has thrown no light on the intellectual shortcomings of the common run of mathematicians, so signally displayed in their wretched treatment of the generalities of their own science. He finds hardly anything to say to their disadvantage but things so trite and obvious, that the greatest zealot for mathematics could afford to pass them by, insisting only on the inestimable benefits which are to be set against them, and which alone are really to the purpose; for it is no objection to a harrow that it is not a plough, nor to a saw that it is not a chisel.

For instance, are we much the wiser for being once more told, at great length, and with a cloud of witnesses brought to back the assertion, that mathematics, being concerned only with demonstrative evidence, does not teach us, either by theory or practice, to estimate probabilities? Did any mathematician, or eulogist of mathematics, ever pretend that it did? Does the science to which Sir W. Hamilton assigns a place above all others as an intellectual discipline — does Metaphysics enable us to judge of probable evidence? If such a claim has ever been made in its behalf, I am not aware of it; Sir W. Hamilton certainly was too well acquainted with the subject to make any such pretension. Metaphysics, like Mathematics, and all the rest of the fundamental sciences, demands, not probable, but certain evidence. The province of Probabilities in science is not the abstract, but what M. Comte terms the concrete sciences; those which treat of the combinations actually realized in Nature, as distinguished from the general laws which would equally govern any other combinations of the same elements : zoölogy and botany, for example, as contrasted with physiology; geology, as opposed to thermology and chemistry. In an abstract science a probability is of no account; it is but a momentary halt on the road to certainty, and a hint for fresh experiments.

Inasmuch as abstract science in general, and mathematics in particular, afford no practice in the estimation of conflicting probabilities, which is the kind of sagacity most required in the conduct of practical affairs, it follows that, when made so exclusive an occupation as to prevent the mind from obtaining enough of this necessary practice in other ways, it does worse than not cultivate the faculty — it prevents it from being acquired, and *pro tanto* unfits the person for the general business of life. It is natural that people who are bad judges of probability, should be, according to their temperament, unduly credulous or unreasonably sceptical; both which charges our author, with great earnestness and a heavy artillery of authorities, drives home against the mathematicians. But he would have made little progress towards proving his case, even by a much more complete catalogue of the intellectual defects of a mathematician who is nothing but a mathematician. A person may be keenly alive to these, and may hate them, as M. Comte did, with a perfect hatred, while upholding mathematical instruction as not only a useful but the indispensable first stage of all scientific education worthy of the name.* Nor can any reasonable view of the subject refuse to recognize, in the very faults which our author imputes to mathematicians, the excesses of a most valuable quality. Let us be assured that for the formation of a well-trained intellect, it is no slight recommendation of a study, that it is the means by which the mind is earliest and most easily brought to maintain within itself a standard of complete proof. A mind thus furnished, and not duly instructed on other subjects, may commit the error of expecting in all proof too close an adherence to the type with which it is familiar. That type may and ought to be widened by greater variety of culture; but he who has never acquired it has no just sense of the difference between what is proved and what is not proved: the first foundation of the scientific habit of mind has not been laid. It

* I do not know that the logical value of mathematics has ever been more finely and discriminatingly appreciated than by M. Comte in his latest work, "*Synthèse Subjective*" (p. 98). "Bornée à son vrai domaine, la raison mathématique y peut admirablement remplir l'office universel de la saine logique: induire pour déduire, afin de construire. Renonçant à de vaines prétentions, elle sent que ses meilleurs succès restent toujours incapables de nous faire, partout ailleurs, induire, ou même déduire, et surtout construire. Elle se contente de fournir, dans le domaine le plus favorable, un type de clarté, de précision, et de consistance, dont la contemplation familière peut seule disposer l'esprit à rendre les autres conceptions aussi parfaites que le comporte leur nature. Sa réaction générale, plus négative que positive, doit surtout consister à nous inspirer partout une invincible répugnance pour le vague, l'incohérence, et l'obscurité, que nous pouvons réellement éviter envers des pensées quelconques, si **nous y faisons assez d'efforts.**"

has long been a complaint against mathematicians, that they are hard to convince: but it is a far greater disqualification both for philosophy, and for the affairs of life, to be too easily convinced; to have too low a standard of proof. The only sound intellects are those which, in the first instance, set their standard of proof high. Practice in concrete affairs soon teaches them to make the necessary abatement: but they retain the consciousness, without which there is no sound practical reasoning, that in accepting inferior evidence because there is none better to be had, they do not by that acceptance raise it to completeness. They remain aware of what is wanting to it.

Besides accustoming the student to demand complete proof, and to know when he has not obtained it, mathematical studies are of immense benefit to his education by habituating him to precision. It is one of the peculiar excellences of mathematical discipline, that the mathematician is never satisfied with an *à peu près*. He requires the *exact* truth. Hardly any of the non-mathematical sciences except chemistry has this advantage. One of the commonest modes of loose thought, and sources of error both in opinion and in practice, is to overlook the importance of quantities. Mathematicians and chemists are taught by the whole course of their studies, that the most fundamental differences of quality depend on some very slight difference in proportional quantity; and that from the qualities of the influencing elements, without careful attention to their quantities, false expectations would constantly be formed as to the very nature and essential character of the result produced. If Sir W. Hamilton's mind had undergone this improving discipline, we should not have found him employing the most precise mathematical terms with the laxity which is habitual in his writings. For instance: whenever he means that one of two things diminishes while another increases, he says that they are in the inverse ratio of one another. He affirms this of the Extension and Comprehension of a general notion;* of the number of objects among which our attention is divided, and the intensity with which it is applied to each;† of the knowledge-giving and the sensation-giving properties of an impression of sense;‡ and of the intensity and the prolongation of an energy.§ That an inverse ratio is the name of a definite relation between quantities, seems never to have occurred to him.

Neither is it a small advantage of mathematical studies, even in their poorest and most meagre form, that they at least habituate the mind to resolve a train of reasoning into steps, and make sure of each step before advancing to another. If the practice of mathematical reasoning gives nothing else, it gives wariness of mind; it accustoms us to demand a sure footing: and though it leaves us no better judges of ultimate premises than it found us (which is no more than may be said of almost all metaphysics), at least it does not suffer us to let in, at any of the joints in the reasoning, any assumption which we have not previously faced in the shape of an axiom, postulate, or definition. This is a merit which it has in common with Formal Logic, and is the chief ground on which some have thought that it could perform the func-

* See, among other passages, Lectures, iii. 146, 147.
† Ibid. i. 246.   ‡ Ibid. ii. 98.   § Ibid. p. 439.

tions and supply the place of that science; an opinion in which I by no means agree.

That mathematics "do not cultivate the power of generalization,"* which to our author appears so obvious a truth that he need not give himself the trouble of proving it, will be admitted by no person of competent knowledge, except in a very qualified sense. The generalizations of mathematics are, no doubt, a different thing from the generalizations of physical science; but in the difficulty of seizing them, and the mental tension they require, they are no contemptible preparation for the most arduous efforts of the scientific mind. Even the fundamental notions of the higher mathematics, from those of the differential calculus upwards, are products of a very high abstraction. Merely to master the idea of centrifugal force, or of the centre of gravity, are efforts of mental analysis surpassed by few in our author's metaphysics. To perceive the mathematical law common to the results of many mathematical operations, even in so simple a case as that of the binomial theorem, involves a vigorous exercise of the same faculty which gave us Kepler's laws, and rose through those laws to the theory of universal gravitation. Every process of what has been called Universal Geometry — that great creation of Descartes and his successors, in which a single train of reasoning solves whole classes of problems at once, and demonstrates properties common to all curves or surfaces, and others common to large groups of them — is a practical lesson in the management of wide generalizations, and abstraction of the points of agreement from those of difference among objects of great and confusing

* Discussions, p. 282.

diversity, to which the most purely inductive science cannot furnish many superior. Even so elementary an operation as that of abstracting from the particular configuration of the triangles or other figures, and the relative situation of the particular lines or points, in the diagram which aids the apprehension of a common geometrical demonstration, is a very useful, and far from being always an easy, exercise of the faculty of generalization so strangely imagined to have no place or part in the processes of mathematics.

Sir W. Hamilton allows no efficacy to mathematical studies in the cultivation of any valuable intellectual habit, except the single one of continuous attention. "Are mathematics then," he asks,* "of no value as an instrument of mental culture? Nay, do they exercise only to distort the mind? To this we answer: That their study, if pursued in moderation and efficiently counteracted, may be beneficial in the correction of a certain vice, and in the formation of its corresponding virtue. The vice is the habit of mental distraction; the virtue the habit of continuous attention. This is the single benefit, to which the study of mathematics can justly pretend, in the cultivation of the mind." He adds, truly enough,† "But mathematics are not the only study which cultivates the attention; neither is the kind and degree of attention which they tend to induce, the kind and degree of attention which our other and higher speculations require and exercise." So that, according to him, there is no purpose answered by mathematics in general education, but one which would be better fulfilled by something else.

* Discussions, pp. 313, 314. † Ibid. p. 322.

Without stopping to express my amazement at the assertion that the student of mathematics exercises no mental faculty but that of continuous attention, I will avail myself of an admission which Sir W. Hamilton cannot help making, but the full force of which he does not perceive. "We are far," he says,* "from meaning hereby to disparage the mathematical genius which *invents* new methods and formulæ, or new and felicitous applications of the old. . . . Unlike their divergent studies, the inventive talents of the mathematician and philosopher in fact approximate." Was, then, Sir W. Hamilton so ill-acquainted with everything deserving the name of mathematical tuition, as to suppose that the inventive powers which, in their higher degree, constitute mathematical genius, are not called forth and fostered in the process of teaching mathematics to the merest tyro? What sort of mathematical instruction is it of which solving problems forms no part? We come, within a page afterwards, to the following almost incredible announcement: † "Mathematical demonstration is solely occupied in deducing conclusions; probable reasoning, principally concerned in looking out for premises." Sir W. Hamilton thinks he can never be severe enough upon Cambridge for laying any stress on mathematics as an instrument of mental instruction. Did he ever turn over, I do not say a volume of Cambridge Problems, for these, it may be said, test the knowledge of the pupil rather than his inventive powers, and may be an exercise chiefly of memory: but did he ever see two such volumes as Bland's Algebraical and Geometrical Problems? Did he really imagine that working these

---

* Discussions, p. 290. † Ibid. p. 291.

was not "looking out for premises"? He seems actually to have thought that learning mathematics meant cramming it; and apparently believed that a mathematical tutor resolves all the equations himself, and merely asks his pupil to follow the solutions. For in every problem which the pupil himself solves, or theorem which he demonstrates, not having previously seen it solved or demonstrated, the same faculties are exercised which, in their higher degrees, produced the greatest discoveries in geometry. Mathematical teaching, therefore, even as now carried on, trains the mind to capacities, which, by our author's admission, are of the closest kin to those of the greatest metaphysician and philosopher. There is some color of truth for the opposite doctrine in the case of elementary algebra. The resolution of a common equation can be reduced to almost as mechanical a process as the working of a sum in arithmetic. The reduction of the question to an equation, however, is no mechanical operation, but one which, according to the degree of its difficulty, requires nearly every possible grade of ingenuity: not to speak of the new, and in the present state of science insoluble, equations, which start up at every fresh step attempted in the application of mathematics to other branches of knowledge. On all this, Sir W. Hamilton never bestows a thought. It is hardly necessary to point out that any other study, pursued in the manner in which he supposes mathematics to be, would as little exercise any other faculty than that of "continuous attention" as mathematics would. Next to metaphysics, the study he most patronizes is that of languages; of which he has so lofty an opinion, as to say *

---

* Discussions, note to p. 268.

that "to master, for example, the Minerva of Sanctius with its commentators, is, I conceive, a far more profitable exercise of mind than to conquer the Principia of Newton:" we may at least say that he was a better judge of the profit that might be derived from it. I, also, rate very highly the value, as a discipline to the mind, of the thorough grammatical study of any of the more logically constructed languages: but if the study consisted in learning the Minerva of Sanctius, or its commentators either, by rote, I believe the benefit derived would be about the same with that which Sir W. Hamilton considered to result from the exercise of "continuous attention" in mathematics.

It is a characteristic fact, that when the paper "on the Study of Mathematics" originally appeared as an article in the *Edinburgh Review*, no mention was made in it of Mixed or Applied Mathematics; the little which now appears on that subject being a subsequent addition, called forth by Dr. Whewell's reply. Dr. Whewell must have looked down from a considerable height upon an assault on the utility of Mathematics, in which the part of it that, in the opinion of its rational defenders, constitutes three fourths of its utility, was silently overlooked. When Sir W. Hamilton's attention was called to what he had previously omitted to think of, this is the way in which he disposes of it:* "Mathematics can be applied to objects of experience only in so far as these are measurable; that is, in so far as they come, or are supposed to come, under the categories of extension and number. Applied mathematics are, therefore, equally limited and equally unimproving as pure. The sciences,

* Discussions, pp. 334, 335.

indeed, with which mathematics are thus associated, may afford a more profitable exercise of mind; but this is only in so far as they supply the matter of observation, and of probable reasoning, and therefore *before* this matter is hypothetically subjected to mathematical demonstration or calculus."

This passage amounts to proof that the writer simply did not know what applied mathematics mean. The words are those of a person who had heard that there was such a thing, but knew absolutely nothing about what it was.

Applied mathematics is not the measurement of extension and number. It is the measurement, *by means* of extension and number, of other quantities which extension and number are marks of; and the ascertainment by means of quantities of all sorts, of those qualities of things which quantities are marks of.

For the information of readers who are no better informed than Sir W. Hamilton, and the reminding of those who are, I will illustrate this general statement by bringing it down to particulars; which a person, himself of very slender mathematical acquirements, can do, provided he has studied the science as every philosophical student ought to study it, but as Sir W. Hamilton has not done, with especial reference to its Methods.

The first, and typical example of the application of mathematics to the indirect investigation of truth, is within the limits of the pure science itself; the application of algebra to geometry; the introduction of which, far more than any of his metaphysical speculations, has immortalized the name of Descartes, and constitutes the greatest single step ever made in the progress of the exact sciences. Its rationale is simple. It is grounded on the general truth, that the position of every point, the direction of every line, and consequently the shape and magnitude of every enclosed space, may be fixed by the length of perpendiculars thrown down upon two, or (when the third dimension of space is taken into account) upon three, straight lines, meeting one another at right angles in the same point. A consequence, or rather a part, of this general truth, is that curve lines and surfaces may be determined by their *equations*. If from any number of points in a curve line or surface, perpendiculars are drawn to two (or three) rectangular axes, there exists between the lengths of these perpendiculars a relation of quantity, which is always the same for the same curve, or surface, and is expressed by an equation in which these variable are combined with certain constant quantities. From this relation, every other property of the curve or surface may always be deduced. In this way, numbers become the means of ascertaining truths not numerical. The periphery of an ellipse is not a number; but a certain numerical relation between straight lines is a mark of an ellipse, being proved to be an inseparable accompaniment of it. The equation which expresses this characteristic mark of any curve, may be handed over to algebraists, to deduce from it, through the properties of numbers, any other numerical relation which depends on it; with the certainty that when the conclusion is translated back again from symbols into words, it will come out a real, and perhaps previously unknown, geometrical property of the curve.

In such an example as this, the application of algebra

to geometry appears only in its most elementary form: but its extent is indefinite, and its flights almost beyond the reach of measurement. Its general scheme may be thus stated: In order to resolve any question, either of quality or quantity, concerning a line or space, find something whose magnitude, if known, would give the solution required, and which stands in some known relation to the rectangular co-ordinates (for instance, in the problem of Tangents, the length of the subtangent). Express this known relation in an equation: if the equation can be resolved, we have solved the geometrical problem. Or if the question be the converse one — not what are the properties of a given line or space, but what line or space is indicated by a given property; find what relation between rectangular co-ordinates that property requires: express it in an equation, and this equation, or some other deducible from it, will be the equation of the curve or surface sought. If it be a known curve or surface, this process will point it out; if not, we shall have obtained the necessary starting point for its study.

This application of one branch of mathematics to another branch, ranks as the first step in Applied Mathematics. The second is the application to Mechanics. The object-matter of Mechanics is the general laws, or theory, of Force in the abstract, that is, of forces, considered independently of their origin. As an extension is not a number, though a numerical fact may be a mark of an extension, so a force is neither a number nor an extension. But a force is only cognizable through its effects, and the effects by which forces are best known are effects in extension. The measure of a force, is the space through which it will carry a body of given magnitude in a given time. Quantities of force are thus ascertained, through marks which are quantities of extension. The other properties of forces are, their direction (a question of extension, which has already been reduced to a numerical relation between co-ordinates), and the nature of the motion which they generate, either singly or in combination; which is a mixed question of direction and of magnitude in extension. All questions of Force, therefore, can be reduced to questions of direction and of magnitude; and as all questions of direction or magnitude are capable of being reduced to equations between numbers, every question which can be raised respecting Force abstractedly from its origin, can be resolved if the corresponding algebraical equation can.

While the laws of Number thus underlie the laws of Extension, and these two underlie the laws of Force, so do the laws of Force underlie all the other laws of the material universe. Nature, as it falls within our ken, is composed of a multitude of forces, of which the origin (at least the immediate origin) is different, and the effects of which on our senses are extremely various. But all these forces agree in producing motions in space; and even those of their effects which are not actual motions, nevertheless travel; are propagated through spaces, in determinate times: they are all, therefore, amenable to, and conform to, the laws of extension and number. Often, indeed, we have no means of measuring these spaces and times; nor, if we could, are the resources of mathematics sufficient to enable us, in cases of great complexity, to arrive at the quantities of things we cannot directly measure, through those which we can.

Fortunately, however, we can do this, sufficiently for all practical purposes, in the case of the great cosmic forces, gravitation and light, and, to a less but still a considerable extent, heat and electricity. And here the domain of Applied Mathematics, for the present, ends. To it we are indebted, not only for all we know of the laws of these great and universal agencies, considered as connected bodies of truth, but also for the one complete type and model of the investigation of Nature by deductive reasoning; the ascertainment of the special laws of nature by means of the general. I will not offer to the understanding of any one who knows what this operation is, the affront of asking him if it is all performed "before" the matter is "hypothetically subjected to mathematical demonstration or calculus."

In being the great instrument of Deductive investigation, applied mathematics comes to be also the source of our principal inductions, which invariably depend on previous deductions. For where the inaccessibility or unmanageableness of the phænomena precludes the necessary experiments, mathematical deduction often supplies their place, by making us acquainted with points of resemblance which could not have been reached by direct observation. Phænomena apparently very remote from one another, are found, in the mode of their accomplishment, to follow the same or very similar numerical laws; and the mind, grasping up seemingly heterogeneous natural agencies which have the same equation, and classing them together, often lays a ground for the recognition of them as having either a common, or an analogous, origin. What were previously thought to be distinct powers in Nature, are identified with each other, by ascertaining that they produce similar effects according to the same mathematical laws. It was thus that the force which governs the planetary motions was shown to be identical with that by which bodies fall to the ground. Sir W. Hamilton would probably have admitted that the original discovery of this truth required as great a reach of intellect as has ever yet been displayed in abstract speculation. But is no exercise of intellect needed to apprehend the proof? Is it like an experiment in chemistry or an observation in anatomy, which may require mind for its origination, but to recognize which, when once made, requires only eyesight? Is "continuous attention" the only mental capacity required here? If Sir W. Hamilton could think so, his ignorance of the subject must have been greater than can be imputed to any educated mind, not to speak of a philosopher.

In the achievements which still remain to be effected in the way of scientific generalization, it is not probable that the direct employment of mathematics will be to any great extent available: the nature of the phænomena precludes such an employment for a long time to come — perhaps forever. But the process itself — the deductive investigation of Nature; the application of elementary laws, generalized from the more simple cases, to disentangle the phænomena of complex cases — explaining as much of them as can be so explained, and putting in evidence the nature and limits of the irreducible residuum, so as to suggest fresh observations preparatory to recommencing the same process with additional data; *this* is common to all science, moral and metaphysical included; and the greater the difficulty, the more needful is it that the inquirer should come prepared with an exact understanding of the requisites of this mode of investigation, and a mental type of its perfect realization. In the great problems of physical generalization now occupying the higher scientific minds, chemistry seems destined to an important and conspicuous participation, by supplying, as mathematics did in the cosmic phænomena, many of the premises of the deduction, as well as part of the preparatory discipline. But this use of chemistry is as yet only in its dawn; while, as a training in the deductive art, its utmost capacity can never approach to that of mathematics: and in the great inquiries of the moral and social sciences, to which neither of the two is directly applicable, mathematics (I always mean Applied Mathematics) affords the only sufficiently perfect type. Up to this time, I may venture to say that no one ever knew what deduction is, as a means of investigating the laws of nature, who had not learned it from mathematics; nor can any one hope to understand it thoroughly, who has not, at some time of his life, known enough of mathematics to be familiar with the instrument at work. Had Sir W. Hamilton been so, he would probably have cancelled the two volumes of his Lectures on Logic, and begun again on a different system, in which we should have heard less about Concepts and more about Things, less about Forms of Thought, and more about grounds of Knowledge.

Nor is even this the whole of what the inquirer loses, who knows not scientific Deduction in this its most perfect form. To have an inadequate conception of one of the two instruments by which we acquire our knowledge of nature, and consequently an imperfect comprehension even of the other in its higher forms, is not all. He is almost necessarily without any sufficient conception of human knowledge itself as an organic whole. He can have no clear perception of science as a system of truths flowing out of, and confirming and corroborating, one another; in which one truth sums up a multitude of others, and explains them, special truths being merely general ones modified by specialities of circumstance. He can but imperfectly understand the absorption of concrete truths into abstract, and the additional certainty given to theorems drawn from specific experience, when they can be affiliated as corollaries on general laws of nature — a certainty more entire than any direct observation can give. Neither, therefore, can he perceive how the larger inductions reflect an increase of certainty even upon those narrower ones from which they were themselves generalized, by reconciling superficial inconsistencies, and converting apparent exceptions into real confirmations.* To see these things requires more than a mere mathematician; but the ablest mind which has never gone through a course of mathematics, has small chance of ever perceiving them.

In the face of such considerations, it is a very small

---

* Ignorance of this important principle of the logic of induction, or want of familiarity with it, continually leads to gross misapplications, even by able writers, of the logic of ratiocination. For instance, we are constantly told that the uniformity of the course of nature cannot be itself an induction, since every inductive reasoning assumes it, and the premise must have been known before the conclusion. Those who argue in this manner can never have directed their attention to the continual process of giving and taking, in respect of certainty, which reciprocally goes on between this great premise and all the narrower truths of experience; the effect of which is, that, though originally a generalization from the more obvious of the narrower truths, it ends by having a fulness of certainty which overflows upon these, and raises the proof of them to a higher level; so that its relation to them is reversed, and instead of an inference from them, it becomes a principle from which any one of them may be inferred.

achievement to fill thirty octavo pages with the ill-natured things which persons of the most miscellaneous character, through a series of ages, have said about mathematicians, from a sneer of the cynic Diogenes, to a sarcasm of Gibbon, or a colloquial platitude of Horace Walpole; without any discrimination as to how many of the persons quoted were entitled to any opinion at all on such a subject, and with such entire disregard of all that gives weight to authority, as to include men who lived and died before algebra was invented, before the conic sections had been defined and studied by the mathematicians of Alexandria, or the first lines of the theory of statics had been traced by the genius of Archimedes; men whose whole mathematical knowledge consisted of a clumsy arithmetic, and the mere elements of geometry. Had there been twenty times as many of these testimonies, what proportion of them would have been of any value? Until quite recently, the professors of the different arts and sciences have made it a considerable part of their occupation to cry down one another's pursuits; and men of the world and *littérateurs* have been, in all ages, ready and eager to join with every set of them against the rest: the man who dares to know what they neither know nor care for, and to value himself on the knowledge, having always and everywhere been regarded as the common enemy. Did Sir W. Hamilton suppose that a person of half his reading would have any difficulty in furnishing, at a few hours' notice, an equally long list of amenities on the subject of grammarians or of metaphysicians? When our author does get hold of a witness who has a claim to a hearing, the witness is pressed into the service without any sifting of what he really says; it makes no difference whether he asserts that the study of mathematics does harm, or only that it does not simply suffice for all possible good. One of the authorities on whom most stress is laid is that of Descartes. I extract the important part of the quotation as our author gives it, partly from Descartes himself and partly from Baillet, his biographer.* The italics are Sir W. Hamilton's. "It was now a long time, says Baillet, since he had been convinced of the *small utility* of the *mathematics*, especially when studied on their own account, and not applied to other things. There was nothing, in truth, which appeared to him *more futile* than to occupy ourselves with simple numbers and imaginary figures, as if it were proper to confine ourselves to these *trifles* (bagatelles) without carrying our view beyond. There even seemed to him in this something *worse than useless*. His maxim was, that *such application insensibly disaccustomed us to the use of our reason*, and made us run the danger of losing the path which it traces. The words themselves of Descartes deserve quotation : Revera nihil *inanius* est, quam circa nudos numeros figurasque imaginarias ita versari, ut velle videamur in talium *nugarum* cognitione conquiescere, atque superficiariis istis demonstrationibus, quæ casu sæpius quam arte inveniuntur, et magis ad oculos et *imaginationem* pertinent, quam ad intellectum, sic incubare, ut quodammodo *ipsa ratione uti desuescamus;* simulque nihil intricatius, quam tali probandi modo, novas difficultates confusis numeris involutas expedire . . . Baillet goes on: In a letter to Mersenne, written in 1630, M. Descartes recalled to him that *he*

* Discussions, pp. 277, 278.

had renounced the study of mathematics for many years: and that he was anxious not to lose any more of his time in the barren operations of geometry and arithmetic, studies which never lead to anything important." Finally, speaking of the general character of the philosopher, Baillet adds: — "In regard to the rest of mathematics" (he had just spoken of astronomy — which Descartes thought, "*though he dreamt in it himself, only a loss of time*") "in regard to the rest of mathematics, those who know the rank which he held above all mathematicians, ancient and modern, will agree that he was the man in the world best qualified to judge them. We have observed that, after having studied these sciences to the bottom, *he had renounced them as of no use for the conduct of life and solace of mankind.*"

Whoever reads this passage as if it were all printed in Roman characters, and declines to submit his understanding to the italics which Sir W. Hamilton has introduced, will perceive the following three things. First, that Descartes was not speaking of the study of mathematics, but of its exclusive study. His objection is to stopping there, without proceeding to anything ulterior: *conquiescere, incubare.* Secondly, that he was speaking only of pure mathematics, as distinguished from its applications, and under the belief, how prodigiously erroneous we now know, that it did not admit of applications of any importance. Finally, that his disparagement of the pursuit, even as thus limited — his representation of it as "*nugæ,*" as "a loss of time," rested mainly on a ground which Sir W. Hamilton gave up, the unimportance of its object-matter. It was a repetition of the objection of Socrates, whom also our author thinks it worth while to cite as an authority on such a question, and who "did * not perceive of what utility they" (mathematical studies) "could be, calculated as they were to consume the life of a man, and to turn him away from many other and important acquirements." Such an opinion, in the days of Socrates, and from one whose glorious business it was to recall the minds of speculative men to dialectics and morals, reflects no discredit on his great mind. But the objection is one which Sir W. Hamilton, with every thinker of the last two centuries, disclaims. "The question," he expressly says,† "does not regard the value of mathematical *science*, considered in itself, or in its objective results, but the utility of mathematical *study*, that is, in its subjective effect, as an exercise of mind." All that Descartes said against it in this aspect (at least in the passage quoted, which we may suppose to be one of the strongest) is, that by affording other objects of thought, it diverts the mind from the use of *ipsa ratio*, that is, from the study of pure mental abstractions; which Descartes, to the great detriment of his philosophy, regarded as of much superior value to the employment of the thoughts upon objects of sense, which "magis ad oculos et imaginationem pertinent."

It was by his example, rather than by his precepts, that Descartes was destined to illustrate the unfavorable side of the intellectual influence of mathematical studies: and he must have been a still more extraordinary man than he was, could he have really understood a kind of mental perversions of which he is himself,

* Discussions, p. 323.   † Ibid. p. 266.

in the history of philosophy, the most prominent example.
Descartes is the completest type which history presents
of the purely mathematical type of mind — that in which
the tendencies produced by mathematical cultivation
reign unbalanced and supreme. This is visible not only
in the abuse of Deduction, which he carried to a greater
length than any distinguished thinker known to us, not
excepting the schoolmen; but even more so in the character of the premises from which his deductions set out.
And here we come upon the one really grave charge
which rests on the mathematical spirit, in respect of the
influence it exercises on pursuits other than mathematical.
It leads men to place their ideal of Science in deriving
all knowledge from a small number of axiomatic premises,
accepted as self-evident, and taken for immediate intuitions of reason. This is what Descartes attempted to
do, and inculcated as the thing to be done: and as he
shares with only one other name the honor of having
given his impress to the whole character of the modern
speculative movement, the consequences of his error
have been most calamitous. Nearly everything that is
objectionable, along with much of what is admirable,
in the character of French thought, whether on metaphysics, ethics, or politics, is directly traceable to the
fact that French speculation descends from Descartes
instead of from Bacon.* All reflecting persons in

* It is but just to add, that the English mode of thought has suffered in
a different, but almost equally injurious manner, by its exclusive following
of what it imagined to be the teaching of Bacon, being in reality a slovenly
misconception of him, leaving on one side the whole spirit and scope of
his speculations. The philosopher who labored to construct a canon of
scientific Induction, by which the observations of mankind, instead of remaining empirical, might be so combined and marshalled as to be made
the foundation of safe general theories, little expected that his name would

England, and many in France, perceive, that the chief infirmities of French thinking arise from its geometrical spirit; its determination to evolve its conclusions, even on the most practical subjects, by mere deduction from some single accepted generalization; the generalization, too, being frequently not even a theorem, but a practical rule, supposed to be obtained directly from the fountains of reason; a mode of thinking which erects one-sidedness into a principle, under the misapplied name of logic, and makes the popular political reasoning in France resemble that of a theologian arguing from a text, or a lawyer from a maxim of law. If this be the case even in France, it is still worse in Germany, the whole of whose speculative philosophy is an emanation from Descartes, and to most of whose thinkers the Baconian point of view is still below the horizon. Through Spinoza, who gave to his system the very forms as well as the entire spirit of geometry; through the mathematician Leibnitz, who reigned supreme over the German speculative mind for above a generation; with its spirit temporarily modified by the powerful intellectual individuality of Kant, but flying back after him to its uncorrected tendencies, the geometrical spirit went on from bad to worse, until in Schelling and Hegel the laws even of physical nature were deduced by ratiocination from subjective deliverances of the mind. The whole of German philosophical speculation has run from the beginning in this wrong groove, and having only recently become aware of the fact, is at present making convulsive efforts to get out

become the stock authority for disclaiming generalization, and enthroning empiricism, under the name of experience, as the only solid foundation of practice.

of it.* All these mistakes, and this deplorable waste of time and intellectual power by some of the most gifted and cultivated portions of the human race, are effects of the too unqualified predominance of the mental habits and tendencies engendered by elementary mathematics. Applied mathematics in its post-Newtonian development does nothing to strengthen, and very much to correct, these errors, provided the applications are studied in such a manner that the intellect is aware of what it is about, and does not go to sleep over algebraical symbols; a didactic improvement which Dr. Whewell, to his honor be it said, was earnestly and successfully laboring to introduce, thus practically correcting the real defects of mathematics as a branch of general education, at the very time when Sir W. Hamilton, who had not the smallest insight into those defects, selected him for the immediate recipient of an attack on mathematics, which, as it only included what Sir W. Hamilton knew of the subject, left out everything which was much worth saying.

It is not solely to mathematical studies that Sir W. Hamilton professes and shows hostility. Physical investigations generally, apart from their material fruits, he holds but in low estimation. We have seen in a former chapter how singularly unaware he is of the power and exertion of intellect which they often require. Touching

* The character here drawn of German thought is, I hardly need say, not intended to apply to such a man as Goethe, or to those who received their intellectual impulse from him. In him, indeed, not to speak of his almost universal culture, the intellectual operations were always guided by an intense spirit of observation and experiment, and a constant reference to the exigencies, outward and inward, of practical human life. Such criticism as can justly be made on Goethe as a thinker, rests on entirely different grounds.

their effect on the mind, he makes two serious complaints, which come out at the very commencement of his Lectures on Metaphysics.* The first is, that the study of Physics indisposes persons to believe in Free-will. To this accusation it must plead guilty: physical science undoubtedly has that tendency. But I maintain that this is only because physical science teaches people to judge of evidence. If the free-will doctrine could be proved, there is nothing in the habits of thought engendered by physical science that would indispose any one to yield to the evidence. A person who knows only one physical science, may be unable to feel the force of a kind of proof different from that which is customary in his department; but any one who is generally versed in physical science is accustomed to so many different modes of investigation, that he is well prepared to feel the force of whatever is really proof. Metaphysicians of Sir W. Hamilton's school, who pursue their investigations without regard to the cautions suggested by physical science, are equally catholic and comprehensive in the wrong way; they can mistake for proof anything or everything which is not so, provided it tends to form an association of ideas in their own minds.

The other objection of Sir W. Hamilton to the scientific study of the laws of Matter, is one which we should scarcely have expected from him, namely, that it annihilates Wonder.

"Wonder,† says Aristotle, is the first cause of philosophy; but in the discovery that all existence is but mechanism, the consummation of science would be an extinction of the very interest from which it originally

* Lectures, i. 35–42.   † Ibid. p. 37.

sprang. 'Even the gorgeous majesty of the heavens,' says a great religious philosopher,* 'the object of a kneeling adoration to an infant world, subdues no more the mind of him who comprehends the one mechanical law by which the planetary systems move, maintain their motion, and even originally form themselves. He no longer wonders at the object, infinite as it always is, but at the human intellect alone which in a Copernicus, Kepler, Gassendi, Newton, and Laplace, was able to transcend the object, by science to terminate the miracle, to reave the heaven of its divinities, and to exorcise the universe. But even this, the only admiration of which our intelligent faculties are now capable, would vanish, were a future Hartley, Darwin, Condillac, or Bonnet, to succeed in displaying to us a mechanical system of the human mind, as comprehensive, intelligible, and satisfactory as the Newtonian mechanism of the heavens.'" We may be well assured that no Hartley, Darwin, or Condillac will obtain a hearing, if the "great religious philosopher" can prevent it.

I shall not enter into all the topics suggested by this remarkable argument. I shall not ask whether, after all, it is better to be "subdued" than instructed; or whether human nature would suffer a great loss in losing wonder, if love and admiration remained; for admiration, *pace tantorum virorum*, is a different thing from wonder, and is often at its greatest height when the strangeness, which is a necessary condition of wonder, has died away. But I do wonder at the barrenness of imagination of a man who can see nothing wonderful in the material universe, since Newton, in an evil hour, partially unravelled a

* F. H. Jacobi. The entire passage is in Discussions, p. 312.

limited portion of it. If ignorance is with him a necessary condition of wonder, can he find nothing to wonder at in the *origin* of the system of which Newton discovered the laws? nothing in the probable former extension of the solar substance beyond the orbit of Neptune? nothing in the starry heavens, which, with a full knowledge of what Newton taught, Kant, in the famous passage which Sir W. Hamilton is so fond of quoting (and quotes in this very lecture) placed on the same level of sublimity with the moral law? If ignorance is the cause of wonder, it is downright impossible that scientific explanation can ever take it away, since all which explanation does, in the final resort, is to refer us back to a prior inexplicable. Were the catastrophe to arrive which is to expel Wonder from the universe — were it conclusively shown that the mental operations are dependent upon organic agency — would wonder be at an end because the fact, at which we should then have to wonder, would be that an arrangement of material particles could produce thought and feeling? Jacobi and Sir W. Hamilton might have put their minds at ease. It is not understanding that destroys wonder, it is familiarity. To a person whose feelings have depth enough to withstand that, no insight which can ever be attained into natural phænomena will make Nature less wonderful. And as for those whose sensibilities are shallow, did Jacobi suppose that *they* wondered one iota the more at the planetary motions, when astronomers imagined them to take place by the complicated evolutions of "cycle on epicycle, orb on orb"? A spectacle which they saw every day, had, we may rely upon it, as little effect in kindling their imaginations then, as now. Hear the opinion of a great poet;* not speaking particularly of wonder, but of the emotions generally which the spectacle of nature excites, and in words which apply to that emotion equally with the rest.

"Some are of opinion that the habit of analyzing, decomposing, and anatomizing, is inevitably unfavorable to the perception of beauty. People are led into this mistake by overlooking the fact that such processes being to a certain extent within the reach of a limited intellect, we are apt to ascribe to them that insensibility of which they are, in truth, the effect, and not the cause. Admiration and love, to which all knowledge truly vital must tend, are felt by men of real genius in proportion as their discoveries in natural philosophy are enlarged; and the beauty, in form, of a plant or an animal, is not made less, but more apparent, as a whole, by more accurate insight into its constituent properties and powers."

Hear next one of the most illustrious discoverers in physical science. Instead of regarding understanding as antithetical to wonder, Dr. Faraday complains that people do not wonder sufficiently at the material universe, because they do not sufficiently understand it.

"Let us now consider, for a little while, how wonderfully we stand upon this world. Here it is we are born, bred, and live, and yet we view these things with an almost entire absence of wonder to ourselves respecting the way in which all this happens. So small, indeed, is our wonder, that we are never taken by surprise; and I do think that to a young person of ten, fifteen, or twenty years of age, perhaps the first sight of a cataract or a mountain would occasion him more surprise than

* Wordsworth, in the Biography by his nephew, ii. 159.

he had ever felt concerning the means of his own existence; how he came here; how he lives; by what means he stands upright; and through what means he moves about from place to place. Hence, we come into this world, we live, and depart from it, without our thoughts being called specifically to consider how all this takes place; and were it not for the exertions of some few inquiring minds who have looked into these things, and ascertained the very beautiful laws and conditions by which we *do* live and stand upon the earth, we should hardly be aware that there was anything wonderful in it." *

If any additional authority be desired, the greatest poet of modern Germany was also the keenest scientific naturalist in it.

---

* Lectures on the Forces of Matter, pp. 2, 3. The philosophy of this is well given by Mr. Lewes, in his valuable work on Aristotle (p. 212). "Surprise starts from a background of knowledge, or fixed belief. Nothing is surprising to ignorance, because the mind in that state has no preconceptions to be contradicted."

CHAPTER XXVIII.

CONCLUDING REMARKS.

In the examination which I have now concluded of Sir W. Hamilton's philosophical achievements, I have unavoidably laid stress on points of difference from him rather than on those of agreement; the reason being, that I differ from almost everything in his philosophy on which he particularly valued himself, or which is specially his own. His merits, which, though I do not rate them so high, I feel and admire as sincerely as his most enthusiastic disciples, are rather diffused through his speculations generally, than concentrated on any particular point. They chiefly consist in his clear and distinct mode of bringing before the reader many of the fundamental questions of metaphysics; some good specimens of psychological analysis on a small scale; and the many detached logical and psychological truths which he has separately seized, and which are scattered through his writings, mostly applied to resolve some special difficulty, and again lost sight of. I can hardly point to anything he has done towards helping the more thorough understanding of the greater mental phænomena, unless it be his theory of Attention (including Abstraction), which seems to me the most perfect we have: but the subject, though a highly important, is a comparatively simple one.*

* Even on this subject he has not been able to avoid some fallacies in

With regard to the causes which prevented a thinker of such abundant acuteness, and more than abundant industry, from accomplishing the great things at which he aimed, it would ill become me to speak dogmatically. It would be a very unwarrantable assumption of superiority over a mind like Sir W. Hamilton's, if I attempted to gauge and measure his faculties, or give a complete theory of his successes and failures. The utmost I venture on, is to suggest, as simple possibilities, some of the causes which may have partly contributed to his shortcomings as a philosopher. One of those causes is so common as to be the next thing to universal, but requires all the more to be signalized for its unfortunate consequences; over-anxiety to make safe a foregone conclusion. The whole philosophy of Sir W. Hamilton seems to have had its character determined by the requirements of the doc-

---

reasoning. Thus, in maintaining against Stewart and Brown that we can attend to more than one object at once, he defends this true doctrine by some very bad arguments. He says (Lectures, i. 252), that if the mind could "attend to, or be conscious of, only a single object at a time," the conclusion would be involved, "that all comparison and discrimination are impossible." This assumes that we cannot compare and discriminate any impressions but those which are exactly simultaneous. May not the condition of discrimination be consciousness not at the same, but at immediately successive instants? May not discrimination depend on *change* of consciousness; the transition from one state to another? This is a tenable opinion; it was actually maintained by the philosophers against whom our author was arguing; and if he thought it erroneous, he should have disproved it. Unless he did, he was not entitled to treat a doctrine shown to involve this consequence, as reduced to absurdity. Another of his proofs of our ability to attend to a plurality of things at once, is our perception of harmony between sounds. He argues (Lectures, i. 244) that to perceive a relation between two sounds implies a comparison, and that if this comparison is not between the sounds themselves, simultaneously attended to, it must be a comparison of "past sound as retained in memory, with the present as actually perceived;" which still implies attending to two objects at once. His opponents, however, might say, that if there be a comparison, it is not between two simultaneous impressions, either sensations or mem-

trine of Free-will ; and to that doctrine he clung, because he had persuaded himself that it afforded the only premises from which human reason could deduce the doctrines of natural religion. I believe that in this persuasion he was thoroughly his own dupe, and that his speculations have weakened the philosophical foundation of religion fully as much as they have confirmed it.

A second cause which may help to account for his not having effected more in philosophy, is the enormous amount of time and mental vigor which he expended on mere philosophical erudition, leaving, it may be said, only the remains of his mind for the real business of thinking. While he seems to have known, almost by heart, the voluminous Greek commentators on Aristotle, and to have read all that the most obscure schoolman or fifth-rate German transcendentalist had written on the sub-

---

ories, but between two successive sounds in the instant of transition. They might add, that the perception of harmony does not necessarily involve comparison. When a number of sounds in perfect harmony strike the ear simultaneously, we have but a single impression ; we perceive but one mass of sound. Analyzing this into its component parts is an act of intelligence, not of direct perception, and is performed by fixing our attention first on the whole, and then on the separate elements, not all at once, but one after another. The perception of the parts is so far from being distinctly present in our feeling of the harmony, that in proportion as we consciously realize it we injure the general effect. These objections to his doctrine our author seems not to have thought of, because those of Stewart, whom as an opponent he principally had in view, were different. (Lectures, ii. 145.) But they ought to have occurred to him without prompting, being in complete unison with his doctrine that consciousness of wholes usually precedes that of their parts ; that " instead of commencing with minima, perception commences with masses." (Lectures, ii. 327, and many similar passages.)

Sir W. Hamilton is also inconsistent in affirming (Lectures, i. 237) that attention is " an act of will or desire," and afterwards (247, 248) that it is in some cases automatic, " a mere vital and irresistible act." This, however, is only a verbal inaccuracy. He doubtless meant that attention is generally voluntary, but occasionally automatic.

jects with which he occupied himself; while, not content with a general knowledge of these authors, he could tell with the greatest precision what each of them thought on any given topic, and in what each differed from every other; while expending his time and energy on all this, he had not enough of them left to complete his Lectures. Those on Metaphysics, as already remarked, stopped short on the threshold of what was, especially in his own opinion, the most important part of it, and never reached even the threshold of the third and last of the parts into which, in an early lecture, he divided his subject.* Those on Logic he left dependent, for most of the subordinate developments, on extracts strung together from German writers, chiefly Krug and Esser; often not destitute of merit, but generally so vague, as to make all those parts of his exposition in which they predominate, unsatisfactory;† sometimes written from points of view different from Sir W. Hamilton's own, but which he never found time or took the trouble to re-express in adaptation to his own mode of thought.‡ In the whole circle of

* Lectures, i. 123-125. This third part is "Ontology, or Metaphysics Proper;" "the science conversant about inferences of unknown being from its known manifestations;" things not manifested in consciousness, but legitimately inferrible from those which are.

† This is strikingly the case, among many others, with the Lectures on Definition and Division. On those subjects our author lets Krug and Esser think for him. Those authors stand to him instead, not merely of finding a fit expression for his thoughts, but apparently of having any thoughts at all.

‡ For example (Lectures, iii. 159-162), his own idea of Clearness as a property of concepts, is that "a concept is said to be clear when the degree of consciousness is such as to enable us to distinguish it" (the concept) "as a whole from others;" but this idea is expounded by a passage from Esser, in which it is not the concept, but the objects thought through the concept, which, if sufficiently distinguished from all others, constitute the conception a clear one. I confess that Esser has here greatly the advantage over Sir W. Hamilton, who might have usefully corrected his own theory from the borrowed commentary on it.

psychological and logical speculation, it is astonishing how few are the topics into which he has thrown any of the powers of his own intellect; and on how small a proportion even of these he has pushed his investigations beyond what seemed necessary for the purposes of some particular controversy. In consequence, philosophical doctrines are taken up, and again laid down, with perfect unconsciousness, and his philosophy seems made up of scraps from several conflicting metaphysical systems. The Relativity of human knowledge is made a great deal of in opposition to Schelling and Cousin, but drops out or dwindles into nothing in Sir W. Hamilton's own psychology. The validity of our natural beliefs, and the doctrine that the incogitable is not therefore impossible, are strenuously asserted in this place and disregarded in that, according to the question in hand. On the subject of General Notions he is avowedly a Nominalist, but teaches the whole of Logic as if he had never heard of any doctrine but the Conceptualist; what he presents as a reconcilement of the two being never adverted to afterwards, and serving only as an excuse to himself for accepting the one doctrine and invariably using the language of the other. Arriving at his doctrines almost always under the stimulus of some special dispute, he never knows how far to press them: consequently there is a region of haze round the place where opinions of different origin meet. I formerly quoted from him a felicitous illustration drawn from the mechanical operation of tunnelling; that process affords another, justly applicable to himself. The reader must have heard of that gigantic enterprise of the Italian Government, the tunnel through Mont Cenis. This great work is carried on simultaneously from both ends, in well-grounded confidence (such is now the minute accuracy of engineering operations) that the two parties of workmen will correctly meet in the middle. Were they to disappoint this expectation, and work past one another in the dark, they would afford a likeness of Sir W. Hamilton's mode of tunnelling the human mind.

This failure to think out subjects until they had been thoroughly mastered, or until consistency had been attained between the different views which the author took of them from different points of observation, may, like the unfinished state of the Lectures, be with great probability ascribed to the excessive absorption of his time and energies by the study of old writers. That absorption did worse; for it left him with neither leisure nor vigor for what was far more important in every sense, and an entirely indispensable qualification for a master in philosophy — the systematic study of the sciences. Except physiology, on some parts of which his mental powers were really employed, he may be said to have known nothing of any physical science. I do not mean that he was ignorant of familiar facts, or that he may not, in the course of his education, have gone through the curriculum. But it must have been as Gibbon did, who says, in his autobiography, " I was content to receive the passive impressions of my professor's lectures, without any active exercise of my own powers." For any trace the study had left in Sir W. Hamilton's mind, he might as well never have heard of it.*

---

* The signs of Sir W. Hamilton's want of familiarity with the physical sciences meet us in every corner of his works. One, which I have not hitherto found a convenient place for noticing, is the singular view he takes of analysis and synthesis. He imagines that synthesis always pre-

It is much to be regretted that Sir W. Hamilton did not write the history of philosophy, instead of choosing, as the direct object of his intellectual exertions, philosophy itself. He possessed a knowledge of the materials such as no one, probably, for many generations, will take the trouble of acquiring again; and the erudition of philosophy is emphatically one of the things which it is good that a few should acquire for the benefit of the rest. Independently of the great interest and value attaching to a knowledge of the historical development

supposes analysis, and that unless grounded on a previous analysis, synthesis can afford no knowledge. "Synthesis without a previous analysis is baseless; for synthesis receives from analysis the elements which it recomposes." (Lectures, i. 98.) "Synthesis without analysis is a false knowledge, that is, no knowledge at all. . . . A synthesis without a previous analysis is radically and *ab initio* null." (Ibid. 99.) This affirmation is the more surprising, as the example he himself selects to illustrate analysis and synthesis is a case of chemical composition; a neutral salt, compounded of an acid and an alkali. Did he suppose that when a chemist succeeds in forming a salt by synthesis merely, putting together two substances never actually found in combination, he does not make exactly the same addition to chemical science as if he had met with the compound first, and analyzed it into its elements afterwards? Did Sir W. Hamilton ever read a memoir by a chemist on a newly-discovered elementary substance? If so, did he not find that the discoverer invariably proceeds to ascertain by synthesis what combinations the new element will form with all other elements for which it has any affinity? Sir W. Hamilton, though he drew his example from physics, forgot all that related to the example, and thought only of psychological investigation, in which it does commonly happen that the compound fact is presented to us first, and we have to begin by analyzing it; our synthesis, if practicable at all, taking place afterwards, and serving only to verify the analysis. Therefore, in spite of his own example, Sir W. Hamilton defines synthesis as being always a recomposition and "reconstruction." (Lectures, i. 98.) Could any one who had the smallest familiarity with physical science have committed this strange oversight?

Another example, to which I shall content myself with referring, is the incapacity of understanding an argument respecting a principle of Mechanics, shown in his controversy with Dr. Whewell respecting the law that the pressure of a lever on the fulcrum, when the weights balance one another, is equal to the sum of the two weights. (Discussions; pp. 338, 339.)

of speculation, there is much in the old writers on philosophy, even those of the middle ages, really worth preserving for its scientific value. But this should be extracted, and rendered into the phraseology of modern thought, by persons as familiar with that as with the ancient, and possessing a command of its language; a combination never yet so perfectly realized as in Sir W. Hamilton: It is waste of time for a mere student of philosophy, to have to learn the familiar use of fifty philosophic phraseologies, all greatly inferior to that of his own time; and if this were required from all thinkers, there would be very little time left for thought. A man who had done it so thoroughly as Sir W. Hamilton, should have made his contemporaries and successors, once for all, partakers of the benefit; and rendered it unnecessary for any one to do it again, except for verifying and correcting his representations. This, which no one but himself could have done, he has left undone; and has given us, instead, a contribution to mental philosophy which has been more than equalled by many not superior to him in powers, and wholly destitute of erudition. Of all persons, in modern times, entitled to the name of philosophers, the two, probably, whose reading on their own subjects was the scantiest, in proportion to their intellectual capacity, were Dr. Thomas Brown and Archbishop Whately: accordingly they are the only two of whom Sir W. Hamilton, though acknowledging their abilities, habitually speaks with a certain tinge of superciliousness. It cannot be denied that both Dr. Brown and Archbishop Whately would have thought and written better than they did, if they had been better read in the writings of previous thinkers: but I am not afraid that posterity will contradict me when I say, that either of them has done far greater service to the world, in the origination and diffusion of important thought, than Sir W. Hamilton with all his learning; because, though indolent readers, they were, both of them, active and fertile thinkers.

It is not that Sir W. Hamilton's erudition is not frequently of real use to him on particular questions of philosophy. It does him one valuable service: it enables him to know all the various opinions which can be held on the questions he discusses, and to conceive and express them clearly, leaving none of them out. This it does, though even this not always; but it does little else, even of what might be expected from erudition when enlightened by philosophy. He knew, with extraordinary accuracy, the ὅτι of every philosopher's doctrine, but gave himself little trouble about the διότι. With one exception, I find no remarks bearing upon that point in any part of his writings.* I imagine he

* This solitary exception relates to Hume. Respecting the general scope and purpose, the pervading spirit, of Hume's speculations, Sir W. Hamilton does give an opinion, and, I venture to think, a wrong one. He regards Hume's philosophy as scepticism in its legitimate sense. Hume's object, he thinks, was to prove the uncertainty of all knowledge. With this intent he represents him as reasoning from premises "not established by himself," but "accepted only as principles universally conceded in the previous schools of philosophy." These premises Hume showed (according to Sir W. Hamilton) to lead to conclusions which contradicted the evidence of consciousness; thus proving, not that consciousness deceives, but that the premises generally accepted on the authority of philosophers, and leading to these conclusions, must be false. (Discussions, pp. 87, 88, and elsewhere.)

This is certainly the use which has been made of Hume's arguments, by Reid and many other of his opponents. Admitting their validity as arguments, Reid considered them, not as proving Hume's conclusions, but as a *reductio ad absurdum* of his premises. That Hume, however, had any foresight of their being put to this use, either for a dogmatical or a purely

16

would have been much at a loss if he had been required to draw up a philosophical estimate of the mind of any great thinker. (He never seems to look at any opinion of a philosopher in connection with the same philosopher's other opinions.) Accordingly, he is weak as to the mutual relations of philosophical doctrines. He seldom knows any of the corollaries from a thinker's opinions, unless the thinker has himself drawn them; and even then he knows them, not as corollaries, but

sceptical purpose, appears to me supremely improbable. If we form our opinion by reading the series of Hume's metaphysical essays straight through, instead of judging from a few detached expressions in a single essay (that "on the Academical or Sceptical Philosophy"), I think our judgment will be that Hume sincerely accepted both the premises and the conclusions. It would be difficult, no doubt, to prove this by conclusive evidence, nor would I venture absolutely to affirm it. In the case of the freethinking philosophers of the last century, it is often impossible to be quite certain what their opinions really were; how far the reservations they made, expressed real convictions, or were concessions to supposed necessities of position. Hume, it is certain, made such concessions largely: insincere they can hardly be called, being so evidently intended to be φωνήεντα, at least συνετοῖσι. I have a strong impression that Hume's scepticism, or rather his professed admiration of scepticism, was a disguise of this description, intended rather to avoid offence than to conceal his opinion; that he preferred to be called a sceptic, rather than by a more odious name; and having to promulgate conclusions which he knew would be regarded as contradicting on one hand the evidence of common sense, on the other the doctrines of religion, did not like to declare them as positive convictions, but thought it more judicious to exhibit them as the results we *might* come to, if we put complete confidence in the trustworthiness of our rational faculty. I have little doubt that he himself did feel this confidence, and wished it to be felt by his readers. There is certainly no trace of a different feeling in his speculations on any of the other important subjects treated in his works; and even on this subject, the general tenor of what he wrote pointing one way, and only single passages the other, it is most reasonable to interpret the latter in the mode which will least contradict the expression of his habitual state of mind in the former.

I cannot but believe, therefore, that Sir W. Hamilton has misunderstood the essential character of Hume's mind; but his hearty admiration and honest vindication of him as a thinker are highly honorable to Sir W. Hamilton, both as a philosopher and as a man.

only as opinions. One of the most striking examples he affords of this inability is in the case of Leibnitz; and it is worth while to analyze this instance, because nothing can more conclusively show, how little capable he was of entering into the spirit of a system unlike his own.

If there ever was a thinker whose system of thought could without difficulty be conceived as a connected whole, it was Leibnitz. Hardly any philosopher has taken so much pains to display the filiation of all his main conceptions, in a manner at once satisfactory to his own mind and intelligible to the world. And there is hardly any one in whom the filiation is more complete, these various conceptions being all applications of one common principle. Yet Sir W. Hamilton understands them so ill, as to be able to say, after giving an account of the Pre-established Harmony, that "its author himself probably regarded it more as a specimen of ingenuity than as a serious doctrine." * And again: "It is a disputed point whether Leibnitz was serious in his monadology and pre-established harmony." † To say nothing of the injustice done, by this surmise, to the deep sincerity and high philosophic earnestness of that most eminent man, it is obvious to those who study opinions in their relation to the mind entertaining them, that a person who could thus think concerning the Pre-established Harmony and the Monadology, however correctly he may have seized many particular opinions of Leibnitz had never taken into his mind a conception of Leibnitz, himself as a philosopher. These theories

* Lectures, i. 304. † Foot-note to Reid, p. 309.

were necessitated by Leibnitz's other opinions. They were the only outlet from the difficulties of the fundamental doctrine of his philosophy, the Principle of Sufficient Reason.

All who know anything of Leibnitz, are aware that he affirmed it to be a principle of the universe, that nothing exists which has not an antecedent ground in reason, and cognizable by reason; a ground which, when known, gives all the properties of the thing by natural and necessary consequence. This Sufficient Reason might be some abstract property of the thing, serving as the pattern on which it was constructed, and being the key to all its other attributes. Such, for example, is the property by which mathematicians define the circle or the triangle, and from which, by mere reasoning, the remaining properties of those figures are deducible. In other cases, the Sufficient Reason of a phænomenon is found in its physical cause. But the mere existence of the cause as an invariable antecedent, does not constitute it the Sufficient Reason of the effect. There must be something in the nature of the cause itself, something capable of being detected in it, which, once known, accounts for its being followed by that particular effect; something which explains the character of the effect, and had it been known beforehand, would have enabled us to foretell the precise effect that would be produced. To so great a length did Leibnitz carry this doctrine, as to affirm that God (saving actual miracle, which as a highly exceptional fact he was willing to admit) could not, in the exercise of his ordinary providence, conduct the government of the world except *par la nature des créatures;* through second causes, each containing, in its own properties, wherewithal to furnish a complete explanation of the phænomena to which it gives rise.

Setting out with this *à priori* conception of the order of the universe, Leibnitz found Mind apparently acting upon Matter and Matter upon Mind, and was utterly unable to discover in the nature and attributes of either, any Sufficient Reason for this action. The two substances seemed wholly disparate: there was nothing in them from which action of any kind upon one another could have been presumed to be so much as possible. He saw in this one case, what is true, though he did not see it, in all cases whatever — that there is no *nexus*, no natural link, between agent and patient, between cause and effect, and that all we know or can know of their relation is, that the one always follows the other. But to accept the mere fact as ultimate, without craving for a demonstration, could not enter into Leibnitz's geometrical mind; and was positively forbidden by his Principle of Sufficient Reason. Here was a dilemma! Happily, however, the difficulty of admitting that Mind could act upon Matter, disappeared in the case of an Infinite Mind. In the Omnipotence of the Deity there lay a Sufficient Reason for the possibility of anything which the Deity might be pleased to do. It must be God, therefore, and no subordinate agency, that directly produces the effects on Matter which seem owing to Mind, and the effects on Mind which seem owing to Matter. This being admitted, there were only two possible theories to choose from. Either God, from the beginning, wound up Mind and Matter to go together like two clocks, though without any connection with one another; and I see an object, not because the object is before my eyes, but because it was prearranged from eternity that the presence of the object and the fact of my seeing should occur at the same instant; or else, at the moment when the object appears, God intervenes, and gives me the perception of sight, exactly as if the object had caused it. The former theory is the Pre-established Harmony; the latter is the doctrine of Occasional Causes, to which, as rather the less grotesque supposition of the two, the Cartesians had been driven by the pressure of the same difficulty. But this hypothesis, as it supposed nothing less than a standing miracle, was wholly inadmissible by Leibnitz. It was inconsistent with the idea which he had formed to himself of the perfections of the Deity. He considered it as assimilating Providence to a bad workman, whose engines will not work unless he himself stands by, and gives them a helping hand; "a watchmaker, who, having constructed a timepiece, would still be obliged himself to turn the hands, to make it mark the hours."* Leibnitz could not find, in the idea of God, any Sufficient Reason why so roundabout a mode of governing the universe should have been chosen by him. He was thus thrown upon the hypothesis of a Pre-established Harmony, as his only refuge; and there can be no doubt that he accepted it, with the full conviction of an intellect accustomed to pursue given premises to their consequences with all the rigor of geometrical demonstration.

* Quoted from Leibnitz by Sir W. Hamilton, Lectures, i. 303.

The doctrine of Monads was as necessary a corollary from Leibnitz's first principle as the Pre-established Harmony. Everything, whether physical or spiritual, which has an individual existence, is a compound of innumerable attributes, between many of which we cannot seize any connection, but on Leibnitz's theory it was not admissible to suppose that no connection exists. There must be something, somewhere, which contains in its own nature the complete theory and explanation of the combination of attributes, and is the reason of its being that combination and no other: and what could this be unless a sort of kernel of the entire Being — the Soul in the case of a spiritual being, a kind of Essence of the Individual in that of a merely physical object? The Monads of Leibnitz do not really differ from the imaginary Essences of the schoolmen, except in not being abstractions, but objective realities in the completest meaning of the word; which, indeed, the Substantiæ Secundæ of the Realists already were, only that they were essences of classes, and were conceived as inhering simultaneously in numerous individuals, while the Monads of Leibnitz were lively little beings, the principles of animation and activity, each of them the real agent or Force at the bottom of one individual. All this may seem poor stuff, and a melancholy exhibition of a great intellect. But as there is nothing in experience which directly disproves these theories, they are not really more absurd than many a one which has not so quaint an appearance: and it is the strength, not the weakness, of a systematic intellect, that it does not shrink from conclusions because they have an absurd look, when they are necessary corollaries from premises which the thinker, and probably most of those who criticise him, have not ceased to regard as true. Leibnitz was led to the Monads and the Pre-established Harmony by the same logical necessity, which made Descartes, far more absurdly, affirm the automatism of animals; and we might as reasonably doubt the seriousness of the latter opinion, as of the former. The same logical consistency made him a Necessitarian, and an Optimist; since the doctrine of Sufficient Reason made God the author of all that happens, consequently of all human actions; and God's attributes could not be a Sufficient Reason for any world but the best possible.

Other examples may be given, though none greater than this, of Sir W. Hamilton's inability to enter into the very mind of another thinker. Is it not, for instance, a surprising thing, that one who knew Socrates, Plato, and Aristotle so well, should attribute* to all of them his own opinion, that not truth but the search for truth is the important matter, and that the pursuit of it is not for the sake of the attainment, but of the mental activity and energy developed in the search? If there have been three men since speculation began who would have vehemently rejected such a doctrine, they are the three who are here placed at the head of the authorities in its support. Our author arrives at this strange misunderstanding, by giving a meaning to single expressions, derived from his own mode of thought, and not from theirs. In Aristotle's case the assertion rests on a mistake of the meaning of the Aristotelian word $\dot{\epsilon}\nu\dot{\epsilon}\rho\gamma\epsilon\iota\alpha$, which did not signify energy, but fact as opposed to pos-

* Lectures, i. 11, 12.

sibility, *actus* to *potentia*.* One hardly knows what to say to a writer who understands Τέλος οὐ γνῶσις ἀλλὰ πρᾶξις, to mean, " The intellect is perfected not by knowledge but by activity."

We see, from such instances, how much even Sir W. Hamilton's erudition wanted of what we have a right to expect from erudition in a superior mind — that it should enter into the general spirit of the things it knows, not know them merely in their details. Sir W. Hamilton studied the eminent thinkers of old, only from the outside. He did not throw his own mind into their manner of thought; he did not survey the field of philosophic speculation from their standing point, and see each object as it would be seen with their lights, and with their modes of looking. The opinion of an author stands an isolated fact in Sir W. Hamilton's pages, without foundation in the author's individuality, or connection with his other doctrines. For want of this elucidation one by another, even the opinions themselves are, as in the case last cited, very liable to be misunderstood. Yet, such as his expositions of the opinions of philosophers are, it is greatly to be regretted that we have not more of them; and that his unrivalled knowledge of all the antecedents of Philosophy, has enriched the world with nothing but a few selections of passages on topics on which circumstances had led Sir W. Hamilton to write. He is known to have left copious common-place books,

---

* The very passage quoted from Aristotle in support of this representation of him, shows that he was using the word in his own and not in Sir W. Hamilton's sense. Τέλος δ' ἡ ἐνέργεια, καὶ τούτου χάριν ἡ δύναμις λαμβάνεται. ... καὶ τὴν θεωρητικὴν (ἔχουσιν) ἵνα θεωρῶσιν· ἀλλ' οὐ θεωρῶσιν ἵνα θεωρητικὴν ἔχωσιν.

without which indeed it would have been hardly possible that such stores of knowledge could be kept within easy reference. Let us hope that they are carefully preserved; that they will, in some form or other, be made accessible to students, and will yet do good service to the future historian of philosophy. Should this hope be fulfilled, future ages will have greater cause than, I think, Sir W. Hamilton's published philosophical speculations will ever give them, to rejoice in the fruits of his labors, and to celebrate his name.

THE END.

www.ingramcontent.com/pod-product-compliance
Lightning Source LLC
Chambersburg PA
CBHW021942240426
43668CB00037B/483